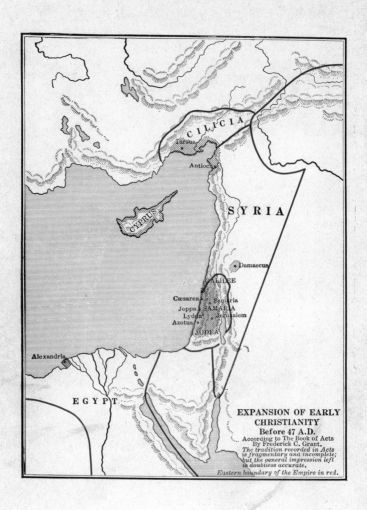

CILICIA

Tarsus

Antioch

SYRIA

CYPRUS

Damascus

GALILEE

Cæsarea
Joppa   SAMARIA
Lydda   Jerusalem
Azotus
JUDEA

Alexandria

EGYPT

**EXPANSION OF EARLY
CHRISTIANITY
Before 47 A.D.**
According to The Book of Acts
By Frederick C. Grant.
*The tradition recorded in Acts
is fragmentary and incomplete;
but the general impression left
is doubtless accurate.*
Eastern boundary of the Empire in red.

The Abingdon Religious Education Texts
David G. Downey, General Editor
WEEK-DAY SCHOOL SERIES   GEORGE HERBERT BETTS, Editor

THE EARLY DAYS OF CHRISTIANITY

BY
FREDERICK C. GRANT

THE ABINGDON PRESS
NEW YORK   CINCINNATI

Copyright, 1922, by
FREDERICK C. GRANT

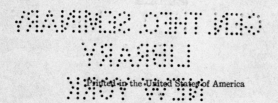
Printed in the United States of America

For the sake of clearness, the Biblical text used in this volume has in many places been paraphrased in modern English. Though adhering closely to the current versions, the original has been consulted and a new translation made where obscurities occur.

TO MY
FIRST TEACHERS OF RELIGION
FATHER   MOTHER
AUNT ISABEL

TABLE OF CONTENTS

	PAGE
CHRONOLOGY OF THE NEW TESTAMENT	8
FOREWORD	11

CHAPTER

I.	THE ROMAN WORLD	13

PART ONE: THE EARLY CHURCH IN PALESTINE

II.	THE DISCIPLES AT JERUSALEM	25
III.	THE DAY OF PENTECOST	33
IV.	PETER AND JOHN IN THE TEMPLE	42
V.	THE GROWTH OF THE CHURCH	51
VI.	THE FIRST CHRISTIAN MARTYR	60
VII.	PHILIP THE EVANGELIST	68
VIII.	PAUL OF TARSUS	76
IX.	PAUL'S CONVERSION	85
X.	CORNELIUS THE CENTURION	92
XI.	CHRISTIANITY REACHES ANTIOCH	100

PART TWO: THE WORK OF PAUL

XII.	THE GOSPEL IN CYPRUS AND GALATIA	113
XIII.	MISTAKEN FOR GODS	121
XIV.	FOES WITHIN THE FOLD	129
XV.	THE GOSPEL IN MACEDONIA	137
XVI.	BEFORE THE AREOPAGUS	146
XVII.	PAUL AT CORINTH	156

CONTENTS

CHAPTER   PAGE

XVIII. THREE YEARS AT EPHESUS 164
  XIX. TWO IMPORTANT LETTERS 172
   XX. IN JERUSALEM AGAIN 181
  XXI. PAUL'S ARREST 191
 XXII. THE APPEAL TO CÆSAR 200
XXIII. PAUL IN ROME 210

PART THREE: THE CHURCH AFTER PAUL

  XXIV. CHRISTIANITY IN THE DAYS OF NERO 223
   XXV. THE CHURCH IN PALESTINE 235
  XXVI. THE MAKING OF THE NEW TESTAMENT . . 245
 XXVII. THE BLOOD OF THE MARTYRS 256
XXVIII. TWO CENTURIES OF GROWTH 266
  XXIX. CHURCH WORSHIP AND MEMBERSHIP 277
   XXX. THE FATHERS OF THE EARLY CHURCH . . . 289
  XXXI. THE LAST PERSECUTION 300
 XXXII. "BY THIS SIGN CONQUER" 311

LIST OF ILLUSTRATIONS

FACING PAGE

Jaffa (Joppa): Traditional Home of Simon the Tanner 94

The Site of Antioch at the Present Time. . . 104

Thessalonica (Modern Saloniki)............ 146

Cæsarea: The Ruins of Saint Paul's Prison. . 198

The Last Prayer.......................... 224

Christ or Artemis....................... 260

Arch of Constantine in Rome............. 318

MAPS

Expansion of Early Christianity..... *Frontispiece*
(Before 47 A.D.)

FACING PAGE

Relative Density of Population First Century A.D 15

The Routes of Saint Paul............... 114

The Expansion of Early Christianity...... 270
(First, Second, and Third Centuries)

CHRONOLOGY OF THE NEW TESTAMENT

ROMAN HISTORY	CHRISTIAN HISTORY	CHRISTIAN LITERATURE
31 B.C.-14 A.D. AUGUSTUS, Emperor	5-4 B.C. JESUS born	
	27 Preaching of JOHN the Baptist	
14-37 TIBERIUS, Emperor	27-29 Ministry of JESUS	
26-36 PILATE, Procurator of Judaea and Samaria	29 The Crucifixion	(Oral accounts of Jesus' ministry and teaching)
	35 PAUL'S Conversion	
	38 PAUL visits Jerusalem	
37-41 CALIGULA, Emperor	38-47 PAUL in Syria and Cilicia	
41-54 CLAUDIUS, Emperor	42 Martyrdom of JAMES (and John?)	
44 Death of HEROD AGRIPPA	46 Relief visit to Jerusalem	
	47-48 First Miss. Journey	
	48-49 Council at Jerusalem	
49 Jews expelled at Rome	49-52 Second Miss. Journey	50 1-2 Thessalonians
51 GALLIO, Proconsul of Achaia	50 PAUL reaches Corinth	51 Galatians
		(Oral accounts of the early church in Palestine)
54-68 NERO, Emperor	52-56 Third Miss. Journey	55 1-2 Corinthians
	52-55 Three years in Ephesus	56 Romans
	55-56 Winter in Corinth	
	56 PAUL at Jerusalem	? Special documents used by Luke (Luke 1-2; Acts 1-12)
58 FESTUS succeeds FELIX	56-58 In Prison at Caesarea	59-61 Philippians, Philemon, Colossians, Ephesians
	59 PAUL reaches Rome	

Events	Writings
	? *"Sayings of Jesus"*
	65 *"Letters to the Seven Churches"* (Rev. 1-3) etc.
	66 *"Little Apocalypse"* (Mark 13)?
64 Nero's persecution	? Gospel of Mark (70+)
	? Epistle of James
61-64 PETER and PAUL martyred at Rome	? Gospel of Matthew (80+)
	? Gospel of Luke (85+)
66 Revolt in Palestine	? I Peter ? Jude
	? Epistle to Hebrews
	? Acts of Apostles (90+)
68-69 GALBA, OTHO, VITELLIUS	95 Apocalypse of John
69-79 VESPASIAN, Emperor	? *I Clement*
70 Fall of Jerusalem	? 1-2 Timothy, Titus
79-81 TITUS, Emperor	? 1-2-3 John
81-96 DOMITIAN, Emperor	? Gospel of John (90-110)
	115 *Letters of Ignatius*
95 Domitian's persecution	117 *Epistle of Polycarp*
96-98 NERVA, Emperor	120 *"Teaching of the Twelve Apostles"*
98-117 TRAJAN, Emperor	120 Quadratus' *Apology*
112 PLINY in Bithynia	130 *"Epistle of Barnabas"*
115 Martyrdom of IGNATIUS	135 *"Shepherd"* of Hermas
	140 Aristides' *Apology*
117-138 HADRIAN, Emperor	? *Epistle to Diognetus*
120 Rescript of Hadrian	? 2 Peter (about 150)
	150 Tatian's *"Oration"*
138-161 ANTONINUS PIUS, Emperor	150 Justin's *Apology and Dialogue*

FOREWORD

ALTHOUGH an independent work, the present volume forms a sequel to *The Life and Times of Jesus*, already published in this series. Together they provide an elementary outline of the rise of the Christian religion, from the birth, ministry, and passion of Jesus to the triumph of Christianity under Constantine. Their aim is to enable the pupil to realize vividly the historical facts and personalities, and to appreciate the chief factors in this immensely important development. This can only be accomplished if the pupil himself takes serious interest in the course, faithfully prepares the lessons, and goes over with notebook at his side the Study Topics assigned.

As with the earlier volume, the principles involved in teaching this course and suggested methods of treatment are discussed in the *Teacher's Manual* which is to accompany it.

CHAPTER I

THE ROMAN WORLD

THE world in which Christianity arose was almost entirely under the dominion of the Roman Empire. From about the middle of the third century before Christ, as a result of the wars with Carthage, the Roman rule had been gradually extended beyond the borders of Italy until the whole Mediterranean coast was under its control. At the death of the Emperor Augustus (14 A. D.) this vast empire, divided into provinces, stretched from the Atlantic Ocean on the west to the Euphrates River, the Arabian Desert, and the shores of the Red Sea on the east: and from the English Channel, the Rhine and the Danube Rivers and the Black Sea on the north to the Sahara Desert and the first cataract of the Nile on the south. The rest of the known world was made up of the uncivilized or savage tribes living north of the Rhine and the Danube, the nomads of the deserts south and east, the fierce and turbulent Parthians beyond the Euphrates, the independent kingdom of Armenia, and the remote and little-known lands of Ethiopia, India, and China. Thus the world in which Christianity arose—the known and civilized world of the west—was almost completely under Roman dominion.

PHYSICAL FEATURES AND POPULATION

A glance at the map shows the empire divided throughout its length by the Mediterranean Sea, and divided throughout its breadth by both the Mediterranean and the lesser seas, the Tyrrhenian, Ionian, Adriatic, and Ægean; by two deep gulfs on the north coast of Africa, another between Cilicia and Syria, and the straits of Gibraltar, the Dardanelles, the Sea of Marmora and the Bosphorus. In consequence, although the Romans were not naturally good sailors, their empire was a "maritime" one—like the modern "empire" of Great Britain.

A sea empire.—Although in extent about the same length and breadth as the United States, and lying in almost the same degrees of latitude (30° to 50° north), no vast expanse of fertile plain and prairie, like the central part of our country, was anywhere to be found within this empire. For north of Italy lay the Alps; north of Greece and extending down into the peninsula lay the Carpathians and the Balkan ranges; the heart of Asia Minor was a high, thinly populated table-land; Arabia and all of north Africa (except the valley of the Nile and a thin fringe of coastland) were desert. Hence this maritime empire was made up chiefly of peoples who dwelt along the shores of the great inland sea. All the important cities were either upon or near its coast.

But if the sea divided, it also united the empire, for it was the greatest highway of the ancient world. Voyages were easily and quickly made in every direction. The islands Sardinia, Sicily, Crete, Cyprus, and scattered groups in the Ægean, almost formed stepping-stones—at least they afforded convenient stopping-places—on the routes across the Great Sea.

The subject peoples.—The most diverse races and peoples met and mingled in the population of this vast *Imperium Romanum:* Spaniards, Italians, Greeks, Macedonians, Illyrians, Gauls, Celts, Phœnicians, Syrians, Arabs, Egyptians, Jews, and many from the uncivilized

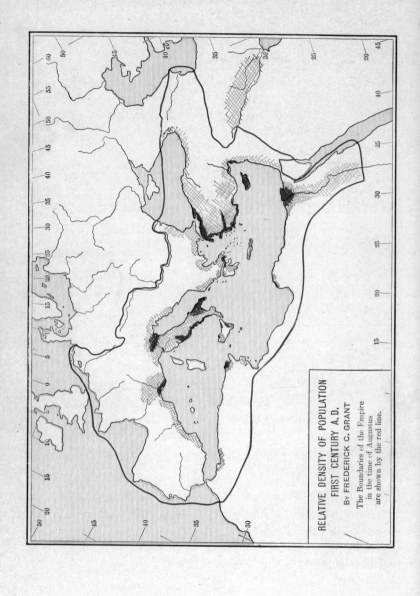

RELATIVE DENSITY OF POPULATION
FIRST CENTURY A.D.
BY FREDERICK C. GRANT

The Boundaries of the Empire
in the time of Augustus
are shown by the red line.

peoples of the north (brought in as slaves), together with numberless traders from Armenia, Persia (Parthia), and the Orient. It is true, Alexander the Great (who died 323 B. C.) had begun three centuries before the process of welding the eastern peoples into one. But Alexander's empire was short-lived, and the process had gone on but slowly until Rome took over the administration of world-government.

Population.—It is estimated that between sixty-five and one hundred million people lived under the empire in the first century—considerably less than the population of the United States to-day. The great centers of population were, as they had been for many centuries, Egypt (the valley of the Nile), Palestine and Syria, Cilicia and the south and west coasts of Asia Minor, Greece (though much more sparsely populated than in the days of Pericles and Plato), Italy, and the islands —especially Sicily and Cyprus. Next in rank, perhaps, stood the regions immediately back of Carthage and Cyrene, and southern Gaul (back of Marseilles and along the lower Rhone).

GOVERNMENT

Over this scattered but yet firmly united empire stood the emperor, supreme. Theoretically, he was only the *imperator*, or head of the army, and therefore responsible to the Roman Senate for his actions; actually, his power was unlimited. It is only because Augustus was a man conservative by nature and afraid of unpopularity that he took great care not to overstep the traditional limits of his office, and deferred to the Senate again and again. His successor, Tiberius, had no such fear of unpopularity; and from his time onward the imperial power was practically absolute.

The provinces.—Over the separate provinces into which the empire was divided were appointed governors (who had charge of the administration of law and order) and procurators (who had charge of collecting and forwarding the taxes). No uniform system of law was established for the whole empire. The old, traditional laws of the various peoples were allowed to remain in force, often administered by some local assembly (like the Sanhedrin in Jerusalem); the governor interfered only in cases of life and death, or when the prestige or authority of the empire was at stake. In such actions he was required to use great tact and skill, for the first object of the imperial administration was the maintenance of peace and prosperity, which insured a steady flow of tribute from the provinces. We shall see again and again how this policy affected the attitude of the government and its agents toward the early Christians.

At the same time the emperors and their subordinates were anxious to *Romanize* their subjects, that is, to bring them all to one standard of culture, education, religion, industrial well-being, and political loyalty, for a common civilization alone would guarantee the unity and permanence of the empire. We shall see how this policy also affected the fortunes of the Christian Church.

The legions.—Throughout the empire were stationed the legions which composed the Roman army. Especially in the northern and eastern provinces, along the borders where Germans, Celts, or Parthians threatened to invade, were found their barracks and camps. Turbulent and unruly districts required special garrisons. Important cities, such as those where the governors and procurators resided, often had troops stationed to guard the treasury and enforce the administration of justice.

INDUSTRIES, COMMERCE AND TRAVEL

This vast Mediterranean basin, bordered on the north by unpenetrated forests and mountain ranges, on the east and south by deserts, on the west by the unknown and boundless western ocean, had more or less a common industrial life. The peasant in the valley of the Po, the Greek farmer on the banks of the Mæander, the sailor unlading a ship at Marseilles or Corinth or Alexandria, the muleteer of Antioch or Cyrene or Tarentum, ate almost the same kind of food, wore almost the same kind of clothes, slept in almost the same kind of bed, used almost the same Greek slang. It was the world of the olive tree and its products, of the vine, of Egyptian wheat and cotton, of Cilician wool, of Italian flax and barley. Just as the whole United States uses Georgia cotton and Minnesota flour and Chicago beef and California fruit and New England shoes, so the people throughout the Roman Empire exchanged their products. Ship-builders and riggers, masons, carpenters, road-builders, tanners, leather-workers, wagon-makers, spinners, weavers, dyers, farmers, sheep-grazers, brass-founders, silversmiths, jewelers, potters, oil-pressers, vintners, tent-makers were to be found in nearly every province.

Trade.—The trade, both by sea and land, was immense and constantly increasing. After Pompey had driven the pirates from the open seas, regular routes were mapped for freight and passenger vessels, as well as the imperial triremes, and one had no trouble in securing passage from one port to another (save during the winter season). Good harbors were dredged and protected with breakwaters; lighthouses were built and harbor police appointed. Month after month, from early spring to late autumn, great wheat barges plied between Alexandria and Rome. Across the isthmus at Corinth were transported thousands of tons of food-stuffs and manufactured articles. One merchant in western Asia Minor, according to the inscription found on his tomb, visited Rome no less than seventy-two times. Traders and merchants, tourists and pilgrims traveled everywhere.

Highways.—By land, great roads were laid out, kept in repair by highway commissioners (*curatores*) and patrolled by guards. Across Macedonia, for example, connecting its Adriatic and Ægean coasts, lay the famous and much-traveled *Via Egnatia*. Across Asia Minor, east and west, ran several routes; one, from Sardis to the Euphrates, was the old horse-road used since the days of the Persians; another, leading from Ephesus to the east, joined this and carried the bulk of travel and transport. Others ran north and south along the coast or spread out like spiders' webs from Dorylaion, Ancyra, Laodicea. Through the Cilician and Syrian gates, past Antioch, Sidon and Cæsarea, lay the coast road to Alexandria. Over these highways passed the soldiers and couriers of the emperor. A regular postal system was maintained, the post traveling between twenty-five and fifty miles a day. A letter mailed in Ephesus on Tuesday would be delivered in Troas on Friday. One sent to Rome would be there in less than three weeks.

EDUCATION, SOCIAL LIFE, RELIGION

Although the government of the empire was Roman, its culture or civilization, especially in its eastern half, was thoroughly Hellenistic. That is to say, the common language was Greek, the customs and social usages, the ideals and beliefs of the people were those which had either survived or grown up during the three centuries since Alexander's conquest. Schools were found in all but the smallest villages; grammar, music, geometry, rhetoric, philosophy, were among the subjects taught— invariably in Greek. Public libraries were found in many cities; public baths and gymnasiums almost everywhere. Cities like Alexandria, Antioch, Athens, Ephesus, were centers of learning made famous by the brilliant teachers at their "universities."

Slaves and workmen.—Everywhere were found the slaves, the lowest class of laborers, bought and sold by their masters. They were usually captives taken in the wars, or kidnaped in childhood from the islands or remote districts in the country. Some of them were highly educated men, teachers, physicians, or trusted stewards on the great estates. And most of them, as a rule, were treated more humanely, in the opening years of the empire, than ever before in history.

Above the slaves were the free craftsmen, often banded together into guilds, or "labor unions," for purposes of mutual aid in sickness or when out of work.

Religion.—Everywhere were found the temples of the ancient gods of the cities, together with new temples in honor of the chief Greek deities, Apollo, Athena, Zeus, and also in honor of the *genius* of the empire—which men naturally looked upon, in those days, as worthy of worship. For had not the establishment of the Roman power brought with it an era of prosperity and peace such as was never known before? The Augustan Peace, the *pax romana* or *pax augusta*, was the promise of a new age now dawning upon the world. Men could scarcely help being stirred religiously by the situation in which they found themselves. As the poet Virgil expressed it,

> "Now comes the last age, foretold by the Sibyl of
>   Cumæ;
> Once more is renewed the procession of centuries:
>   Justice
> Returns to the earth, and the Golden Era of
>   Saturn."
> —Eclogue 4: 4-6.

In addition to the official worship of the old gods in the public temples, there were growing up new cults of every sort. The empire tolerated them, though not on the same terms as the older religions. Isis, Serapis, Attis, the Great Mother Cybele, were worshiped in every port and capital of the east. The Jews of the Dispersion (*Diaspora*), whose synagogues were found everywhere from east to west, were ardent missionaries, and had undertaken to convert the Gentile world to the religion of one God and the Law of Moses.

The "preparation for the gospel."—All these factors in the life of the early Roman Empire were of very great significance for the rise of Christianity. Its political unity, its guarantee of public order and safety, its prudent administration of justice, its good roads and harbors, its vast shipping and its postal system, its common language (Greek), its widespread common education, its tolerance of new religions, its more humane treatment of the slaves and peasants, its associations for the betterment of certain classes (mostly laborers), and the widespread spirit of hopefulness and anticipation which had spread abroad (like the "era of good feeling" in America)—all this had, as we shall see, a wonderful bearing upon the spread of the Christian gospel and the founding of the Christian Church. Christians have always looked upon it as the work of God's providence, the divine preparation for the gospel. The words of Saint Paul were wholly justified,

> **"When the fullness of the time had come, God sent forth his Son."—Galatians 4: 4.**

STUDY TOPICS

1. Look up, in your ancient history, the maps which show the gradual expansion of the Roman Empire between the third century B. C. and the reign of Augustus. Locate the places named in the opening paragraphs of this chapter.
2. What was the official title of Augustus? What did it mean? How did he receive it? (See your ancient history, for example, Breasted's *Ancient Times*.)
3. Define legion, province, *procurator, curator, pax romana*, in your notebook.
4. What was the common language of at least the eastern half of the Roman Empire? In what language was the New Testament written?
5. Who was Virgil? Find out what he meant by the "Sibyl of Cumæ" and the "Golden Era of Saturn."
6. What was the condition of the slaves in this period?
7. Read in your ancient history the chapters on the civilization of the early Roman Empire (for example, Breasted's *Ancient Times*, §§91–93).
8. Are there any conditions in the modern world favorable to the spread of the Christian religion, which may be compared with those in the first century? If so, how ought we to seize the opportunity?

PART ONE

THE EARLY CHURCH IN PALESTINE

CHAPTER II

THE DISCIPLES AT JERUSALEM

CHRISTIANITY arose in one of the new eastern provinces of the Roman Empire. Since the year 63 B. C., when Pompey entered Jerusalem, the Romans had been gradually taking over the administration of Palestine. Herod the Great (40-4 B. C.) had been a *rex socius* or "allied king"—that is, an ally of the Romans. His sons were "tetrarchs," ruling under the supervision of the legate of Syria stationed at Antioch. But when Herod's son Archelaus was deposed in the year 6 A. D., on account of his unfitness for office, the emperor appointed a *procurator* for Judæa and Samaria; and from that time onward (save for one brief interval) Judæa was a full-fledged province of the Roman Empire, albeit a province of second rank.

It was under one of these Roman procurators, Pontius Pilate, that John the Baptist appeared as the herald of the Messiah, and our Lord himself fulfilled his ministry. It was Pilate who gave permission for Jesus' crucifixion, yielding to the demand of Jesus' enemies and hoping in this way to keep peace at a crucial hour during Passover week in the spring of the year 29 A. D.

EVENTS FOLLOWING THE PASSOVER

Jesus and his disciples had come to Jerusalem to keep the Passover, as did every faithful Jew unless he lived too far from Palestine. The Master himself had realized, even before he came up from Galilee for the feast, that this would be his last visit to the Holy City, that persecution, suffering, death awaited him there. But he went, nevertheless, undaunted by the prospect.

And as he had anticipated, so events turned out. He was seized at midnight on the very eve of the Passover, while praying in the Garden of Gethsemane. After a hasty and illegal "trial" by his enemies, he was denounced before Pilate as an insurrectionist against the Roman government. After a weak and half-hearted attempt to save him, Pilate yielded to popular clamor —artfully roused outside the *prætorium* by the priests— and Jesus was led away to be crucified.

The resurrection.—Meanwhile, the disciples remained in Jerusalem, hiding, fearful to venture out lest they too should be mobbed by some fanatical crowd of fellow pilgrims now in the city. Only a few faithful women followers of Jesus, and his "acquaintances," looked on from a distance while he was hanging upon the cross (Luke 23:49). As soon as the Sabbath following the Passover had ended, some of the disciples started for their homes, disappointed, disillusioned, compelled to admit that the hope of the kingdom of God and their faith in Jesus' Messiahship had all been a tragic mistake. Others, like the women who went early on Sunday morning (the morning after the Sabbath) to the sepulcher, remained in Jerusalem to do what they could to give Jesus a suitable burial; for on Friday afternoon, as sunset approached (which meant the arrival of the Sabbath), Jesus' body had been very hastily taken down from the cross and temporarily laid, unwrapped and unprepared for burial, in the new tomb of Joseph of Arimathæa, a secret disciple. Going early to the tomb, as it began to dawn on the first day of the week, with spices and linen in which to wrap the body, they were amazed to find the great stone door of the tomb rolled away and the body of Jesus gone.

Just then appeared two men in dazzling apparel, bidding them go and tell the other disciples that Jesus was risen from the dead! But the disciples when they heard it could not believe. Peter and one of the others ran to the tomb, found it, as the women had found it, empty, but saw no vision nor heard any words. It was too good to be true, that Jesus was not dead but still living, still their Master, still Messiah. Someone must have taken away his body during the night!

But that very day Jesus himself appeared to them, convincing them beyond any doubt that he was risen from the dead, really alive, and their Master still. To Peter, to the faithful eleven, to the devoted women, to two disciples on their way home to Emmaus, Jesus appeared and proved that he was still alive, still Messiah, still continuing his work for God and God's kingdom.

This was the turning-point in the disciples' faith, and the most important hour in all Christian history. Only this conviction that Jesus was still living, still present with them, still preparing for the coming of God's kingdom "in power and great glory," enabled them to conquer their doubts and fears and carry out the mission which he had for them to perform as his representatives.

The ascension.—Several times after that they saw him, singly or in groups, and always he was the same. Though "glorified," and possessing a "spiritual body" which entered the room where they were gathered even though the doors and windows were barred, it was the same Jesus they had known in the happy, hopeful days in Galilee, which now seemed so long ago. Not only in

the final chapters of the Gospels do we find accounts of
Jesus' appearances after the resurrection; but also in
one of the letters of Paul, written long before any of the
Gospels, there is a list of his appearances—to Cephas
(Peter), to the Twelve, to more than five hundred
brethren at once, to James, then to all the apostles, and
last of all to Paul himself (1 Corinthians 15: 4–8).

For several weeks, therefore, the disciples remained
in Jerusalem, sharing these experiences, and, in obedience
to Jesus' command, waiting for the "baptism of the
Holy Spirit" which had been promised since the days
of John and was expected to precede the coming of the
Kingdom.

At last, one day, as they were gathered on the Mount
of Olives (where Jesus had been seized by the high
priest's servants on the night before he died), the Master
appeared to them once more, and they asked him, "Lord,
are you now about to restore the kingdom to Israel?"
In spite of all that had taken place, in spite of all that
Jesus had taught them, they still expected the reign of
God to be an earthly kingdom, with a throne set up in
Jerusalem, and with armies and captains and collectors
of tribute to serve under Jesus as king! But he replied
to them,

> "It is not for you to know the times or seasons,
> which the Father has fixed by his own authority.
> But you shall receive power, when the Holy Spirit
> has come upon you, and you shall be my witnesses,
> not only in Jerusalem but in all Judæa and Samaria,
> and to the very ends of the earth."—Acts 1: 7-8.

While they looked and listened to these words he
vanished from them. He went up, and a cloud hid him
from their sight. And there appeared two men in white

apparel—as in the vision of the women at the sepulcher
—who said, "Men of Galilee, why do you stand gazing
up into heaven? This Jesus, who has been received up
into heaven, shall come again in the same manner as
you have seen him go."

And so they returned to Jerusalem, to the upper room,
where Jesus had eaten the Passover with them, and
engaged in prayer and waited for the fulfillment of
Jesus' promise.

THE CHOICE OF MATTHIAS

There were now only eleven disciples, since Judas, the
betrayer, had committed suicide.

The "Eleven."—These were Peter and James and
John and Andrew, Philip and Thomas, Bartholomew
and Matthew, James the son of Alphæus, Simon the
zealot, and Jude the son (or perhaps brother) of James.
These all, Luke says, "with one accord continued sted-
fast in prayer, together with certain women (who had
come up with them from Galilee, and some who lived in
Jerusalem), and Mary the mother of Jesus, and his
brethren (who had at last been convinced of Jesus'
Messiahship, and followed him to the Passover) (Acts
1: 14).

A new apostle.—For some reason—probably because
Jesus had chosen just twelve men, no more and no less,
to be his disciples—it was felt that some one must be
chosen to fill Judas' place. The Kingdom, as they
expected it, was to be the restoration of the ancient
monarchy of David; and the twelve disciples were,
therefore, to be twelve "judges" set over the tribes.
This may be the reason why the number twelve was so
carefully preserved. Or it may have been because each
apostle was expected to be a witness for Jesus to one

of the Jewish tribes dispersed throughout the world. In some such way they may have understood the requirement. Whichever it was, Peter arose at one of the meetings of the disciples and other followers of Jesus (about one hundred and twenty persons in all), and proposed that another "witness" be chosen.

> **"Of the men who have been with us all the time that the Lord Jesus went in and out among us, beginning from the baptism of John and until the day when he was received up from us, one must be chosen to be a witness with us of his resurrection."**
> **—Acts 1: 21, 22.**

There were two nominations, Joseph Barsabbas (who had still another name, *Justus*) and Matthias—disciples who are not mentioned elsewhere in the New Testament, and of whom, therefore, we know nothing. But instead of voting, as we should do, they followed the usual Jewish custom of prayer and casting lots: for they felt that the choice was not theirs but God's, and he would show his preference in this way. "Thou, Lord," they prayed, "who knowest the hearts of all men, show which of these two is the one whom thou hast chosen, to take the place in this ministry and apostleship of Judas, who fell away" (Acts 1: 24, 25). Then they cast lots; and the lot fell to Matthias. "And he was numbered with the Twelve."

Witnesses for Jesus.—This, then, was the very beginning of the Christian Church—when these few disciples, mostly Galileans and not at home in Jerusalem, but held there for a purpose and united by an absolute conviction of Jesus' resurrection and continued life and Messiahship and coming reign—when these men calmly set about their task of "witnessing" to Jesus, and chose one more to fill out their band. Their backs were now turned forever upon their homes in Galilee, their business, their old associations and friendships. Their task was one, and their whole purpose in life was to accomplish it. Their fears had vanished: it did not matter that the authorities were hostile and would certainly oppose their movement. They were men under command, and they were obedient. Jesus was their Master still, and he had a work for them to do.

Out of that tiny group, hiding at first in fear in an upper room in the ancient city of Jerusalem, grew in time the great Christian Church, the church of the empire, and the leading religion of the Western world— a religion still making conquests, and bent upon bringing the whole world to Christ, our religion to-day, twenty centuries after the apostles. Twelve men! —and most of them Galileans, scarcely able to speak their own language well; men despised as ignorant and crude by the learned priests and Pharisees of the capital; uncouth fishermen and peasants, one a publican and one a fanatic, a "zealot"—these were the "weak ones of the earth" whom God chose and used in accomplishing the holiest of his purposes.

STUDY TOPICS

1. Review the first part of Chapter II of *The Life and Times of Jesus*. Describe the relation of Palestine to the Roman Empire at the beginning of the first century. Find Syria and Palestine on a map of the empire. Locate them on an outline map in your notebook.
2. Read the last chapter of Saint Luke and the first chapter of the book of Acts, and see how they fit together. Make a brief outline of the two chapters.

3. Look up the list of Jesus' appearances in 1 Corinthians 15. Copy it in your notebook.
4. Where was the Mount of Olives? How far was it from Jerusalem? What is "a Sabbath day's journey," and why is it so called? (Acts 1 : 12.)
5. Describe the great change which took place in the minds of the disciples between the crucifixion and the ascension. What produced this change?
6. Who were "the women"? See Luke 8 : 1-3; 23 : 27-28, 49, 55; John 19 : 25; Mark 16 : 1.
7. Why was Matthias chosen "by lot"?
8. In what sense are Christians to-day to be "witnesses for Jesus"? Does God still bless the testimony even of poor and uneducated disciples?

CHAPTER III

THE DAY OF PENTECOST

As the disciples continued waiting for the fulfillment of "the promise," the festival of Pentecost drew near. As its name implies in Greek, this was fifty days after the Passover, and was the occasion of special services at the Temple. It was the old "Feast of Weeks," or "Feast of First Fruits" (of the wheat harvest), described in the Old Testament; and it was the second of the three great festivals to be celebrated at the national sanctuary, the temple, by all Jewish men and boys over twelve. Its importance was further enhanced by a growing belief that the sacred Law had been given to Moses at Sinai on the sixth or seventh day of the month Siwan, the day on which Pentecost fell.

The disciples, as Luke said at the end of his Gospel, "were continually in the temple blessing God." That is, they attended the services at the regular hours of worship, the morning and evening sacrifices, and the "hours of prayer" through the day. But they also had meetings of their own for prayer, held probably in the upper room where they were staying (Acts 1: 13–14). It was here that the Master "showed himself alive after his passion by many infallible proofs, appearing to them (from time to time) during a space of forty days, and speaking the things concerning the kingdom of God" (Acts 1: 3).

THE COMING OF THE SPIRIT

The promise whose fulfillment they awaited was the one which John the Baptist had proclaimed, in announcing the coming of the Messiah: "There comes one mightier than I, the latchet of whose shoes I am not worthy to unloose; he shall baptize you with the Holy Spirit and with fire . . ." (Luke 3: 16). Jesus had repeated and renewed it when he charged the disciples "not to depart from Jerusalem, but to wait for the promise of the Father, which, said he, you have heard from me. For John indeed baptized with water; but you shall be baptized with the Holy Spirit not many days hence" (Acts 1: 4–5).

The wind and the fire.—As they waited, earnestly engaged in prayer in the quiet upper chamber on the morning of the day of Pentecost, a strange, mysterious event occurred. Of a sudden there "came a sound from heaven like the rushing of a mighty wind, filling the whole house where they were sitting"—such a sound as one hears sometimes at the beginning of a storm; first the intense calm, broken by a faint, far-off rustling, then the rush and roar of a wind growing stronger every second till the house shakes and the windows rattle, so that it can only be described as coming from a distance, out of the sky, "from heaven" (Acts 2: 2; compare 4: 31).

Then, as in the manifestation of Yahweh to the ancient prophet Elijah (1 Kings 19: 9–13), the wind was followed by an appearance resembling fire. "There appeared to them[1] tongues which were being distributed among them, like flames of fire, and rested upon each one of them."

Speaking with tongues.—But strange as was this experience, it was at once followed by one still more striking. The disciples, who were mostly Galilæans and had attracted attention in Jerusalem by their uncouth pronunciation of the mother tongue (Matthew 26: 73),

---

[1] "Appeared" as in a vision: the words are ordinarily used of visions.

now "began to speak with different tongues, as the Spirit gave them utterance."

> "Now there were dwelling at Jerusalem Jews, devout men, from every nation under heaven. And when this sound was heard, the multitude came together and were confounded, for every man heard them speaking in his own language. And they were all amazed and marveled, saying, Behold, are not all these which speak Galilæans? And how hear we every man in his own language wherein we were born?—Parthians and Medes and Elamites, and the dwellers in Mesopotamia, in Judæa and Cappadocia, in Pontus and Asia, in Phrygia and Pamphylia, in Egypt and the parts of Libya about Cyrene, and sojourners from Rome, both Jews and proselytes, Cretans and Arabians, we do hear them speak in our own tongues the mighty works of God! And they were all amazed and perplexed, saying one to another, 'What does this mean?' But others said, 'They are full of new wine.' "—Acts 2: 5-13.

This story, taken from one of the earliest records of the church, presents a clear and vivid picture of the scene: the Jews and proselytes gathered at Jerusalem; Passover pilgrims still lingering after the feast; visitors come up to keep Pentecost or the Feast of Weeks; others who had settled in the holy city of Judaism to spend their remaining years under the very shadow of the Temple; the exultant disciples, speaking in a strange, new manner, a group of men all speaking in other "tongues."

PETER'S SERMON

We can understand the surprise of the multitude as they listened to the words of the Twelve. It seems strange to us, if the disciples were heard speaking in various foreign languages, that some in the crowd supposed them intoxicated with new wine. Yet this helps us to imagine more clearly the picture. The disciples were jubilant, and felt exalted, free and happy. "The promise" had at last been fulfilled! They could scarcely contain their joy. Their hearts overflowed. It was an hour of strange, mysterious rejoicing, and the men in the street could not understand it since they did not share in its cause.

Prophecy fulfilled.—Peter, who was the spokesman for the band of disciples, rose up to explain their strange words and actions to the crowd. His address is the earliest Christian sermon of which we have any record, outside the teaching of Jesus, and it is well worth while to study it carefully. We must remember that Peter was a fisherman, a plain man of the people. His words were few, like Lincoln's, and went straight to the heart of his subject.

> "Men of Judæa, and all who dwell in Jerusalem, listen while I explain to you what has happened. These men are not drunk, as you suppose—impossible! for this is only nine o'clock in the morning. Rather, what you see before you is the fulfillment of the words of Joel the prophet,
>> 'And it shall be in the last days, saith God,
>> I will pour forth my Spirit upon all flesh;
>> And your sons and your daughters shall prophesy,
>> And your young men shall see visions,
>> And your old men shall dream dreams;
>> Yea, and on the very slaves and handmaids in those days
>> Shall my Spirit be outpoured. . . .
>> Before the Day of the Lord arrives,

That great and notable Day—
And it shall come to pass
That whosoever calls on the name of the Lord
    shall be saved.' "

—Acts 2: 14-21.

Jesus the Messiah. —We now begin to see the meaning of "the promise" for the disciples themselves. Jesus their Master, still living, risen from the dead, ascended to God's right hand, was about to return in glory and hold the Last Judgment, and set up his reign on earth as Messiah, as Prince in the kingdom of God over a renewed and purified world. The outpouring of the Spirit was one of the events which prophecy was understood to reveal as preceding this "great and notable Day of the Lord."

Now Peter turns from the immediate experience of the day and its explanation to the real cause lying back of it all—Jesus' Messiahship, resurrection, and present glory.

> "Men of Israel, hear these words. Jesus of Nazareth, a man approved by God unto you through mighty works and wonders and signs which God did through him in your very midst, as you yourselves know—he, being delivered up by the determinate counsel and foreknowledge of God, was crucified and put to death at the hands of lawless men. But God raised him up, having loosed the pangs of death: for it was not possible that death should restrain him."—Acts 2: 22-24.

Peter then proves this point by a long quotation from the Psalms, the words, "Thou wilt not leave my soul in Sheol," being understood of Jesus' death and burial. "This Jesus," he continues, "did God raise up; and we all are witnesses to the fact." Quoting another Psalm, with the words,

> **"The Lord said unto my Lord,**
> **Sit thou on my right hand**
> **Until I make thine enemies thy footstool,"**

(this was understood of Jesus' exaltation to God's right hand in glory) he concluded,

> **"Being exalted, therefore, at the right hand of God, and having received from the Father the promise of the Holy Spirit, he has poured forth this, which you yourselves see and hear. . . . Let all the house of Israel know for certain that God has made him both Lord and Christ, this Jesus whom you crucified!"—Acts 2: 33-36.**

The effect of the sermon.—We scarcely realize the power of these simple words, reinforced as they were by appeal to the sacred and familiar writings of the Old Testament, reinforced still more strongly by the strange events of the morning which all had witnessed. Awe filled the hearts of Peter's hearers. His plain, straightforward talk convinced them. "Brethren, what shall we do?" was their eager response. And Peter replied,

> **"Repent, and be baptized every one of you in the name of Jesus Christ for the remission of sins; and you too shall receive the gift of the Holy Spirit. For the promise is to you—not to us alone—to you and your children, and to all that are afar off, even as many as the Lord our God shall call to him."—Acts 2: 37-39.**

With these and other words of exhortation he urged his hearers to repentance. "Then they that received his word," Luke adds, "were baptized. And there were added to them that day about three thousand souls."

Beginning of the church's growth.—Such was the success of the first day's preaching of the gospel by the apostles, the first-fruits of "the promise" of the Spirit. Into that strange experience of the Spirit's coming and his power, the sound like a wind from heaven, the fire which "distributed itself" into tongue-like flames above the head of each apostle, the "talking with tongues"— into that strange and mystical experience we cannot enter. We cannot explain it, because we have never experienced it; possibly no one can explain ecstasy of that sort. There were other experiences somewhat like it (see Acts 4: 31, and many references to "prophesying" or "speaking with tongues" in Saint Paul's letters—for example, 1 Corinthians 12–14). Usually, the prophet or speaker with a strange tongue required an interpreter to explain his utterances. The strange gift died away gradually, and disappeared by the end of the second century. Occasionally since those days, persons have been said to "speak with tongues," either in ecstasy, when they spoke words that no one could understand, or when repeating by some strange trick of memory words in foreign languages which they had some time heard. This is not identical with the apostles' experience on Pentecost, but it at least helps us to understand the impression their words made upon the minds of their hearers.

At the same time we must not overlook the fact that what converted in one day three thousand Jews and proselytes to the Christian faith was not the strange events, the mystical experiences of the apostles, alone; rather it was Peter's plain, straightforward, reasoned appeal to the consciences of men who had known Jesus of Nazareth and had seen him innocently put to death, and were now told that he had risen from the dead and ascended to the throne of God. The outpouring of the Spirit was only the latest proof of his exaltation and power. That is what brought three thousand men to their knees in penitence, and started the church on its wonderful, expansive growth.

STUDY TOPICS

1. What was a proselyte? Look up in the Bible dictionary. Define "mystical," "ecstasy," "pentecostal."
2. Recall from your study of the life of Christ the description of the Temple services. Look up "Pentecost" in the Bible dictionary.
3. Read the story of Elijah at Horeb (in First Kings), and note any resemblances to the story of Pentecost.
4. Locate on the map the peoples represented in the throng at Jerusalem described in Acts 2:9-11. Note that Luke lists them in a general order from east to west—but not very far west.
5. How did Peter refute the charge that the disciples were drunk with new wine?
6. Name some of the "mighty works" of Jesus which would be known to Peter's hearers (see Chapters IX, X, etc., of *The Life and Times of Jesus*).
7. Read the whole passage in Joel, and study it as a prediction of the "signs" to precede "the Day of the Lord."
8. Look up "speaking with tongues" in the Bible dictionary.
9. Is repentance still essential to becoming or remaining a Christian? Show how Saint Peter's words are true to-day. How do they apply to us?

A great many, probably the majority of modern scholars hold that the disciples' experience on the day of Pentecost was simply the "glossolalia," or ecstatic "speaking with (another) tongue" common in the apostolic age—at least in the Gentile churches. What this was we know fairly well from the letters of Paul—semi-articulate cries of rejoicing, prayers, blessings, confessions of sin, "prophecies," and so on. It is noteworthy that Paul himself laid no great weight on this strange experience. Then in the course of time the "glossolalia" was forgotten, and the tradition was recorded as in the second chapter of Acts—as the "gift of divers languages," equipping the apostles to "preach the gospel to every creature," and "make disciples of all nations." The essential thing, of course, is an experience which *convinced the disciples themselves* that the Holy Spirit had been given them, that God was with them, that Jesus was coming "in power." The strange phenomenon itself had little if any effect upon the multitude (see verses 12, 13), which is just what happened later on when the Christians in Corinth "spoke with tongues" (1 Corinthians 14: 23). The gift was useful only to its possessor (1 Corinthians 14: 2–4): in this case it was just the kind of proof the disciples awaited that God approved their course and that he was actually present with them, through his Spirit.

It is most wonderful how God accommodates himself to the limitations and necessities of men. We do not need such proof to-day because we have other proofs of his presence and power (do we sufficiently recognize them?). No doubt this is one reason for the absence, or infrequency, of miracles in modern times.[1]

---

[1] See Dr. Hayes' book on *The Gift of Tongues.*

CHAPTER IV

PETER AND JOHN IN THE TEMPLE

THE accounts which have come down to us regarding the disciples in Jerusalem after the resurrection are among the oldest traditions of the Christian Church. Like the early narratives of the Old Testament, like the traditional histories of other religions, these accounts were circulated "orally"—that is, by word of mouth, not written down—for many years before the New Testament was written. Although the New Testament was written in Greek, there is evidence that these narratives were originally handed down in Aramaic, the language of Palestine, of Jesus and the Twelve.

"THE ACTS OF THE APOSTLES"

Our only authority for the history of these early years is the book of *Acts*, the fifth writing contained in our New Testament.

The author of Acts.—This book was written by the author of the third Gospel, the evangelist Saint Luke (compare Luke 1: 1–4 and Acts 1: 1, 2), who wrote it as a continuation of the narrative of Jesus' life, and dedicated it to his friend Theophilus. Luke wrote, probably, about the year 85, though there are some scholars who hold that the date was much earlier. Luke was the friend of Paul, his traveling companion on several journeys, and "the beloved physician" who was with him even as a prisoner in Rome.

Luke's Gospel has been pronounced "the most beauti-

ful book in the world," and the *Acts* is its fitting sequel.
Writing at the late date of, say, 85 A. D., fifty years
after the events described, Luke delved deeply into the
history of the past, as a historian to-day would do in
writing an account of the Civil War, and searched out
the most trustworthy records, and oral or written, in
order to "trace the course of all things accurately from
the first."   Just as the first two chapters of the Gospel,
so also the first twelve chapters of *Acts* were probably
translated by Luke (or for him) out of the Aramaic
language in the most charming, simple style of the
whole Greek New Testament.   In addition to this, he
used, in the later chapters, where he describes Paul's
journeys, his own diary written down at the time (see
Acts 16: 10ff., and note the use of "we" and "us").

Its trustworthiness and its purpose.—Thus although
the *Acts* is our only "source" for the earliest period of
the church's history, we have great confidence in its
narratives, for its author, Luke, was a careful, accurate,
faithful student and historian of the period, who loved
the church whose story he tells, and who himself shared
in the great movement which brought it out of an
upper room in the city of Jerusalem and planted it in
the very heart of the empire.   Moreover, he personally
knew the great men who led this movement.   As a
Gentile, a physician, a student and lover of literature, a
citizen of the world, he was able to see the events of the
past generation in true perspective; and he was proud
to trace the great expansion of Christianity in those
fifty years since the crucifixion.

For that was his object in writing—to show Christianity expanding as the new world-religion, divinely
revealed, spreading until it filled every part of the
known world, deserving the esteem and protection of

the emperor rather than the persecution which was then
breaking out, in the days of Domitian.

Condition of the church described.—And although
"Acts of the Apostles" is its title, it does not give all of
the acts of all of the apostles. Peter and Paul are the
chief characters in the story; John and James and the
others take very minor parts. Nevertheless, it gives us
enough to present a fairly clear picture of the condition
of the church in those far-off days of its existence. For
instance, at the conclusion of the account of the day of
Pentecost, the following picture is sketched:

> "And they continued stedfastly in the apostles'
> teaching and fellowship, in the breaking of bread
> and in prayers.
>
> "And fear came upon every soul; and many won-
> ders and signs were performed through the apos-
> tles. And all they that believed were together and
> had all things common; and they sold their posses-
> sions and goods and parted them to all, according as
> any man had need. And day by day, continuing
> stedfastly with one accord in the temple, and break-
> ing bread at home, they partook their food with
> gladness and singleness of heart, praising God and
> having favor with all the people. And the Lord
> added to them day by day those that were being
> saved."—Acts 2: 42-47.

The simplicity of life, the earnestness and devotion of
the early Christians in Jerusalem are quite apparent in
this picture.

THE BEGGAR AT THE BEAUTIFUL GATE

One of their visits to the Temple is described in the
very next chapter—a visit which had important consequences for the disciples.

Not alms but restoration.—Peter and John were going up to the Temple at one of the hours of prayer, about three in the afternoon. Now there was a man who had been lame from birth who was laid each day beside the "door of the temple which is called Beautiful," to ask alms of those who passed through. Seeing Peter and John about to enter, he asked them for alms. But the apostles had no money; and, moreover, the lame man really needed something else far more than money. Peter remembered the way in which Jesus had restored the helpless, instead of doling out alms; he remembered also the Master's command to "heal the sick." So he turned and, gazing directly at him, commanded, "Look at us!" The beggar of course expected to receive some money and readily complied. Instead, Peter said to him: "Silver and gold have I none; but such as I have will I give you! In the name of Jesus Christ of Nazareth, walk!" Then, taking him by the right hand, he raised him up. At once his feet and ankles grew strong, and leaping up he first stood, then began to walk freely, and entered the Temple, walking and leaping and praising God. The people were amazed when they saw him, for everyone recognized him as the man who had sat for years begging alms beside the Temple gate—and now he was walking about and praising God for his restoration!

Peter's address to the people.—Filled with wonder and amazement, the people crowded into the portico called Solomon's Porch, along the eastern side of the outer court, and waited to see what would happen next. Then Peter, as usual seizing the occasion, addressed them in simple, outspoken language.

"Men of Israel, why do you marvel at this, as if it were some portent? Or why gaze at us, as if by our

own power or piety we had made the man walk?
The God of Abraham, of Isaac and of Jacob, the
God of our fathers, has glorified his Servant Jesus—
whom you delivered up and denied before Pilate,
when he was determined to release him. You denied the Holy and Righteous One (the Messiah),
asking for a murderer to be released in his stead.
You killed the Prince of Life! But God raised him
from the dead, whose witnesses we are. And it
was by faith in his name that this man was made
strong, whom you yourselves see and know; yes,
that faith which is through him has brought this to
pass in your very presence!"—Acts 3 : 12-16.

Then he continues with an appeal to the consciences of
his hearers.

"Brethren, I know that it was in ignorance that
you crucified Jesus, as did your rulers. Therefore
repent, and turn again, that your sins may be blotted
out . . . and that God may send you the Messiah
who has been appointed, even Jesus: who must
remain in heaven until the times of restoration of
all things, foretold by the prophets. . . . And instead of a curse, for your rejection of the Messiah.
God has in fact raised up his Servant and sent him
to bless you, in turning away every one of you from
your iniquities."—Acts 3 : 17-26.

BEFORE THE COUNCIL

At this moment the chief priests and captain of the
Temple (the head of the Temple police) and certain of
the Sadducees, having heard the commotion, came upon
them. These were members of the same group which
had put Jesus to death. They were determined to stamp
out the growing movement of his followers before any-

thing further came of it. Now to find his disciples still in the Temple, actually addressing and teaching the people (this was the priests' prerogative), and telling them about his resurrection from the dead (which seemed nonsense to the Sadducees)—this was too much! So they laid hands upon Peter and John and shut them up in prison for the night.

Nevertheless, Peter's words had not been without effect. "Many of them that heard the word believed; and the number of the believers came to be about five thousand." All men "glorified God for that which was done," for the lame man was over forty years old, and the story of his restoration had a great effect upon all who heard it.

"By what power or in what name?"—The next morning the "rulers and elders and scribes" held a meeting to consider what should be done with Peter and John. "Annas the high priest was there, and Caiphas and John and Alexander, and as many as were of the kindred of the high priest"—the very ones who had conducted the false "trial" at which Jesus had been condemned to death.

The first question which they asked the apostles was this: "By what power or in what name have you done this?" That is, they assumed the apostles to be workers of magic, possessed of some supernatural "power" made effective by pronouncing some particular "name" or formula over people. To this question Peter, being naturally the spokesman, answered boldly,

> **"Rulers of the people, and elders, if we are now to be brought into court and publicly examined for doing a good deed to a helpless man, let it be known to you and to all Israel that in the 'name' of the**

Messiah, Jesus of Nazareth, whom you crucified, and
whom God raised from the dead—in his name this
man stands here before you sound and well."—Acts
4: 9-10.

The boldness of the apostles.—This was a brave
answer as well as a true one. The two Galilæan fishermen stood helpless in the presence of their bitterest and
most powerful enemies, the enemies who had put their
Master to death only a short time ago and were now
determined to spare no pains in annihilating the faith of
his followers. "When they beheld the boldness of Peter
and John," Luke says, "and perceived that they were
unlearned and ignorant men, they marveled; and they
took knowledge of them, that they had been with Jesus"
(Acts 4: 13). Moreover, seeing that the man who had
been healed was even then standing beside them, grateful for their goodness to him, they could say nothing
against it.

So they ordered the prisoners taken out of the court,
and conferred among themselves. It was impossible to
deny that the miracle had taken place, for everyone in
Jerusalem now knew about it. Nor was there any
charge which could be brought against the disciples, such
as magic or witchcraft or an injury done to the lame
man. Their only course was to threaten the apostles
and order them to cease teaching in the name of Jesus
or using his name to heal the sick.

Recalling Peter and John into the council, they gave
them this charge. But the apostles immediately answered: "Whether it is right in the sight of God to
obey you rather than God, you must judge. For our
part, we cannot but speak the things that we have seen
and heard."

The prayers of the church.—Being released, the two apostles returned to the upper room and reported all that had occurred in the council chamber. When the story had been told, the whole band knelt down and prayed for strength and guidance in the persecution which seemed presently coming upon them. "And now, Lord, look upon their threatenings; and grant unto thy servants to speak thy word with all boldness, while thou stretchest forth thy hand to heal; that signs and wonders may be done through the name of thy holy Servant Jesus" (Acts 4: 29–30).

And when they had prayed, the place was shaken wherein they were gathered together, and they were all filled with the Holy Spirit, and spoke the word of God with boldness. It was another Pentecost, with the power of the Spirit manifest among them. In the midst of danger and threatened persecution they had the assurance of God's favor and presence. If their enemies could "take knowledge of them, that they had been with Jesus," they themselves were no less conscious of being in his presence still, through the Holy Spirit. This gave them courage in proclaiming "the word."

STUDY TOPICS

1. Tell how the history of the earliest days of Christianity has come down to us.
2. Turn to the diagram in *The Life and Times of Jesus*, facing page 193, and locate the Beautiful Gate, Solomon's Porch, and the Sanhedrin's Council Chamber.
3. Recall the reference to the Beautiful Gate in "The Vision of Sir Launfal." Can you quote it?
4. Who were the Sadducees? Recall from your study of the Life of Christ, or look up in the Bible dictionary. What distinguished them from the Pharisees?

5. Read carefully Peter's sermon at the Temple, and analyze it in the way his first sermon was treated in Chapter III.
6. Study carefully the prayer of the apostles (Acts 4: 24–30). Note that quotations from the Old Testament are found in all the apostles' utterances: their minds were steeped in scripture. Note that the current Jewish belief in predestination is taken for granted, and compare Peter's words in Acts 2: 23. What did they ask for in this prayer, personal safety or the spread of God's work? Of what value were "signs and wonders" in their situation?
7. Read Acts 3 and 4 and make a list of the titles given to Jesus therein.
8. How did men explain the boldness of the apostles in testifying for their faith? Should their example inspire us to like courage? And does the explanation of their "boldness" suggest how we too may become courageous? Name some ways in which we ought to be bold witnesses for Christ.

CHAPTER V

THE GROWTH OF THE CHURCH

THE church in Jerusalem had a remarkably sudden growth at the first. From the one hundred and twenty who were gathered together between Passover and the day of Pentecost the number had grown until now it included thousands (Acts 1: 15; 2: 41; 4: 4). There was no better place than Jerusalem, with its sojourners and proselytes from every nation, in which to proclaim the message of Jesus' Messiahship; there was no better time than those weeks in spring and early summer when vast throngs of pilgrims filled the city. Moreover, in Jerusalem people had either heard Jesus himself teach in the Temple, or had at least heard about him and his message and his unjust condemnation by the authorities. It is not surprising, then, that "the multitude of the disciples multiplied in Jerusalem exceedingly"—even some of the priests were converted (Acts 6: 7) and Levites (Acts 4: 36).

"ALL THINGS COMMON"

In a city filled with strangers, a holy city of pilgrims, without sufficient natural industries to support it and not well located for commerce, it was only natural that there should be many poor. Old persons who had saved barely enough to keep them till they died, and who had come here to live near the Temple (Luke 2: 25, 36, 38); priestly families returning from the Dispersion, or those whose land had been sold or confiscated by the government—such people were found in abundance in the city.

The care of the poor.—Many such persons were found among the "multitude of the disciples"; and it is noteworthy that the Christian Church, which has taught the world the practice of charity, was even thus early busy with the care of its poorer members.

> "And the multitude of them that believed were of one heart and soul; and not one of them said that any of the things which he possessed was his own; but they had all things in common. And with great power gave the apostles their witness to the resurrection of the Lord Jesus; and great grace was upon them all. For neither was there any among them that lacked; for as many as were possessors of lands or houses sold them, and brought the price of the things sold and laid it at the apostles' feet; and distribution was made unto each, according as any had need."—Acts 4: 32-35.

This was not "communism," such as has been practiced in Russia under the Bolshevists and elsewhere from time to time in human history. It was not an attempt to carry out an economic "program." It was, rather, simple charity, under the strong impulse of a feeling of brotherhood as the disciples of a common Master, and with the expectation of the immediate return of Jesus in glory (when earthly property would be no longer valuable). That the condition did not long continue is seen from the fact that a few years later Saint Paul took up a collection of money in the churches of Asia and Greece for the poor "saints which are at Jerusalem" (Romans 15: 26). Failure no doubt resulted from the using up of all money derived from the sale of property, so that in the end the Jerusalem Christians were left with neither property nor funds. But who shall

say that their charity was mistaken? It was not long
before the property, and, indeed, the lives, of disciples
were jeopardized by persecution. Their wealth, such as
it was, was better spent upon the poor, as the Master
counseled (Luke 18: 22), than hoarded and finally lost.

Barnabas' gift.—Among those who sold their land
and brought the money to the apostles for distribution
to the needy was Joseph Barnabas. Though a native
of Cyprus, he was a Levite, that is, a descendant of the
house of Levi, whose office it was to assist the priests in
the Temple, to sing or blow trumpets at the sacrifices,
and to serve as wardens or guards of the sacred edifice.
The Levites had received, after the exile, an apportion-
ment of land to the north and west of Jerusalem; and
Barnabas' field must have been his patrimony, inherited
by his family from those far-off days. It was the generous
gift of a man sincerely in earnest. We shall not be surprised, therefore, to hear more of him later on.

Ananias and Sapphira.—In contrast to the generosity of Barnabas and others like him, the story continues with the incident of two persons, Ananias and
his wife Sapphira, who sold some property and kept
back part of the price, pretending to have given it all.
Peter knew of their deception, and when Ananias came
in he rebuked him sternly. He did not censure him for
selling the land, or for keeping back part of the money,
but for pretending to have given the whole when in
truth he gave only a part: "How is it that you have
conceived this scheme? You have not lied to men but
to God!"

So great was the shock of discovery that the man fell
to the ground and died. Not long afterward Sapphira
came in. Peter asked her if she had sold the land for
such-and-such a price. She answered, "Yes, for so

much." Peter sternly rebuked her also—"Why have you agreed to tempt the Spirit of the Lord in this way? Behold, the feet of them that have carried your husband out dead are at the door—and they shall carry you out too!" At that she likewise fell down and died.

This event filled with awe the hearts of the believers. It seemed the very beginning of the divine judgment upon deceivers. It was the miraculous and immediate punishment, wrought by the Holy Spirit, upon those who had tried to "play too safe," to worship both God and Mammon, to deceive the brotherhood, playing false to the spirit of charity, aiming to get credit for generosity and unselfishness and at the same time enjoy the possession of at least a part of their property should the Kingdom finally fail to appear. The crime and its swift punishment left a deep impression upon the early church, as we must infer from the preservation of this anecdote among the earliest stories of the community in Jerusalem.

Healing the sick.—Jesus had not only commanded his disciples to preach the gospel; he had also bidden them heal the sick (Luke 9: 1–6; 10: 9; etc.). It now seemed that the ministry of the Master himself was being continued through the apostles.

> "By the hands of the apostles were many signs and wonders wrought among the people; and they were all of one accord in Solomon's Porch. But of the rest durst no man join himself to them. Howbeit the people magnified them, and believers were the more added to the Lord, multitudes both of men and women; insomuch that they even carried out the sick into the streets, and laid them on beds and couches, that, as Peter came by, at least his shadow might fall over some of them. And there

> also came together the multitude from the cities
> round about Jerusalem, bringing sick folk and those
> who were vexed with unclean spirits; and they were
> all healed."—Acts 5: 12-16.

Nothing convinced men more completely of the truth
of the gospel than the manifest power which accompanied its preaching, power to heal the sick and exorcize
evil spirits.

RENEWED OPPOSITION

The movement was now spreading so rapidly, the
popularity of the apostles was increasing to such a wide
extent, that the high priest and the party of the Sadducees (who had, as we said, direct oversight of the
Temple) "were filled with jealousy, and laid hands on
the apostles and put them in public ward" once more.

Preaching in the Temple.—But in the night they
were mysteriously released—the story says, "An angel
of the Lord opened the prison doors, and brought
them out and said, 'Go, stand and speak to the people
in the temple all the words of this Life.'" As soon as
the Temple gates were opened in the morning, therefore,
the apostles entered and began to teach.

Meanwhile the Sanhedrin had been assembled by the
high priest and his associates, in order that legal process
might be taken against the leaders of the new movement,
for if this enthusiastic new faith progressed, the time
would come, they felt, when the nation would be further
embroiled with Rome. For "Messianism," the dream of
the coming kingdom of God, meant nothing to the
Sadducees but social unrest, refusal of the tribute, and
armed revolt.

Sending for the prisoners, what was their surprise to
find the jail locked and guarded but empty! The

apostles had escaped during the night! And what was their further surprise to find that the men, instead of fleeing the city, were actually once more in the Temple, teaching the people their forbidden doctrine!

The Temple police were at once dispatched to bring them into court, which they did without show of violence —for fear the people might stone them.

Once more before the council.—The high priest reminded them of his former charge: "We strictly commanded you not to teach in this name; and behold, you have filled Jerusalem with your teaching and intend to bring this man's blood upon us!" To this Peter and the others replied, just as on their former appearance before the council, "We must obey God."

> **"We must obey God rather than men. The God of our fathers raised up Jesus, whom ye slew, hanging him on a tree. Him did God exalt at his right hand to be Prince and Saviour, to give repentance to Israel, and remission of sins. And we are witnesses of these things; and so is the Holy Spirit, whom God has given to them that obey him."—Acts 5:30-32.**

This was their simple, straightforward teaching, and it furnished their answer to the court. This is what they had been teaching the people in the Temple. And they had nothing different to offer the learned rabbis when brought to trial for their preaching.

Gamaliel's advice.—The Sadducees were completely incensed by their simple statement. The mention of Jesus' Messiahship, his resurrection and exaltation, the "remission of sins" through him and not through the Temple sacrifices, the experience of the Holy Spirit—all this was contrary to the authoritative teaching of Judaism as the Sadducees understood and taught it. Above all, the assertion that the one whom God raised from the dead and exalted was the one whom they had put to death—this "cut them to the heart, and they were minded to slay them."

But there was one sane and prudent man on the council, the great Pharisaic scholar Gamaliel, the teacher of Saul of Tarsus, a man not only learned in the Law but also honored by all the people. He asked the removal of the prisoners from the court and then made an address to the council. It was an appeal for clemency and moderation. He reminded them that all such movements as this one seemed to be died away of their own accord in time. Theudas, with his four hundred followers, Judas of Galilee in the days of the census, were examples of misguided enthusiasts who, sooner or later, brought themselves and their followers to disaster.

> "And now I say, refrain from these men and let them alone. If this movement is of human origin [let us assume that it is] it will end soon enough, but if it is from God, you will not be able to hinder it— and beware lest you are found opposing him!"— Acts 5: 38-39.

To this the Sanhedrin partly agreed. When they had called the apostles and beaten them with stripes, they charged them once more to cease teaching in the name of Jesus, and let them go. "They therefore departed from the presence of the council, rejoicing that they were counted worthy to suffer dishonor for the Name. And every day, in the Temple and at home, they ceased not to teach and preach Jesus as the Messiah" (Acts 5: 41, 42).

It is evident that persecution, suffering, even the danger of death was not to hinder the testimony of the apostles, or destroy their faith in their Lord. Upon such a rock of courage and faith, strong as granite, the Christian Church was built: and "the gates of death" were not going to "prevail against it."

STUDY TOPICS

1. Look up "Levites" in the Bible dictionary. What were their duties?
2. Who was Barnabas? Where was he born? Find the place on the map.
3. How does the story in Acts explain the modern epithet "Ananias"? What must have been the man's state of mind to be so violently affected by Peter's rebuke?
4. Have you ever heard of any modern parallels to the "faith healing" of the apostles' days?—for example, at the grotto of Lourdes; Sainte Anne de Beaupré; or the work of Mr. Hickson and other Christian healers. Remember that Jews and Christians look upon the physician's skill as a gift from God, just as important as the faith which makes for health. See Ecclesiasticus 38.
5. What especially angered the Sadducees, and incensed them against the teaching of the apostles? Was this the same party that had opposed our Lord in his ministry? How had they taken action against him?
6. The Pharisee Gamaliel was a representative of the better side of Judaism in the first century. Look up some other examples described in the New Testament: John the Baptist's parents (Luke 1–2); Simeon and Anna; the scribe "not far from the kingdom of God" (Mark 12: 28–34); the widow in the Temple (Luke 21: 1–4); Joseph of Arimathæa, "a councilor" (Luke 23: 50–52). We must not forget these

examples, or the fact that the earliest Christians, the apostles and their followers, were—like Jesus himself—of Jewish blood. How should this affect our attitude toward members of their race to-day? And does the principle hold true of our attitude toward still other races?

7. Name some ways in which your church cares for the poor and the sick. Do you have a share in this work?

CHAPTER VI

THE FIRST CHRISTIAN MARTYR

AN important part of the care of the poor in the early church consisted in the support of poverty-stricken widows. There were no Homes for the Aged in those days, no life insurance companies, no Societies for the Care of Widows and Orphans. Consequently, when a man died and left a wife and family, they were cast upon the charity of their relatives or neighbors—unless the family happened to be rich. Among the Jews, a systematic provision for needy widows and orphans had been undertaken by the synagogues, and "charity" in the sense of benefaction was a recognized and highly praised virtue, called "almsgiving."

THE CHOICE OF THE SEVEN

As the body of disciples and believers in Jesus continued to increase, there naturally were added many who had heretofore been dependent upon the benevolence of their neighbors. These the church undertook to provide for, even as the synagogue had done.

The "daily ministration."—But with several thousand believers now gathered together in Jerusalem it is not strange that the apostles found difficulty in caring for the poor in this number. It was not long before the "Hellenists"—Jews who had been born in other provinces than Judæa, in the Greek world outside the Holy Land—complained that the widows in their group were being neglected in favor of the "Hebrews" (those born in Palestine). This slight may have been as natural

60

as it was unintentional: the foreign-born Jews, not feeling quite at home in Jerusalem, perhaps not speaking Aramaic fluently (and there may even have been proselytes from other races among them), would not make their needs known as readily as those familiar with the methods of distribution.

Seven helpers appointed.—This complaint soon reached the ears of the Twelve. They at once called a meeting of the disciples and said,

> "It is not right for us to abandon the preaching of the word of God and serve tables! Therefore, brethren, choose from among you seven men of good report, men full of the Spirit and of wisdom, whom we may give charge of this business. For our part, we will continue stedfastly in prayer and the ministry of the word."—Acts 6: 2-4.

The whole multitude was pleased at this proposal, and chose the following seven: Stephen, "a man full of faith and of the Holy Spirit"; Philip, of whom we shall hear more anon; Prochorus, Nicanor, Timon, Parmenas; and Nicolas, a proselyte from Antioch. As their Greek names imply, these seven men were probably all "Hellenists," men born outside Judæa. They were brought before the apostles, who, when they had prayed, laid their hands on their heads. This was the customary Jewish rite of ordination or appointment to some sacred office.

We do not know whether or not this solution of the difficulty was satisfactory. No doubt it was, for we hear no more of complaints from the friends of the Hellenist widows. Instead, we read that "the word of God increased, and the number of the disciples multiplied in Jerusalem exceedingly and a great company of the priests were obedient to the faith" (Acts 6: 7). It showed great confidence in their fellow believers and a truly Christian spirit of brotherhood for the Jewish-born apostles in Jerusalem to appoint over an important activity of the church men who were either Gentile proselytes or Jews born in foreign lands.

THE MARTYRDOM OF STEPHEN

Nevertheless, new troubles soon developed, troubles of far greater magnitude, but still begun among the "Hellenists."

Disputing in the synagogue.—It seems that the disciples, although they were believers in Jesus, were still worshiping just as they had always done as Jews in the synagogue and Temple. Their worship in the upper room or in other gatherings among themselves was in addition to the strict and faithful observance of the Law and its customs. Now, there were in Jerusalem a number of synagogues where the Hellenists worshiped —such as the synagogues of the Cyrenians, the Alexandrians, the Cilicians, the Ephesians, and so on. Stephen, one of the Seven, aroused great interest in these synagogues with his fiery and convincing addresses and the "great wonders and signs" (probably the healing of sickness, mainly) which he performed among the people. Opponents now arose to dispute with him in the synagogue—it was the Jewish custom to permit debates within the sacred edifice. But his opponents always found themselves beaten by his arguments. The controversy became more and more bitter, and, since they were not able to overcome him in debate, they undertook to discredit him in other ways. They "suborned" certain men, that is, they secretly engaged them as false witnesses, who testified, "We have heard him speak blasphemous words against Moses and against God."

Stephen brought to trial.—They further "stirred up
the people and the elders and the scribes," and seized
him and brought him before the high priest's council, or
Sanhedrin. The "witnesses" now testified that they had
heard him "speak against this holy place (the Temple)
and the Law; for we have heard him say that this Jesus
of Nazareth shall destroy this place and change the
customs which Moses delivered to us." How much of
truth there was in this testimony we cannot say. Stephen
was a zealous young man, full of spirit, enthusiastic and
earnest; but he had probably not been a Christian long,
and his zeal was not tempered by careful consideration
of his words. The "witnesses" may easily have discovered some foundation for their garbled testimony.

The high priest's interrogation was solemn and
dignified: "Are these things so?"

Stephen began his reply in a manner calculated to win
his hearers' approval. It was a defense worthy an
ecclesiastical lawyer. It was a long address, filling most
of chapter seven of the book of Acts. He began with
the beginning of Hebrew history, the call of Abraham
and his journey to Canaan, the story of Joseph in Egypt,
Jacob's journey thither, his death and burial, the oppression in Egypt, Moses' birth, education, flight into
Midian, and so on. One would think he meant to cover
the whole Old Testament in his speech. But we must
remember not only that his hearers loved to be reminded
of the story of their nation's sacred past, and would
not feel wearied at such a narrative;[1] but also that
Stephen in this way very artfully refuted the charge
against him. Instead of blaspheming Moses and the
Law, as the "witnesses" said, he was showing the pro-

---

[1] See Psalm 78, which was sung in temple or synagogue; and, in the New
Testament, as a Christian-Jewish example, Hebrews 11.

foundest respect for both, and the intensest, most loving loyalty to the nation, "the people of the Law." His patriotism was manifest in every word.

But as he went on his tone changed. It may be that Luke has omitted (between verses 50 and 51) something from his source, for the conclusion of the speech is exceedingly abrupt. Or it may be that his hearers refused to listen to a long, oratorical defense when they wanted only to know whether or not he was a conspirator against the Law or the Temple. At least, he went on by pointing out that the nation had repeatedly disobeyed God's commands, and rejected his messengers, the prophets: even Moses they had disobeyed, and a Temple they had built for the God who had no need of it, for "He dwells not in houses made by hands."

Perhaps as he glanced around and saw looks of disapproval, and possibly seeing that the high priest was about to cut short his speech, he suddenly concluded the address with words of bitter invective.

> **"Stiffnecked, and uncircumcised in heart and ears! You always resist the Holy Spirit! As did your fathers, so do you. Which of the prophets did they not persecute? They killed those who announced the coming of the Righteous One—of whom you have now become the betrayers and murderers— you, who received the Law sent from heaven by angels[2] and then did not keep it!"—Acts 7 : 51-53.**

Though this final utterance sounds somewhat like certain sayings of John the Baptist and Jesus, the words are more like those of a man who knows his case is lost, that he is condemned already, that nothing he can possibly say will alter the judgment against him. The

---

[2] This was a Jewish legend.

words were perfectly true; but truth was not what the court wanted.

Stephen is stoned.—The court proceeded no further. The riot which Stephen had perhaps anticipated, just before he spoke his final words, broke out at once. It had been observed that when he began his defense his face shone "as it had been the face of an angel" (Acts 6: 15). And now, still more lifted up in spirit and seeing a vision, even as he stood there facing death, he said, "Behold, I see the heavens opened and the Son of man standing at the right hand of God." He said no more. For the mob, which had been waiting outside the court, broke upon him, shouting and screaming and holding their ears, and rushed him out of the city and stoned him. This was the ancient punishment for blasphemy (the original charge against Stephen). According to custom, the witnesses were required to cast the first stones. This much of a semblance of justice was carried out. And as they did so the "witnesses" laid down their outer garments at the feet of a young man named Saul, one of the "Hellenists" of the synagogue of the Cilicians.

As they stoned him, Stephen called out to his Master whom he beheld at the right hand of God, saying, "Lord Jesus, receive my spirit." Then kneeling down amid the shower of missiles hurled at him, he cried, "Lord, lay not this sin to their charge." And when he had said this, he "fell asleep."

It was the first overt act on the part of the authorities or the multitude, since the crucifixion of Jesus, to get rid of the growing movement. It was a terrible mistake, even from the viewpoint of the authorities, and ought never to have occurred. It was an outburst of fanaticism, of mob rule, of ungovernable passions. It was the first entry in the long annals of bloodshed and persecution which record the progress of that faith which overcame the world. And, as in every age "the blood of the martyrs is the seed of the church," so it was even here in the death of the proto-martyr. Persecution served only to drive the disciples from Jerusalem and spread the new faith in other quarters. In a most true sense, therefore, Stephen's death was not in vain.

STUDY TOPICS

1. Who were the "Hellenists" (Acts 6:1)? the "Hebrews"? Refer again to the list of the peoples among whom the Jews were dispersed, who were represented in Jerusalem (Acts 2:9-11), and compare Acts 6:9. Look up "Libertines" in the Bible dictionary.

2. Does the church to-day perform any function similar to that for which the Seven were appointed? Do you know any ways in which boys and girls can help their pastor in his work?

3. How does their appointment show the spirit of brotherhood and the confidence which the apostles possessed?

4. Compare the charge against Stephen with that brought against Jesus in the high priest's house (Mark 14:58).

5. Read the speech of Stephen (as given in Acts 7:2-53) in the light of what is said above. Note the long historical introduction, the evident reverence for Moses, the emphasis on Israel's age-long disobedience, and the abrupt and apparently disconnected conclusion in verses 51-53.

6. Compare Stephen's dying words with the prayer of Jesus on the cross (Luke 23:34). The spirit of that prayer shows the influence of Jesus upon the first martyr-disciple.

7. Do you know the hymn, "The Son of God Goes Forth

to War"? Write in your notebook the verse referring to the chief figure in this chapter.

8. What qualities in Stephen's character do you admire?
Are there ways in which we ought to imitate him
to-day?

CHAPTER VII

PHILIP THE EVANGELIST

So far the Christian movement had scarcely spread beyond Jerusalem and the nearby villages (see Acts 5: 16). It was increasing so rapidly, however, that sooner or later it must inevitably pass the boundaries of Judæa and then advance into the great world outside. "You shall be my witnesses," the Master had said, "both in Jerusalem and in all Judæa and Samaria, and unto the uttermost parts of the earth" (Acts 1: 8). The martyrdom of Stephen only hastened what was a necessary step in the expansion of the church.

"They were all scattered abroad throughout the regions of Judæa and Samaria, except the apostles."
—Acts 8: 1.

THE GOSPEL IN SAMARIA

It is significant that the first city evangelized outside Jerusalem was Samaria. In one way this was natural and to be expected, for Samaria was the chief city (once the capital) of the district by that name, which together with Judæa formed the new Roman province ruled by the procurator (see Chapter II of this volume). But, on the other hand, there was a strong feeling of antagonism on the part of the Judæans toward their northern neighbors. It dated from the days of Ezra, and had lasted on through the changes and vicissitudes of succeeding generations, until in the days of Jesus it could be said that "Jews had no dealings with Samaritans" (John 4: 9). Jesus had shown the unfairness of this hatred in his great parable of the good Samaritan. And it is most significant that the church's first move outside Jerusalem was not back to Galilee but to Samaria. Christianity was destined from the first (though some failed to recognize it) to overstep the lines and divisions of class and caste, of nationality and sectarianism.

Philip's preaching.—The "scattering" of the Jerusalem church was like the scattering of flames of fire by the wind. Wherever the new believers were driven, there they bore witness to their faith. Persecution, instead of destroying the church, only hastened its growth and spread it farther abroad.

"They therefore that were scattered abroad went about preaching the word. And Philip went down to the city of Samaria, and proclaimed unto them the Christ. And the multitudes gave heed with one accord unto the things that were spoken by Philip, when they heard and saw the signs which he did. For from many of those which had unclean spirits, they came out, shrieking and screaming; and many that were paralyzed and lame were healed. And there was much joy in that city."—Acts 8: 4-8.

We can understand what this joy was like. The gospel message had not been preached there before (see Matthew 10: 5), and when Jesus was on his way through Samaria on the final journey to Jerusalem, one of their villages refused him hospitality (Luke 9: 51–56). Perhaps this only made their welcome of Philip the heartier, and their joy over his message the more intense.

Simon the Magician.—There was in Samaria at that time a notorious magician called Simon. He had a large following, and completely amazed the Samaritans with his tricks and miracles. Letting them think that he was some divine or supernatural being, he called himself "one of the powers of God called The Great Power." Such religious mountebanks were common throughout the world in those days; their books and magical formulas have come down to us by the thousands, written on papyrus or potsherds, and buried in the rubbish heaps of Egypt and elsewhere. We should naturally expect Christianity to come in contact with these self-deceived deceivers sooner or later; and the book of Acts clearly bears evidence to the trustworthiness of the narratives it records, in that it describes such representatives of superstition.

When Simon saw his followers converted by the preaching of Philip; when he saw them baptized, and witnessed the "signs" of spiritual power which Philip performed on the sick and demented, he decided that he too would be baptized, and have some share in the new religion. But though he was baptized, his heart was untouched and his morals unchanged. He was still the same exploiter of the people, the same practicer of the "dark arts." His motive in becoming a Christian was merely to gain control of still more magical powers.

Peter and John sent to Samaria.—When the apostles at Jerusalem heard that the Samaritans had received the gospel they sent down to them Peter and John. When they had arrived they prayed for the new converts, that they might receive the gift of the Holy Spirit,—for, Luke says, "as yet he had come upon none of them; only they had been baptized in the name of the Lord Jesus." Then they laid their hands on them, and they received the Holy Spirit.

Simon thought at once that this rite must be the secret of Philip's power. If only he could gain possession of it, what miracles might he not perform, and regain his old following in Samaria! What expulsion of witches, what sweetening of wells, what averting of blight and mildew from the crops, what exorcism of demons and ghosts might he not accomplish! So he came to the apostles and offered them a sum of money and said, "Give me this power, that on whomsoever I lay my hands, he may receive the Holy Spirit." But Simon had mistaken his man.

With the same stern, almost fierce tone of rebuke which had withered the hypocrite Ananias, Peter turned on him and said: "Your silver perish with you!—trying to obtain the gift of God with money! You have no part nor share in this! For your heart is all wrong before God. Repent of this wickedness and pray God to forgive you this miserable scheme."

Simon, still superstitious and now alarmed, at once cowered before the apostles and begged them to remove any spell their words might have brought upon him. "Pray the Lord for me that none of these things overtake me!"—and with these words he departs from the page of history. We never hear anything more of him. But at least the incident shows what the apostles themselves thought of the "gift of God." It was a power effective only "by the Spirit"; it was not for self-aggrandizement or the fame or influence of those receiving it. Rather, like Jesus' own supernatural powers as Messiah (see Luke 4: 1–13), it was given for the benefit of the poor and helpless and miserable—God's holiest power consecrated to the highest and most unselfish ends.

PHILIP AND THE ETHIOPIAN

For some time the mission in Samaria was continued, the apostles making their way slowly back to Jerusalem, and preaching in various country villages as they passed along.

On the road to Gaza.—Philip, on the other hand, was directed to go to the south of Jerusalem, along the desert road which led to Gaza. "An angel of the Lord," it is said, brought him this command—probably in a vision. So he arose and went, down into the lonely Judæan wilderness. A day or so later the purpose of his mission became apparent.

Down the long road winding southward over the hills came the chariot of some high foreign government official. As it drew near, Philip recognized the traveling retinue of the chief treasurer of Ethiopia, the mountain-kingdom of Queen Candace. The treasurer had been at Jerusalem on a pilgrimage to the Temple, and now was returning home. As he sat in his magnificent chariot he was reading from a scroll the book of the prophet Isaiah. When he saw him, the Spirit prompted Philip, "Go and join that company."

So Philip ran up beside the Ethiopian's chariot, and overheard him reading the familiar passages (it was the ancient custom to read aloud). He made bold to address the officer, and said, "Do you really understand what you are reading?" The officer, perhaps reading Greek only (the Greek translation of the Old Testament called the Septuagint) and unfamiliar with the original—for he was not a Jew but a proselyte—replied, "How can I understand it unless someone interprets it for me?" Seeing that Philip was a Jew, or at least that he spoke as if he understood the book, he invited him to sit beside him and explain it as they went along.

The passage which he had just been reading was the one from the fifty-third chapter of Isaiah describing the great Unknown Sufferer, the Servant of the Lord—a passage which Jesus had often pondered and which meant much to him.

> "He was oppressed,
>   Yet when he was afflicted he opened not his mouth;
> As a lamb that is led to the slaughter,
> And as a sheep that before her shearers is dumb,
> So he opened not his mouth.
> By oppression and judgment he was taken away;
> And as for his generation, who among them con-
>   sidered
> That he was cut off out of the land of the living
> For the transgression of my people to whom the
>   stroke was due?"
>   —Isaiah 53:7-8.

Then the officer asked Philip: "Of whom is this spoken? Of the prophet himself or someone else?" This gave Philip his opportunity, and "beginning from this passage, he preached to him Christ Jesus." For the early Christians understood all Old Testament prophecy as prediction. The prophets had not so much addressed their own times with a message of repentance or consolation as announced beforehand all that the Messiah should do and suffer. It is wonderful, and impresses us still, how closely the picture of the Great Sufferer in Isaiah and the Psalms does resemble our Lord in his passion.

The Ethiopian baptized.—As they went on they came to one of the wadies or seasonal streams in the wilderness, and the officer said, "Here is water; what is to hinder my baptism right here and now?" And so he commanded the chariot to halt, and both of them going down into the water, Philip baptized him in the name of Christ. And so one more messenger was sent forth toward "the uttermost parts of the earth" with the message of Jesus. We do not know what resulted after his return to Ethiopia, for the story has not come down to us. But we know that before many generations there was a strong church in Ethiopia, with its own liturgy, organization, church buildings, and a translation of the Bible into the Ethiopic language. (This translation is often quoted in seeking to establish the early and most correct form of the New Testament text.)

Then Philip, his mission fulfilled, was led by the Spirit into the region along the Mediterranean coast. He was found at Azotus (the ancient Philistine city of Ashdod); and passing on from there "he preached the gospel to all the cities" of the coastal plain, "till he came to Cæsarea" (Acts 8: 40).

STUDY TOPICS

1. Look up the earlier history of the Samaritans (from the fifth century B. C.), and find out why the Jews had no dealings with them (see Bible dictionary).
2. Look up examples of magical formulas used in ancient times (encyclopedia, or Deissmann's *Light From the Ancient East*).
3. Turn to a map of Palestine showing the roads (for example, the frontispiece of *The Life and Times of Jesus* or Crosby's *Geography of Bible Lands*) and trace the road from Jerusalem to Gaza. Where was Ethiopia? Locate Azotus and Cæsarea. Trace Philip's journey from Samaria to Cæsarea.
4. What was the Septuagint? Why was it so named? (See dictionary.) The symbol frequently used in referring to it is "LXX." Why? What was its date?
5. What is a "wady"? A "liturgy"? Look up the word "simony." How does the story told in this chapter explain the original significance of the term?

6. What was the original meaning of Isaiah 53? What meaning did it come to have for the early Christians?

7. Is it possible for people to-day to misunderstand Christianity as Simon the Magician did? How? Does God ever accept money in lieu of repentance and faith and right conduct?

8. Philip must have been a careful Bible student to be able to explain the passage to the Ethiopian. The church always needs teachers of its faith. Have you ever thought of preparing yourself to become a *teacher* of the Christian religion?

CHAPTER VIII

PAUL OF TARSUS

AT the time Christianity arose there were many more Jews living outside Palestine than in it. These formed what was called the Diaspora ("Dispersion" or "Scattering"), and probably numbered between three and four million souls. They were scattered throughout the Roman Empire, from Parthia and the lower valley of the Tigris in the east to Spain and Gaul in the west, and from the bleak northern shores of the Euxine Sea to the borders of the Sahara in Mauretania, Libya and upper Egypt. But chiefly, since the Jew has always (or at least since early times) been a trader and artisan rather than a farmer, grazer or seaman, they settled in the great cosmopolitan cities. Alexandria had so many Jews in the first century that they occupied, according to Philo Judæus (about 50 A. D.), two whole quarters of the city, and were represented by scattered families in other quarters as well. The wealthy cities of the province of Asia—Miletus, Ephesus, Sardis, Pergamum—all had large Jewish populations; and so had Antioch, Tarsus, and even Rome.

Everywhere the Jews built their synagogues, read their sacred Scriptures (including the Greek translation of the Old Testament), and observed their ancestral customs with as much strictness as was possible outside of the Holy Land. Of course, they had not the sacrificial worship of the Temple, but they made up for this in a way by the collection of a tax of one half-shekel (or *didrachma:* worth fifty cents) from every Jew over twenty years old, and by occasional pilgrimages to

Jerusalem to observe the three great festivals—especially
Passover and the Feast of Tabernacles. At the same time
they were zealous missionaries—as Jesus had said, "they
compassed sea and land to make one proselyte." Great
multitudes became adherents of Judaism—"proselytes,"
"those who feared God," throughout the Roman Empire.
They accepted the belief in one God, and respected the
moral provisions of the Law, although they did not
observe to the full its ceremonial requirements. Thus
the Jewish *Diaspora* was one of the most important
factors in the religious situation of the world of the first
century, and it was destined to have an important influence upon the rise and expansion of early Christianity.

PAUL'S EARLY YEARS

In the southeast corner of Asia Minor, just before the
ancient highway from the west swings around into
northern Syria (or the modern Bagdad Railroad, for
that matter, skirting the shores of Alexandretta Bay),
lay in the first century the tiny province of Cilicia. It
had been Roman territory since 103 B. C., but was overrun with pirates until Pompey subdued them and
organized the province in 64. The orator Cicero was one
of its early governors or proconsuls. Its eastern and
southern part was a broad and comparatively fertile
plain, lying between the Taurus and Amanus mountain
ranges, and watered by four abundant rivers. Besides
commerce—the highway from Ephesus to the east which
ran through it was one of the greatest trade routes of
the ancient world—there was a large native industry
engaged in the production and manufacture of a special
kind of heavy cloth made of goat's hair (called *cilicium*),
widely used for tents.

Paul's birth in Tarsus.—Tarsus was the chief city of the province. It lay on the right bank of the Cydnus River, about thirty miles due south of the famous pass through the Taurus Mountains (the Cilician Gates), on the highway of trade and travel to the east. It was between five and ten miles from the seacoast, and enjoyed only such light shipping as could navigate the lower stretches of the river. Ten miles to the north was a range of hills where wealthy families had their villas for refuge from the intense and burning heat of summer on the flat Cilician plain. Even in the days of Xenophon, four centuries earlier, it had been a "large and prosperous city"—as he says in the *Anabasis*.

It was a famous center of learning, and had its own municipal "university." Great teachers, especially teachers of the Stoic philosophy, had gone forth from Tarsus; men educated there were to be found in all the large cities of the empire. It ranked with Athens, Alexandria, and Antioch as a center of education. And among its population were many Jews, attracted thither by the prospect of trade and manufacture.

Here, about the opening years of the present era, was born a boy destined in time to become one of the greatest figures in history. He was "Saul, who is also called Paulus"—it was the custom at that time for Jews to adopt Greek or Roman names (in addition to their Hebrew names) for use in business and other relations with Gentiles. His family was orthodox Jewish, adherents of "the straitest sect of their religion"—Pharisees. They were descendants of the old tribe of Benjamin, and Saul was probably named in honor of the Benjamite son of Kish who became Israel's first king. They were probably in fairly good circumstances, for they not only possessed Roman citizenship—a privilege at that time extended to few families outside Italy—but also they were able to send young Saul to Jerusalem to receive his education in the Law.

His education and early youth.—The earlier years of his life were spent at home. At the synagogue school he learned to read and write the sacred language of his fathers, the Hebrew of the Old Testament. But he also learned Greek, the language of everyday use, and the one in which the Bible was read on the Sabbath during public worship. Like every other Jewish boy, he learned a trade—in his case, the common Cilician one of tent-making. How useful this became to him later on we shall see. Outside his school hours and the time daily spent with the big tentmaker's needle he played in the courtyards or on the streets of his neighborhood. There were other Jewish boys of his age whom he came to know. They were city boys. Unlike Jesus and John the Baptist and the earlier apostles, who grew up in the country or in little villages, these boys were not familiar with rural scenes. Instead, they were familiar with the shops and warehouses, the garrison of Roman soldiers, the race track and gymnasium, the Greek temples, the baths and theaters of a thriving Hellenistic city. It is striking how Paul's letters betray his earliest experiences: their figures of speech are almost wholly chosen from city life. Jesus' figures and parables, on the other hand, were almost all taken from nature.

At the feet of Gamaliel.—At the age of twelve or thirteen it was customary for a Jewish boy to be made a "son of the commandments," or confirmed, as we might say. From then on he was to devote a certain amount of his time to the study of the Torah or Sacred Law, and to begin its complete observance. Hence boys were often sent, at about this age, to study under some

rabbi or teacher of the Torah. Paul's parents sent him
to Jerusalem, to study at the feet of Gamaliel, one of
the most famous rabbis in the whole world (see chapter
V). Here the pupils sat in a circle before the teacher
while he read and expounded the Law of Moses, comparing passage with passage, quoting the observations
and opinions of great teachers in the past, and endeavoring to arrive at the real requirements of the Law as the
expression of the will of God.

PAUL THE PHARISEE

The Jewish religion was legalistic, that is, it was (and
still is) a religion founded upon observance of a sacred
law. This law comprises not only moral rules but also
ceremonial directions—such as those regulating the
temple sacrifices and offerings, and the various cleansings
necessary after touching things "defiled." Strictly to
fulfill its requirements demanded a great deal of time
and the most careful study. The Pharisees were those
whose chief aim in life was to learn the exact requirements of the Law and to observe them scrupulously to
the last detail.

Zeal for the Law.—Into this religious movement of
his teachers and friends Paul plunged with hearty
enthusiasm. He became a Pharisee of the Pharisees,
striving to outdo even the most exacting requirements
of the Law; he became so intolerant of those who failed
to share his scruples that he even persecuted them in
the synagogues. For along with his zeal for the Law he
also shared with the other Pharisees a profound faith in
the coming of the Messiah. The Messiah was to be the
heavenly king of a new and sanctified Israel: sinners,
breakers of the Law, apostates from the Covenant, had
no place in Messiah's kingdom. But they were, never-

theless, delaying Messiah's coming. For he was not to come, as one rabbi said, until all Israel observed perfectly the Law from one Sabbath to the next. Hence Paul's persecution of "the sons of lawlessness," as he would call them, had what seemed to his own mind a really noble excuse. He was hastening, by his zeal, the coming of the Messiah from heaven to be Israel's holy King.

Persecution of the Christians.—It seemed to him that none were more to be blamed for "lawlessness" than the obstinate and fanatical followers of Jesus of Nazareth. Paul completely lacked the gentle spirit of his master, Gamaliel—who had counseled the Sanhedrin to deal fairly with the apostles, lest they might perchance be found opposing God (Acts 5: 35–39). Instead, he felt it his duty to "persecute this Way unto death, binding and delivering into prisons both men and women." He received letters from the high priest and elders in Jerusalem, authorizing him to visit the synagogues as a heresy-hunter, and commanding the synagogue authorities to deliver over to him any who were Christians, in order that they might be brought to Jerusalem and tried for their belief. At the death of Stephen (Chapter VI), the witnesses laid down their garments at the feet of Saul.

Inner dissatisfaction.—It is hard nowadays to conceive such intolerance in the name of religion—at least, in Christian lands. Whatever the spiritual gain or loss of the past two hundred years, at least here in America and in the other enlightened nations we do not persecute one another on account of religious faith.

And it is stranger still to find, as Paul admitted in after years (see Romans 7), that all this time when he was fanatically persecuting the believers in Jesus he was himself growing more and more insecure in his own belief in the Law. Its strictest observance seemed to bring him no nearer God, or to bring down the Messiah from heaven. The ceremonial part was easy enough, once he thoroughly understood it, and had the leisure to observe it; but the moral and spiritual part, that he could never wholly master. The Law said, "Thou shalt not steal"—this also he could obey well enough; but when it said, "Thou shalt not covet," there was implied some control over the very desires of his heart, the deepest ambitions of his soul; and try as he would he could not "kill out desire."

His cruelty as a persecutor may have been in part the very result of his inner unrest. Like the persecutors of heretics in the later Middle Ages, he "thought he did God service" in this way. Let their bodies perish—he was saving their souls in spite of their folly and obstinacy! It satisfied him, in a way, to be doing something —something with a purpose which he told himself was worthy and just.

The examples of the persecuted.—But what must have been the effect upon his troubled conscience of his experience with these poor simple believers in Jesus, uneducated for the most part, but courageous, loyal to their Master, and unafraid to die? What must have been the impression made upon him by the dying martyr Stephen, his face shining with the brightness of an angel's, his eyes glistening with the splendor of a heavenly vision as he knelt and prayed for his persecutors? It might be a long way that Paul had yet to travel before he should "see the Lord" and gain inner peace and confidence. But at least he would not rest content with any half-way measures, with half-truths, and hazy "general beliefs" about religion. Either the Law was wholly true and good or it was positively false and bad. Either the

Christians were utterly wrong, deluded, steeped in sin, so that it was a mercy to save their souls with rod and lash, or they were absolutely in the right. Either Jesus of Nazareth was an impostor and deceiver, a perverter of the people, and accursed (as proved by his death on the cross), or he was the true Messiah, he was the Man from Heaven, he was Israel's King in disguise.

Whether true or false, Paul was soon to discover, and this discovery marked the turning point of his whole life.

STUDY TOPICS

1. Look up on a sequence map (for example, in Breasted's *Ancient Times*, pp. 552, 553) the political changes which took place in Asia Minor during the last two centuries B. C.

2. Cilicia was a famous region in ancient history. Locate the Cilician Gates, Tarsus, Issus. For what were they famous? (See ancient history, encyclopedia, or Bible dictionary.)

3. Read in your ancient history the account of civilization in the eastern Mediterranean world between Alexander the Great and the early Cæsars (for example, Breasted, Chapter XXI, and study the illustrations).

4. Look up the meaning of Roman citizenship in the first century. It was a great protection to travelers all over the world. Why?

5. How do you account for Paul's persecution of the followers of Jesus? Remember that he was an earnestly religious man with a "zeal for God." Is "sincerity" alone enough to justify one's conduct? Or must we be *right* as well as sincere?

6. Look up Acts 22: 3-5; 26: 4, 5, 9-11; and Galatians 1: 13, 14, where Paul himself refers to his youth and early manhood.

7. Why is Paul sometimes called "Saul"?
8. God gives to each one of us certain peculiar advantages, all our own, in our birth-place, our parents and ancestors, our early home, education and experiences. He expects us to measure up to these, and use all our advantages in the best possible way. What are some of your advantages? How ought you to use them in God's service?

CHAPTER IX

PAUL'S CONVERSION

PAUL had not himself known Jesus "in the flesh."
He may have seen him, perhaps after his condemnation
by the priests. He must surely have known something
about him, because the whole city of Jerusalem was
stirred by the events which took place just before Passover in the year 29. But if Paul had known Jesus personally, even in the least degree, we may be sure he
would have mentioned it in his letters. Perhaps his
bitter opposition to the disciples of Jesus would not have
occurred if he had ever known their Master. As it was,
he fanatically persecuted One who was to him only a
name (Acts 26: 9) and the beliefs of whose followers
were only a "Way"—a heresy and delusion (Acts 22: 4).

"For I actually believed it my duty," as he afterward
related this part of his career, "to do all I could against
the name of Jesus of Nazareth. Even in Jerusalem I
did this—and shut up many of the saints in prisons,
having received authority from the chief priests; and
when they were put to death I cast my vote against
them. And by punishing them often in all the synagogues,
I tried to make them blaspheme. And so frantic was I
against them that I persecuted them even in the cities
outside" (Acts 26: 9–11).

ON THE ROAD TO DAMASCUS

Twenty-five miles northeast of the snow-capped summit of Mount Hermon, on the very border of the desert,
lay the old Syrian city Damascus. Here there were

many Jews, and among them followers of Jesus. How there came to be disciples of Jesus in Damascus this early (about 35 A. D.) we do not know. Probably visitors from Jerusalem or pilgrims returning from the feasts had brought the "good news" with them. Or perhaps some of the disciples "scattered abroad" at the time of Stephen's death (Acts 8: 1) settled there. We must remember that the book of Acts does not give us a complete record of the growth of the church, but only a selection from such accounts as had been handed down by tradition to the time of the writer—fifty years later.

The vision and the Voice.—Paul was now carrying on his persecution outside the cities of Palestine. He had secured letters from the hierarchy in Jerusalem authorizing him to bring thither for trial any whom he found professing the new faith. His present destination was Damascus. The road there led down across Samaria and the valley of Esdraelon, across Galilee—where Jesus, whose very name he hated, had spent his ministry— then up into the high, flat, dry wilderness which stretched for fifty miles northeastward to the walls of the city. This last part of the journey took a whole day on horse, from long before dawn until late at night, resting some hours in the heat of the day; and even longer than that by caravan. It led across lonely miles of desert—the desert, where men in all ages have seen visions and heard voices from heaven. Like Moses, Elijah and Amos, and even the Arab, Mohammed, Paul was to pass through a strange, mystical experience before he reached Damascus.

It was midday. Already they were approaching the city and its walls and towers could be made out in the distance ahead. The heat was oppressive, the sun blistering. Suddenly, like a flash of lightning, a stream of light broke over Paul. He fell to the ground, blinded and dazed by the shock. A voice was heard by him saying, "Saul, Saul, why do you persecute me?"—words spoken in Aramaic and addressing him by his familiar Jewish name. Half conscious, he only replied, "Who are you, Sir?" And the voice answered him, speaking out of the light, which now took personal form: "I am Jesus, whom you are persecuting. Rise, and enter the city, and you shall be told what you must do."

His fellow travelers had observed the flash and heard the sound, but they had seen no vision. Paul now rose from the ground and opened his eyes, but he saw nothing: he was blind! So they led him by the hand into Damascus. And for three days he was without sight, and could neither eat nor drink.

The disciple Ananias.—One of the disciples of Jesus in Damascus was a devoted and highly honored man named Ananias. He was now directed in a vision to go to Paul and deliver a message to him from the Lord. "Arise, and go into the street called Straight,[1] and inquire for a man named Saul, of Tarsus; for behold, he is praying, and has seen you in a vision, coming in and laying your hands on him and restoring his sight" (Acts 9: 11, 12).

Ananias naturally hesitated, for he knew what had brought the fierce Tarsian zealot to their city. "Lord, I have heard from many," he answered, "how much evil he has done to thy saints in Jerusalem; and here he has authority from the chief priests to bind all that call upon thy name." But the Lord replied, "Go your way; he is a chosen vessel unto me, to bear my name

---

[1] This was a beautiful colonnaded thoroughfare which ran east and west through the city, with magnificent arched gateways at its ends.

before Gentiles and kings and the children of Israel; for I will show him how many things he too must suffer for my name's sake."

Then Ananias went, found the house, and entering it, said, "Brother Saul, the Lord Jesus, who appeared to you on the way as you came, has sent me to you, in order that you may receive your sight and be filled with the Holy Spirit. Brother Saul, receive your sight!" At once, as if scales had fallen from his eyes, Paul looked up and saw Ananias standing over him. Then Ananias said, "The God of our fathers has appointed you to know his will, and to see the Righteous One (the Messiah), and to hear his voice. For you must be a witness before all men of what you have seen and heard. Why delay? Arise and be baptized, and wash away your sins, and call upon his name in prayer." Then rising up, he was baptized, and took food and was strengthened (Acts 9: 13–18; 22: 13–16).

PAUL THE CHRISTIAN

According to the account which Paul himself wrote, he immediately "conferred not with flesh and blood (that is, with any human being); neither went I up to Jerusalem to consult those who were apostles before me. Instead, I went away into Arabia, and later on returned to Damascus." How long he spent in this retirement, or into what part of Arabia he went, we do not know. Very likely he spent some weeks in a nearby village, convalescing from the weakness which resulted from his stroke on the journey, reading the Scripture in a new light, thinking over his great experience, and making up his mind about questions which his conversion raised.

Preaching in the synagogues.—Then he came back to Damascus, and "proclaimed Jesus in the synagogues,

that he was the Son of God." It was strange that the
very one who had come there to "make havoc of them
that called upon this name" was now preaching that the
Messiah had appeared in Jesus, and many of the disciples were, of course, suspicious. On the other hand,
the orthodox Jews, who refused to accept his teaching,
were violently opposed to him.

> **"But Saul became more and more outspoken in
> his preaching, and refuted the Jews who lived in
> Damascus, proving that Jesus was indeed the Mes-
> siah. It was not long, therefore, before they formed
> a plot to kill him. But Paul got wind of it, and
> though the gates were watched day and night to see
> that he did not escape, his disciples succeeded in
> lowering him down from the wall one night in a
> basket."—Acts 9: 22-25.**

In Jerusalem again.—It was now three years since
Paul left Jerusalem to visit Damascus and stamp out
the Nazarene heresy in its synagogues. The one-time
persecutor was now the most ardent missionary. He
determined to go up to Jerusalem and visit the apostles
—whom he had hitherto not visited, though he was
preaching the faith constantly in the synagogues. The
Jerusalem disciples were naturally fearful, and hesitated
to welcome him into full fellowship. Nevertheless,
Peter and James received him, upon Barnabas' introduction, and he remained there about two weeks (Galatians 1: 18, 19 and Acts 9: 26, 27).

But just as it had been in Damascus, so it was here.
He preached boldly in the synagogues, and, with all
the ardor of a new convert, did not hesitate to engage
in heated argument for the faith. His antagonists, like
Stephen's, seem to have been Hellenist Jews rather

than the orthodox Pharisees or Sadducees. And just as they had murdered Stephen, so they planned to kill Paul. Fearing for his safety, and perhaps anxious lest more persecution be stirred up like that which followed the death of Stephen, the brethren accompanied Paul down to Cæsarea and then sent him on to Tarsus.

In Syria and Cilicia.—Here he was, home again, in the familiar, busy city on the Cilician plain. It was years since he had been back, and how different a man he was now! He had a new outlook on life, a new purpose, and that was to proclaim to his own people Jesus as their Messiah; that the Messiah had at last appeared, and that he was none other than the Jesus whom formerly he had persecuted. Just as he had begun preaching Christ where he once had intended to crush out all faith in him, at Damascus; just as he had boldly proclaimed him in Jerusalem, where formerly he had led in the bitter persecution of the disciples; so here, in his birthplace, he now began his labors as a missionary of the new faith.

For nine years he continued his labors in Syria and Cilicia—years about which we know nothing save that, as he says, he was "still unknown by face to the churches in Judæa. But they only heard it said that 'he who once persecuted us now preaches the faith he formerly destroyed'; and they glorified God in me" (Galatians 1: 22–24). They were years of zealous missionary preaching, years during which the neighboring church in Antioch was founded and steadily growing; years in which, no doubt, Paul was learning to present more calmly and persuasively, and with less of the old passionate rabbinic argument and disputation, the message of the Gospel of Life. And ever and again there rang in his ears, it may be, certain words which he had heard in a vision in the Temple, during those short two weeks he spent with Peter: "Depart, for I will send thee forth far hence unto the Gentiles."

STUDY TOPICS

1. Had Paul known Jesus before his conversion? Give a reason for your answer.

2. How may Christianity have been brought to Damascus between the years 29 (the crucifixion) and 35 (Paul's conversion)?

3. Read Galatians 1:15–24, Paul's own written account of his conversion. Compare it with the accounts in Acts 9:1–30, 22:3–21, and 26:12–20. See also 2 Corinthians 11:32, 33.

4. Harmonize with the data in Galatians 1:11–24 the following chronology:

    35 A. D.—Paul's conversion.

    38 A. D.—Visit to Jerusalem (for fifteen days).

    38 A. D. to 47 A. D.—Paul in Syria and Cilicia.

5. Read Acts 22:17–21. How does it fit in with Acts 9:28–30?

6. Trace on the map Paul's journey to Damascus; to Jerusalem; to Cæsarea and Tarsus.

7. Paul the Pharisee was scrupulously honest with his conscience, though a fanatic and persecutor. Had this anything to do with his discovery of Christ and his conversion? What lesson is there in this for us?

8. Paul said, in after years, "I was not disobedient unto the heavenly vision" (Acts 26:19). What did he mean? Must we always do the right "as God gives us to see the right"? Are there ways for us to obey "the heavenly vision"?

CHAPTER X

CORNELIUS THE CENTURION

It was now some years since the death of Stephen and the intense persecution of those days. Paul, the arch-persecutor, was now himself proclaiming the message of the gospel in the province of Syria and Cilicia. And in Palestine there was a quiet and undisturbed growth of the church. The authorities had either discovered that they could not hinder its progress or else concluded that it was harmless and that its error (as they supposed) would die out in time. And so, Luke says, "the church had peace throughout all Judæa and Galilee and Samaria, and was built up. And walking in the fear of the Lord and by the help of the Holy Spirit, it grew and multiplied" (Acts 9: 31).

PETER AT LYDDA AND JOPPA

There is very little told us of the events of the church in Jerusalem during this period. Indeed, we are fast approaching the end of Luke's narrative of such of its traditions as he incorporates in the book of Acts, for the latter half of the book is almost entirely devoted to the work of Paul. But such anecdotes from these early days as have been preserved tally quite well with what we have already learned. The apostles continued preaching the gospel to their fellow Jews—what the message was, we shall see again from one more sermon of Peter's in this chapter. And wherever the message was preached, the "signs following" continued—wonderful healings of the sick, ecstatic "speaking with tongues," and other proofs of the presence and power of the Spirit.

The healing of Æneas.—Jerusalem was still the headquarters of the Christian movement. Peter and his brother-apostles went down from Jerusalem to visit the other cities and villages to which the gospel had spread, preaching and confirming the faith of the believers. It was on one of these pastoral journeys that Peter visited the ancient village of Lydda in the Philistine plain. Here he found an aged man who had been suffering from paralysis for eight years. Whether he was a disciple or not, we do not know. But on seeing him, Peter said, as he had said long ago to the lame man at the Beautiful Gate: "Æneas, Jesus the Messiah heals you. Arise, and make your bed." At once he arose. "And all that dwelt in Lydda and the plain of Sharon saw him, and they turned unto the Lord" (Acts 9: 32–35).

The restoration of Dorcas.—While Peter was at Lydda the disciples at Joppa, the old seaside city a few miles distant, sent word asking him to come at once. A noble woman of the community, Tabitha by name (they also called her Dorcas, "Gazelle") had fallen sick and died. Peter responded at once, and when he arrived they led him to the upper chamber where her body lay, cold and apparently lifeless. "The widows" stood by, weeping, and showing the garments which Dorcas had made for them while she lived. But Peter, like the ancient prophet Elisha, who restored the Shunammite's son; or, rather, like his Master, who said, "The maid is not dead, but sleeps" (Luke 8: 52), at once bade the mourners withdraw, and knelt down and prayed. Then turning to the body, he said, "Tabitha, arise." And at once she sat up, restored to life and consciousness. The news, of course, spread throughout Joppa, and "many," Luke adds, "believed on the Lord." Peter remained in Joppa several days at the home of a man named, like himself, Simon—a tanner.

The vision of Cornelius.—There is one other story told of this journey of Peter which Saint Luke has narrated in his volume. It is given at considerable length, for the event was extremely important.

We must remember that thus far the gospel had been preached only to Jews—except by Philip to the Ethiopian treasurer (who may have been a proselyte). And we must also remember that the Jews believed that no Gentile could enter God's kingdom and be saved—unless he first became a Jew, through belief in the one God, obedience to his law (the Law of Moses), and observance of the Jewish customs.

Now, there was at that time stationed in Cæsarea, the capital of the province of Judæa and Samaria, a centurion of the Italian cohort (*cohors Italica*) named Cornelius. He was a very "devout man, who feared God with all his household, gave much alms to the people, and always prayed" (Acts 10: 2). He reminds us of the other centurion described by Saint Luke, who built the synagogue at Capernaum (Luke 7: 5). It may be that he had heard of Peter or the other apostles. Possibly he had been to Jerusalem and there heard of the followers of Jesus. Or perhaps he had even heard the preaching of Philip (Acts 8: 40). At any rate he had a vision, one afternoon about three, at the hour of prayer, in which an angel appeared to him and directed him to send to Joppa for Peter. Cornelius at once called two of his servants, and one of the faithful soldiers who formed his bodyguard, told them of the vision, and sent them to Joppa.

JAFFA (JOPPA): TRADITIONAL HOUSE OF SIMON THE TANNER

Peter's vision.—Stranger still was a vision which Peter had the following day. It was about noon, and he had gone up on the housetop to pray. He was hungry, but the light noon meal was not yet ready. (Jews often ate no lunch, only breakfast and dinner; the Greeks and Romans ate three meals like us.) As he prayed he fell into a trance, and saw a strange vessel descending from the sky. It seemed like a vast sheet suspended from heaven by the four corners, and in it were all sorts of animals and fowls. It seemed to him that he heard a voice saying, "Rise, Peter, kill and eat." This was shocking to a faithful Jew, for the Old Testament forbade many kinds of animal food, and the Jews strictly observed the laws about clean and unclean meats (as orthodox Jews still do). Peter replied, "Not so, Lord; for I have never eaten anything common or unclean." And a second time the voice was heard, answering his scruples, "What God has cleansed make not thou common." Three times the vision appeared; and at last it vanished, being "received up into heaven." It was evident that some mysterious significance was to be attached to this vision, something more than a mere matter of food. What it was Peter soon was to learn.

PETER'S VISIT TO CÆSAREA

While he mused over what he had seen and heard the three messengers of Cornelius arrived at the outer gate of Simon's house and called for Peter. He at once went down and welcomed them, and upon learning of their mission prepared to accompany them to Cæsarea the next day.

In Cornelius' house.—Peter's readiness to accompany Gentiles and to accept the hospitality of a Gentile officer's home was not due to his dream on the tanner's housetop; it was the prompting of the Spirit which led him (Acts 10: 19, 20). Otherwise the journey might never have been taken.

It was an overnight journey to Cæsarea, northward along the coast. The next day when they arrived they found Cornelius, with his relatives and close friends, waiting for Peter. The salutation of Cornelius was a profound act of reverence, which Peter refused to accept, as it was worship due only to God. Going into the house, he found a large company gathered together to hear him. Feeling strange in such company, actually a guest in a Gentile home, Peter felt that some apology was necessary—even at the risk of rudeness to his host. So he explained his vision (Acts 10: 28-29).

Then Cornelius related his experience and the command which he had received to send for Peter. "And so we are all present here in the sight of God," he added, "to hear whatever has been commanded you by the Lord."

Peter's sermon.—So Peter began with a simple, straightforward explanation of the disciples' belief in Jesus.

> "Of a truth I perceive that God is no respecter of persons, but in every nation he that feareth him, and worketh righteousness, is acceptable to him. The word which he sent to the children of Israel, preaching good tidings of peace by Jesus Christ (he is Lord of all)—that saying ye yourselves know, which was published throughout all Judæa, beginning from Galilee, after the baptism which John preached; even Jesus of Nazareth, how that God anointed him with the Holy Ghost and with power: who went about doing good, and healing all that were oppressed of the devil, for God was with him. And we are witnesses of all things which he did both in

the country of the Jews and in Jerusalem; whom also they slew, hanging him on a tree. Him God raised up the third day, and gave him to be made manifest, not to all the people, but unto witnesses that were chosen before of God, even to us, who did eat and drink with him after he rose from the dead. And he charged us to preach unto the people, and to testify that this is he who is ordained of God to be the Judge of the quick and the dead. To him bear all the prophets witness, that through his name every one that believes in him shall receive remission of sins."—Acts 10: 34-43.

The gift of tongues.—He had gone no further than this in his sermon when a strange interruption occurred —especially strange it seems to us, though common enough in the early Christian churches. "The Holy Spirit descended on all who heard him," and they began to "speak with tongues" and glorify God. This was not the first time in Peter's experience that this had occurred; but what was most strange was that this was the first time it had ever happened to Gentiles! Heretofore only Jews had "received the gift of the Spirit." Those who accompanied Peter, Jews like himself and disciples of Jesus, were equally amazed to hear Gentiles speaking in this manner, even as orthodox Jewish believers in Jesus.

Peter stopped his sermon and asked, "Can anyone forbid the baptism of these, who have already received the Holy Spirit, even as we?" And so they were baptized then and there—the first Gentiles to be converted to Christianity. Peter remained with them for some time, teaching them no doubt about Jesus and relating the story of the apostles' work in Jerusalem since the day of Pentecost.

Peter's return to Jerusalem.—But as soon as Peter returned to Jerusalem there were some who thought he should not have accepted Gentile hospitality. It was all very well for Gentiles to hear and believe the gospel. But as for fellowship with them, Peter, as a good Jew, should never have accepted it—for it meant giving up the observance of the Law's requirement regarding food. Gentiles paid no attention to the Law's "distinction of meats."

Peter's reply was to relate just what had taken place: his vision and his visit and the prompting of the Spirit; above all the "speaking with tongues" by his Gentile hearers, the gift of God himself.

> "If then God gave unto them the like gift as he did also unto us, when we believed on the Lord Jesus Christ, who was I that I could withstand God?"—Acts 11: 17.

With this their objections were silenced, and they gave thanks to God that even to the Gentiles he had granted "repentance unto life."

It was truly a great moment in Christian history when these words were uttered.

STUDY TOPICS

1. Look up Lydda, Joppa, and Cæsarea on the map. Measure the distance from Joppa to Cæsarea.
2. What did the title "centurion" signify? There were five cohorts of infantry and one ala of cavalry stationed at Cæsarea for the military control of Palestine (that is, the province of Judæa-Samaria). Look up the number of men in cohort and ala, and give the total for the Roman "army of occupation."
3. Look up the story of the restoration of Jairus' daughter

(Luke 8: 40–42, 49–56) and compare it with the restoration of Dorcas (Acts 9: 36–42).

4. Had the form of Peter's vision any connection, do you think, with the fact that he was hungry? The greatest significance of the vision was not, of course, that he saw food, but that he was commanded to eat food hitherto forbidden.

5. What were the main points of Peter's address in Cornelius' house?

6. What was the significance of the "outpouring" of the Spirit on Gentiles as well as Jews?—(To Peter, and those who were with him, and to the "apostles and brethren" in Jerusalem.)

7. Are there any traits in the characters of Saint Peter and Cornelius the Centurion which you especially admire? Describe the two men, and name any other persons of whom they remind you. How may they be imitated to advantage?

8. The Holy Spirit appeared in an unexpected quarter when Gentiles began to "speak with tongues." Are there new ways in which the Spirit moves men to-day, do you think, which many persons do not expect?—for example, good movements begun outside the church. Should we recognize in them the hand of God?

CHAPTER XI

CHRISTIANITY REACHES ANTIOCH

As we have seen, the first twelve chapters of the book of Acts describe the gradual expansion of the church in Palestine, from the eleven disciples gathered in the upper room just after the resurrection to the time when Christianity first began to spread beyond the borders of the Jewish land. The remainder of the book (chapters 13–28) is devoted almost entirely to the work of Paul and shows the further development of the Christian mission in the provinces along the north coast of the Mediterranean until it reached Rome itself and Paul found hearers in the very capital of the empire. In this latter part of the book Luke has made use of a diary written by someone who accompanied Paul on certain of his journeys—most probably, Luke himself, Paul's physician and traveling companion. This is very different from the earlier part of the volume, where his sources were the accounts which had been handed down in Palestine or elsewhere, stories which he had been told by men more closely in touch with the events related, even from the days of the first "eyewitnesses and ministers of the Word." These stories which record the origin and earliest development of our religion can teach us much if we study them carefully and sympathetically.

A religious movement.—In the first place, the church was not a school of philosophy. There were many such schools in the ancient world. Teachers of Stoicism, Epicureanism, Platonism, Cynicism were to be found in every great city—many of them teaching on the street corners or in hired halls to crowds of listeners. But the church was the expression or outward manifestation of a new religion taking powerful hold of the souls of men. And religion in ancient times was always belief in the "supernatural." Without miracles it is difficult to see how the Christian religion could ever have originated or spread abroad in the world in which it arose. Everyone in those days believed in miracles—Jews, Greeks, barbarians. A miracle was the surest proof of the divine authority of a teacher and of God's approval of his teaching.

Its spread among the poor.—In the second place, Christianity arose among the lowly. It was not the educated, or the wealthy, or the socially prominent who crowded into the church by the thousands (Acts 2: 41 and 4: 4) in the first days. "Not many wise, not many noble have part therein; but God has chosen the weak ones of earth to put to shame the strong" (1 Corinthians 1: 26, 27). It was the religion of workingmen and women, poor artisans and peasants, publicans and fishers and villagers, and it was destined soon to win soldiers, tentmakers and dyers, and slaves attached to the great households in the chief cities. The religious authorities of the Jewish people at Jerusalem despised the new sect as "men ignorant of the Law," and therefore having no right to teach the people. It seemed absurd, to the educated priests and rabbis of the capital, for Galilæan peasants and fishermen to be proclaiming the Messiahship and resurrection of Jesus of Nazareth, whom they had put to death. The names of believers mentioned in the first twelve chapters of the Acts are the names of obscure men and women, made great only by their devotion to Jesus and the gospel, or preserved

to later history only by their relation to its earliest
teachers.

Its rapid growth.—In the third place, these old
traditions reflect an exceedingly rapid extension of the
Christian movement. The story of Pentecost with men
from almost every region of the Jewish Dispersion in
the audience of the apostles, and three thousand baptized
on a single day, can scarcely be an exaggeration. Persecution, when it came, served only to extend the preaching of the message. Even martyrdom, as in the death
of Stephen, impressed the persecutors with the courage
and faith of the disciples, and broke down the wall of
bigotry and prejudice. If we make a list of the cities
and districts mentioned in Luke's narrative up to the
first missionary journey of Paul (that is, which were
evangelized in the eighteen years between 29 and 47
A. D.), we discover the following: Jerusalem (Acts 2: 5,
etc.), the cities near by (5: 16), the regions of Judæa
and Samaria (8: 1; 11: 29), the city of Samaria (8: 5),
many villages of Samaria (8: 25), Azotus (8: 40), Cæsarea
(8: 40; 10: 1), Damascus (9: 2, 10, 19), Tarsus (9: 30,
11: 25), Galilee (9: 31), Lydda (9: 32), Sharon (9: 35),
Joppa (9: 36), Phœnicia, Cyprus, Antioch (11: 19)—
fourteen are mentioned by name, not counting "the
cities near by." To these should be added, perhaps,
Ethiopia (8: 39), with its one messenger of the gospel,
the steward of the royal treasury; and Cyrene (11: 20),
if we are to translate "men from Cyrene."

No mention is made of Egypt; but if Ethiopia and
Cyrene were evangelized this early, surely Alexandria
must have heard the good tidings, for there was in the
whole world no greater center of both orthodox and
Hellenistic Judaism than the great cosmopolitan city in
the Nile delta, with its million or more Jews—over half

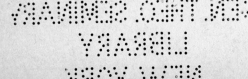

the city's total population. We infer from tradition and from the later strength of the church there that Alexandria received the gospel early; but no records have come down to us, and the early history of the church in Egypt is quite obscure. It is to be noted that Paul, who refused to labor in any other man's field, never even mentions Egypt, though for years he cherished the plan of visiting Rome, and even Spain, on the very "borders of the west." Moreover, Apollos, one of the most gifted preachers of apostolic times, came to Ephesus from Alexandria and taught in the church there (Acts 18: 24, 25). That other cities, not mentioned in Acts, should be added to this list is beyond doubt. The record of Luke is incomplete, and there must have been disciples in the cities and villages visited by Jesus during his ministry and mentioned in the Gospels (for example, Bethany, Emmaus, Jericho, Arimathæa, Nazareth, Sychar, Chorazin, Capernaum, Bethsaida, Cana, Nain).

THE GOSPEL TO THE GENTILES

It was Luke's main purpose in writing the Acts to show how Christianity spread geographically from Jerusalem to Rome, and was gradually planted in all the chief cities of the northern and eastern part of the empire. But he has also shown Christianity overstepping the narrow bounds of the Jewish religion, with its ancient, now antiquated beliefs and conceptions. The Jews believed that no one could be saved without accepting Judaism, and the earliest followers of Jesus in Jerusalem shared this belief. If any but Jews heard the gospel and desired to be baptized, they must also take upon themselves the "yoke of the Law," receive its rites, and share its obligations. Christianity to them was not a new universal religion; it was only a higher, purified and perfected form of Judaism. The baptism of the Ethiopian was no exception, for he was perhaps already a proselyte to the Jewish faith. And Cornelius and his family were "God-fearing"; they leaned strongly toward Judaism, and were Jews in everything but the name. Still, as we have seen, Peter's fellowship with Gentiles, especially in eating at table with them, caused consternation among the orthodox disciples at Jerusalem. His only apology was the fact that the Holy Spirit had been given them, "even as it was given us at the first."

But the day was soon coming when the doors of the church would be thrown wide open to the Gentiles. The man who opened them widest and stood most firmly for the principle of freedom was Saint Paul, who called himself "Apostle to the Gentiles." He was the strongest advocate of religious freedom in all the early church— but he was not the first. Already, tendencies were operative which were leading inevitably in this direction. It would not be long until the church irresistibly broke over the barriers. Luke has indicated this very clearly in his account of the church in Antioch (Acts 11: 19–26).

The Gospel preached in Antioch.—Antioch was the third largest city in the empire. It was formed of four unwalled cities which had grown up side by side at different times on the banks of the Orontes River, eight miles from its mouth at Seleucia, and were later inclosed within one large wall with towers. Its streets and public buildings were among the finest in the world. A large part of its population was Jewish, and in addition there was a large body of proselytes. Although a center of learning, its fame was due, rather, to its luxury and lax ways of living. It was a wealthy city and busy, but

THE SITE OF ANTIOCH AT THE PRESENT TIME

corrupt. It was the queen of the Levant, and was
destined to become a key-city in the expansion of early
Christianity. And at the same time its own need of
the gospel was immense.

How Christianity spread.—On account of the large
Jewish colony it was quite natural that when the church
in Jerusalem was scattered at the time of Stephen's
martyrdom, some of the disciples should take refuge in
Antioch. And so Luke records:

> "They traveled as far as Phœnicia and Cyprus and
> Antioch, speaking the word to none save only to
> Jews. But there were some of them, men from
> Cyprus and Cyrene, who when they were come to
> Antioch spake unto the Greeks also, preaching the
> Lord Jesus. And the hand of the Lord was with
> them, and a great number of them believed and
> turned unto the Lord.
>
> "The report concerning them came to the ears of
> the church in Jerusalem, and they sent forth Barna-
> bas as far as Antioch; who, when he came and saw
> the grace of God, was glad; and he exhorted them
> all that with purpose of heart they should cleave
> unto the Lord. He was a good man and full of the
> Holy Spirit and of faith, and much people was added
> unto the Lord. And he went forth to Tarsus to seek
> for Saul, and when he had found him brought him
> to Antioch. And it came to pass that for a whole
> year they remained there with the church, and
> taught much people; and the disciples were called
> Christians first in Antioch."—Acts 11: 19-26.

Thus Christianity spread, in those far-off days, chiefly
by the word of mouth of anonymous disciples, men
whose hearts overflowed with the message, so that they
could not keep silent but had to speak. It is noteworthy

also, in this narrative, how the mother-church in Jerusalem kept in close touch with the daughter-churches in
other cities. Barnabas was sent down to oversee the
conduct of the church in Antioch, just as Peter and
John had been sent down to Samaria while Philip was
preaching there (Acts 8: 14). Peter had gone on a pastoral tour of the churches in Judæa (Acts 9: 32) and
when he returned gave a report to the "apostles and
brethren" in Jerusalem (Acts 11: 1–18). There were
no settled pastors in these scattered churches, only
"prophets" and "teachers" (Acts 11: 27; 13: 1) who
served as missionaries of the gospel, instructors of the
new converts (as "ministers of the word," teaching the
life of Jesus and repeating his words—Luke 1: 2, 4),
and speakers with tongues. Some of them possessed
extraordinary powers of prophecy—Luke gives a brief
narrative of the prophecy of Agabus, one of the prophets
who came down from Jerusalem to Antioch, and, like
Elijah of old, announced a great famine which was soon
to come over the world, which took place shortly afterward, as Luke says, "in the days of Claudius." When
the famine came the disciples in the other churches
took up a collection, "every man according to his ability,"
for the relief of their poor fellow believers in Judæa.
Paul and Barnabas had charge of this relief fund, and
delivered it to the "elders" in Jerusalem (Acts 11: 30).[1]

The charity of the early church, its care of the poor,
its unity and fellowship, its simple organization under
the oversight and control of the apostles and elders at
Jerusalem, its gradual expansion until it finally reached

---

[1] Note that it was the "elders" who had the care of the poor, as the original
seven "deacons" (Acts 6: 5) were either now dead or scattered over Palestine. Or
it may be that "elders," not "deacons," was the name by which they were commonly known. They are not given any title in Acts 6.

and overstepped the limits both of Jewish territory and Jewish legalism—all this is clearly recognizable from the traditions which Luke records in the early chapters of the Acts.

PETER RELEASED FROM PRISON

There is one more brief narrative, connected with the reign of Herod Agrippa, which Luke inserts in his history before he begins with the epoch-making career of Paul.

A new Jewish king.—Herod Agrippa I was king of all Palestine. He was the grandson of the old King Herod "the Great," who died in 4 B. C., and he was bosom friend of the Emperor Caligula. In 37 A. D. he received from the Emperor the title of king, and for a kingdom the former tetrarchies of Philip and Lysanias in northern and eastern Palestine. When Antipas died in the year 40, Galilee and Peræa were added to his territory. The Emperor Claudius, whom Agrippa used his influence to elect, added in 41 the Province of Judæa (formerly under the rule of procurators) to his kingdom, so that for a time he controlled all Palestine. The Holy Land was thus once more completely under the rule of a Jewish king—as in the days of his grandfather Herod, of Simon the Maccabee, of David and Solomon. The Jewish historian Josephus, writing after the fall of Jerusalem, describes him as a pious and gentle monarch, devoted to the Pharisaic study and observance of the Law, and a great favorite with his people. His reign was brief, for he died in the year 44.

Fresh persecution.—For all his gentleness and legalistic piety, he was a persecutor of the Christians—in order, as Luke relates, to please the (orthodox) Jews (Acts 12:3). James the brother of John was put to death with the sword, and henceforth we find another James, "the brother of the Lord" (that is, Jesus' brother), at the head of the community in Jerusalem. Seeing that this act was approved by the majority of his subjects, Agrippa next ordered Peter imprisoned, about the time of Passover.

The story of Peter's imprisonment, the prayers of the church for his safety, the account of his miraculous release by an angel, his return to the house where the disciples were gathered and the alarm of the maid who answered his knock at the gate and could not believe it was really Peter—this story is related with great detail in the twelfth chapter of Acts. It is almost the last of the traditions of the early Jerusalem church, and one of the most beautiful in all religious literature. What is especially noteworthy for our purpose, as picturing the condition of the primitive church, is the assembly of the Christians at the home of Mary, the mother of John Mark (Acts 12:12)—evidently a well-to-do house, with gateway, porter's door, and inner court. The Christians in Jerusalem still attended the services in the Temple, and observed the hours of prayer; those outside Jerusalem, like their fellow Jews everywhere, went to worship in the synagogues. But in addition, they had their meetings for prayer and instruction and fellowship in the homes of believers, where also they observed the breaking of the bread, after the example of their Lord. The upper room, perhaps in Mary's house, was a place sacred to the apostles and brethren, for here Jesus had eaten the Passover with his disciples before he died. But in their own homes as well they "broke bread," "with gladness and singleness of heart," praising God and telling the good news of Jesus and his kingdom to all who would listen to them—but still for the most part "speaking the word to none save Jews."

STUDY TOPICS

1. Read the story of Peter's release from prison (Acts 12: 1–19). Who were the authorities of the church in Jerusalem, as reflected in this tradition (see verse 17)? What can you say of the organization of the church at this time? What were the duties of the "prophets and teachers"? "the elders"? the apostles?

2. Look up some of the following instances of the "church in the house" among the early Christians: Acts 1: 13; 2: 46; 4: 23; 5: 42; 9: 19, 43; 10: 33; 11: 26; 12: 12. For the expression, see Romans 16: 5. Describe the worship of the early Christians at this date.

3. Draw a map showing the expansion of the church in the first eighteen years of its existence (before Paul's first missionary journey—Acts 1–12), locating the cities and districts evangelized in this period (cities with red dots; districts with fine, red shading).

4. Make a list of the believers mentioned by name in these early chapters of Acts. Of how many of them do you know anything more than their names? See Acts 1: 13, 23; 3: 2; 4: 36; 5: 1; 6: 5; 8: 13, 27; 9: 1, 33, 36, 43; 10: 1; 11: 28; 12: 12, 13, 17; 13: 1. Only thirty-seven are mentioned by name—thirty-seven out of several thousand—and these for the most part obscure men and women. What does this suggest as to the condition of the early Christians, and the class among whom the new faith spread most widely?

5. Recall the sermons described or quoted in the first twelve chapters of Acts. What were the main points of the gospel which the early apostles presented? (See, for example, Acts 2: 22–40; 3: 12–

26; 4: 9–12; 5: 30–32; 10: 34–43.) Note especially what was said regarding (1) the ministry of Jesus and his Messiahship; (2) his death and resurrection; (3) the Holy Spirit; (4) the coming judgment; (5) the need for repentance.

6. What was the importance of miracles in the early church?

7. Why was the earliest preaching of the gospel limited to Jews?

8. If Christianity spread to-day as it did in the first century, what would be some of the features in its expansion? How might it spread in your own town or neighborhood? Imagine the part you yourself might take in it. Is there any reason why the extension of the church should be left entirely to missionaries and clergymen?

PART TWO

THE WORK OF PAUL

CHAPTER XII

THE GOSPEL IN CYPRUS AND GALATIA

It was now nine years (38–47 A. D.) since Paul had gone from Jerusalem to work in Syria and Cilicia. Except for the brief visit at the time of the famine (Acts 11: 30; compare Galatians 1: 22–24) he had not been in Jerusalem all this time. What results he saw from his preaching in Cilicia we do not know. At Antioch, however, the church was growing steadily, and Paul's year there with Barnabas (Acts 11: 25, 26) was a busy one, while he "taught much people" and preached the gospel week after week. Among the leaders of the church in Antioch, the "prophets and teachers" were Barnabas, Simeon Niger (that is, the African?); Lucius of Cyrene; Manaen, the foster brother of Herod the tetrarch; and Paul (Acts 13: 1).

PREACHING IN CYPRUS

Some of these were no doubt the "men of Cyprus and Cyrene" who had come to Antioch and preached to Gentiles (Acts 11: 20). Naturally, they would be anxious to spread the gospel among their own people. We are not surprised, then, to read that "as they ministered to the Lord, and fasted, the Holy Spirit said, 'Separate me Barnabas and Saul for the work whereunto I have called them.'"

The missionaries set apart.—The time had come for another step to be taken in the westward advance of Christianity across the empire. So after the "prophets" had fasted and prayed they laid their hands upon the heads of the two missionaries, thus solemnly consecrating them to their new work, and sent them away.

Paul's plans.—Barnabas was a native of Cyprus (Acts 4:36f.). It was therefore quite natural that he should be chosen for this mission. The choice of Paul was doubtless due both to his success already achieved in Tarsus and Antioch and to his eagerness to spread the message still farther among both Jews and Gentiles. We can easily imagine how he planned his work in order to reach the greatest number in the shortest time. He would visit the great metropolitan key-cities in the various provinces, staying just long enough to get a church started, and then press on to more distant regions. Cyprus, the old home of his companion Barnabas, was only a stepping-stone on the way to Galatia, Asia, and Europe!

At Salamis.—Bidding farewell to the church, the two missionaries went down from Antioch to Seleucia, the seaport, and took ship for Cyprus. Some of the brethren no doubt came to see them off and stood on the great stone pier (fragments of which still remain, running far out beneath the water), and waved good-by as the small wooden coaster got slowly under way. At last only its angular lateen sails could be seen, far out over the blue waters, as it headed west-southwest for Cyprus. The route covered about one hundred and thirty-five or one hundred and forty miles—eighty miles to the northeast tip of the island and the remainder coastwise, with the Olympian range of mountains in full view. The voyage probably took the best part of a day and a night.

Salamis was the eastern port of Cyprus, with roads forking west, northwest and southwest toward the interior of the island. Here Paul and Barnabas disembarked, and preached the gospel in the Jewish

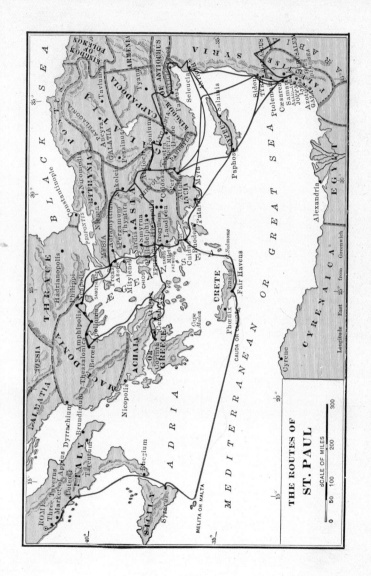

THE ROUTES OF
ST. PAUL

SCALE OF MILES

0   50   100   200   300

synagogues. They must have remained several weeks
in order to preach in more than one. It is not said that
they preached to Gentiles, though they doubtless did,
as well as to Jews. It may even be that Salamis was the
birthplace of Barnabas, and that he had relatives there
with whom the apostles stayed. Luke says that they
"had John as their attendant." This was John Mark,
the cousin of Barnabas, whose mother owned the house
in Jerusalem used by the church (Acts 12: 12), and who
was later to write the Gospel known by his name.

At Paphos.—Leaving Salamis after some weeks, they
journeyed through the island toward Paphos, its port on
the southwest coast. Cyprus was a beautiful island,
populous, and famous from early antiquity as the seat
of the worship of Aphrodite. It had little to boast of in
the way of culture or art or learning, but it was yearly
visited by multitudes of pilgrims, and its shrines were
known throughout the whole world. In the interior the
missionaries would naturally find ample opportunity to
preach to heathen as well as Jews; Luke says that they
went through the "whole island" on their way to the
opposite coast.

At Paphos lived the Roman proconsul, Sergius
Paulus. He was a man of education, but, like most
educated Greeks and Romans of the time, he believed
in sorcery and magic. Few men in Paul's day had the
courage to throw off the old superstitions, handed down
for thousands of years; after all, most persons thought,
there "might be something in them." In Sergius Paulus'
retinue was a Jewish magician and false prophet called
Bar-Jesus, or Elymas.

Unmasking a magician.—Hearing of Paul and Barnabas, the proconsul had them brought before him in
order to learn more about their teaching. What they

said we do not know. But it must have been something which irritated or alarmed the sorcerer, for he at once endeavored "to turn aside the proconsul from the faith." Then Paul, gazing sternly at the impostor, said, in words that sounded to Elymas like the curses he himself was wont to pronounce: "You son of Satan, full of craft and crookedness! You enemy of everything good! How long will you continue to pervert the ways of the Lord? Behold, even now his hand is upon you; you are going blind, and shall not see anything for a long time!"

Elymas was overcome at his own game; and as he felt a mist rising before his eyes, he went out to look for someone to lead him by the hand. Then the proconsul, seeing the magician's discomfiture, believed the apostles' message and became a Christian. The story of this incident, like that of Simon Magus (Acts 8), helps us to realize the conditions under which the gospel was first preached in the Gentile world outside Judæa.

IN PAMPHYLIA AND GALATIA

The narrative of Acts proceeds very abruptly, "Now Paul and his companions set sail from Paphos and came to Perga in Pamphylia" (Acts 13:13). Little as it tells us, that much is significant. It is no longer "Barnabas and Saul"; it is "Paul and his companions" who set out for the mainland provinces—subtly indicating Paul's position as leader in this step.

At **Perga.**—It was a longer voyage than from Antioch to Salamis, for the harbor of Attalia lay a hundred and seventy miles northwest from Paphos, and a round-about coaster would make it nearly two hundred miles. But it is noticeable how Paul avoids the kingdom of Antiochus in his travels—a rough mountainous region west and north of Cilicia, once overrun with pirates and brigands, and possessing no important cities. Pamphylia, on the other hand, was mainly a fertile and prosperous coast plain; and north of it, in the highlands, lay the great province of Galatia with its large cities joined and bound together by a spreading network of highways. We can easily see that it was Paul, with his plan for advancing the gospel "far among the Gentiles," who determined this movement to the north and westward.

What happened at Perga, the capital city of the province, we are not told. John Mark deserted and went home to Jerusalem, and the other two left soon after, pushing on straight north to Antioch of Pisidia (old Pisidia was now a part of the province of Galatia). It has been suggested that Paul became ill of malarial fever in the lowland along the coast, and had to go north for his health's sake into the higher altitudes of the western Taurus ranges. If so, it must have been a great discouragement to Paul for his strength to fail as soon as he had entered his new field. But he was not the only missionary of Christ who has had this experience, and in the end it proved no hindrance to his work. For a few months later he preached in Perga, on his returning journey to Antioch in Syria.[1]

At Antioch of Pisidia.—Antioch was a highland city, nearly four thousand feet above sea-level, and a Roman colony. This gave its citizens certain special rights, including exemption from certain kinds of taxes. Off to the southeast lay a fertile plain, across which passed the old and much-traveled road, already described, which ran across Asia Minor from Ephesus through the cities of Laodicea, Apamea, Antioch,

---

[1] There were two cities called Antioch, one in Pisidia, the other in Syria; be sure to locate them on the map.

Iconium, and Tyana, then through the Cilician Gates to Tarsus and the east. It was, therefore, an important strategic center for the evangelization of all southern Asia Minor, and could be made a base for further advance into the provinces of Asia and Galatia, for it lay almost on the boundary line between the two.

Paul's first step was to preach in the synagogue on the Sabbath following their arrival. After the scripture lessons from the Law and Prophets, as was the custom when notable visitors were present, the "rulers of the synagogue" invited Paul and Barnabas to speak. This was Paul's opportunity. Rising up and beckoning eagerly with his hand, he began by recounting the story of the deliverance from Egypt and the promise of God to send the Messiah to his people. "This Messiah," he said, "has already come, and his name is Jesus. He is the one announced by John the Baptist as close at hand. Nevertheless, the people in Jerusalem and their rulers rejected and put him to death—not knowing the prophets, they fulfilled them by condemning him."

> "But God raised him from the dead, and he was seen for many days by them that came up with him from Galilee to Jerusalem, who are now his witnesses unto the people. And we bring you good tidings of the promise made unto the fathers, how that God hath fulfilled the same unto our children, in that he raised up Jesus; as also it is written in the second psalm, Thou art my Son, this day have I begotten thee. . . .
>
> "Be it known unto you therefore, brethren, that through this man is proclaimed unto you remission of sins; and by him every one that believes is justified from all things, from which ye could not be justified by the Law of Moses. Beware therefore, lest that come upon you which is spoken in the prophets,

'Behold, ye despisers, and wonder, and perish;
For I work a work in your days,
A work which ye shall in no wise believe if one
     declare it unto you.' "
                                   —Acts 13: 30-33, 38-41.

Such was Paul's first recorded sermon. Its effect was
immediate and powerful. The apostles were invited to
speak again on the following Sabbath. Many of the
Jews and devout Gentiles followed them, anxious to
hear more of the message.

The next Sabbath, "almost the whole city" gathered
at the synagogue. This was more than the more orthodox
and conservative of the Jewish congregation could bear
—religion was becoming altogether too popular, and
they at once suspected Paul and Barnabas of sinister
designs. Doing their best to contradict what the apostles
said, they accused them of teaching falsely, until Paul
spoke out and said that they were proving themselves
unworthy of eternal life and from henceforth he and
Barnabas would preach to Gentiles. And as long as
they remained, their preaching was addressed to non-
Jews. Their success in this field is indicated by Luke
when he says, "The word of the Lord was spread about
throughout the whole region."

But not content to be let alone, the members of the
synagogue determined to drive the new teachers from
Antioch. Securing the interest of certain women of high
rank who had leanings toward the Jewish faith, they
worked on the leading men of the city, stirred up a
persecution, and drove Paul and Barnabas from their
territory.

   "But they shook off the dust of their feet against
them, and came unto Iconium. And the disciples

were filled with joy and with the Holy Ghost."—
Acts 13: 51-52.

It was another failure; but in spite of the failure, a
success!

STUDY TOPICS

1. Look up on the map the cities mentioned in this chapter, and trace the route followed by Paul and Barnabas. (If possible, see Murray's "Handy Classical
   Map of Asia Minor.") Trace the road from Ephesus
   through Antioch to Syria and the east. Show both
   the cities and the highway on a sketch-map in your
   notebook.
2. Look up "Cyprus" in the encyclopedia or Bible dictionary. Name some of its products and industries.
3. What light does the story of Elymas throw on the
   early preaching of the gospel?
4. Look up "Asia Minor" in the encyclopedia or Bible
   dictionary, and read the sections on Pamphylia,
   Pisidia, and Galatia. What can you learn of their
   population, products, and industries?
5. Why was Antioch of Pisidia a strategic center for missionary work?
6. Why did Paul begin by preaching in the synagogue,
   instead of turning at once to the Gentiles?
7. Read Paul's sermon in Antioch (Acts 13: 16-41), and
   compare it with other sermons reported in Acts,
   especially those of Peter and Stephen. What were
   Saint Paul's chief points? What was the significance
   of Jesus' resurrection, according to Paul?
8. Paul's ambitious plans for the spread of the gospel
   received a discouraging reception—but he kept right
   on, undismayed. Do we need a similar spirit in our
   work for Christ and righteousness? In the end,
   Paul's life-mission was a magnificent success. Final
   success or failure cannot always be judged by the
   present situation. Give some examples to show this.

CHAPTER XIII

MISTAKEN FOR GODS

It was ninety miles from Antioch to Iconium. Though Paul and Barnabas naturally followed the main highway, this lay through mountainous country, winding and hilly and hard to travel. For three or four days they journeyed along the *Via Sebaste* on foot, between the northern mountain range (now called the Sultan Dagh) at their left and the beautiful Lake Caralis at their right, then turning eastward up through the pass which led to the broad plain of Lycaonia, at whose mouth lay the end of their journey. But imagine how long the journey seemed, after their experience at Antioch! Only a man of dauntless faith and courage, like Saint Paul, would have pressed on undismayed to further toils and dangers.

THE CITIES OF LYCAONIA

Iconium was an important town in the southeastern part of Galatia made up of the ancient territory of the Lycaonians. Streams descended from the hills in the west and watered the plain, making the neighborhood of the city fruitful and even luxuriant. But so high and dry was the district that these streams went no farther, spending themselves, like the "rivers of the desert" near Damascus, in watering the immediate neighborhood.

Opposition from the Jews.—Here was a Jewish synagogue, in which, following his usual custom, Paul and Barnabas began their preaching. So effective was their ministry that "a great multitude both of Jews and

Greeks believed" (Acts 14:1). Luke adds that the divine approval was shown through "signs and wonders" which the apostles were permitted to do, which convinced those who saw them of the truth of the apostles' teaching. But it was not without opposition that their work prospered, for the "disobedient Jews" (that is, those who refused to accept or "obey" the new teaching) stirred up their Gentile neighbors to the point of exasperation, until the city was divided in its opinion, some siding with the Jews, others with the apostles. It was just as it had been in Antioch of Pisidia: the orthodox Jews were at first interested, and some believed; but soon opposition arose, and by intrigue or clever propaganda the Gentiles were roused to frenzy and mob violence. A plot was devised to abuse the apostles and stone them out of the city. But Paul and Barnabas learned of the scheme and fled, going southward toward Lystra and Derbe. There, and in the surrounding country, they continued to preach the gospel.

At Lystra.—At Lystra occurred one of those "signs and wonders" which often accompanied their preaching. A certain cripple, who had never walked but had been lame from birth, sat at the side of the street and heard Paul preaching. Seeing that the man was paying close attention and seemed to have the necessary faith, Paul said to him with a loud voice so that all could hear, "Stand upon your feet!" And the man at once got up and leaped and walked about! The story reminds us of the healing of the beggar at the Beautiful Gate by Peter and John (Acts 3), and helps us to visualize the effect of the apostles' preaching accompanied by such "mighty works" of restoration.

"Zeus" and "Hermes."—In Palestine, such an event was understood to prove the presence of God's Holy

Spirit, and his favor to his people: "A great prophet has arisen among us, and God has visited his people." But among the simple, illiterate, and pagan Lycaonians, who knew nothing of the Holy Spirit, the miracle meant the outward proof that some god was present, appearing incognito and in disguise. Men had believed for thousands of years, in Greece and Asia Minor, that this was what the gods did from time to time—examples are common in the *Iliad* and *Odyssey* of Homer.

Luke tells the story as follows:

> "And when the multitudes saw what Paul had done, they lifted up their voice, saying in the speech of Lycaonia, 'The gods have come down in the likeness of men.' And they called Barnabas, 'Zeus,' and Paul, 'Hermes,' because he was the chief speaker.
>
> "And the priest of Zeus, whose temple was before the city, brought oxen and garlands unto the gates and would have offered sacrifice with the multitudes. But when the apostles heard of it, they tore their clothes (in solemn adjuration) and sprang out among the crowd, crying out, 'Sirs, why do you do this? We also are men of like nature with you, and we bring you good tidings—that you should turn from this empty worship unto the living God, who made the heaven and the earth and the sea, and all that in them is. In the generations gone by he allowed all the nations to walk in their own ways; and yet he left not himself without witness, in that he did good and gave you rain from heaven and fruitful seasons, filling your hearts with food and gladness.' However, even with these words they were scarcely able to restrain the multitudes from offering sacrifice to them."—Acts 14: 11-18.

Paul stoned.—It seems almost impossible to believe that the one whom they were scarcely restrained from worshiping became the next day the object of their angry violence! Yet it is characteristic of all backward and superstitious peoples, and it is just what took place at Lystra. Not content with having driven the apostles from Antioch and Iconium, the unbelieving Jews sent emissaries to warn the other synagogues against the new teachers. These followed the same old tactics, and roused the multitudes by some adverse propaganda— perhaps accusing the apostles of witchcraft and evil designs upon the city. Stirred to violence, like a frenzied, half-insane mob at a lynching, they hurled rocks, bricks, and other missiles at Paul until he fell unconscious under the blows, then dragged him out of the city and left him, supposing that he was dead.

But as the disciples gathered about him he rose up and went with them into the city. The next day he and Barnabas departed for Derbe, fully thirty miles away to the south and east, on the very border of the province. Here they preached, apparently without opposition, and "made many disciples."

THE END OF THE FIRST MISSIONARY JOURNEY

What this journey cost Saint Paul we can only surmise. Thirty miles over a rough mountain road to Derbe on the very day after he was stoned and dragged out of Lystra for dead! Still weak, perhaps, from the fever which developed at Perga, worn with the ceaseless labor of travel afoot and preaching day after day, pursued by fanatics who sought his life and attempted to undo his teaching—these were some of the conditions under which the great apostle to the Gentiles fulfilled his mission and followed in the footsteps of his Master.

"In perils oft."—Seven years later, in one of his letters to the Corinthians, he wrote an account of his trials and difficulties as a missionary:

> "Of the Jews five times received I forty stripes save one. Thrice was I beaten with rods, once was I stoned, thrice I suffered shipwreck, a night and a day have I been in the deep; in journeyings often, in perils of rivers, in perils of robbers, in perils from my own race, in perils from Gentiles, in perils in the city, in perils in the wilderness, in perils in the sea, in perils among false brethren; in labor and toil, in watchings often, in hunger and thirst, in fastings often, in cold and nakedness. And in addition to many things which I omit, there is that which presses upon me daily—anxiety for all the churches."
> —2 Corinthians 11: 24-28.

Must he not have been thinking of this first journey into the interior of Asia Minor when he wrote these words? Some of those terrible experiences are doubtless the ones which he suffered on this long overland circuit of two hundred and fifty miles, from Perga up through the mountains north and east to Derbe, in weakness, pain, and constant persecution.

Results of the journey.—And yet this journey was to be far-reaching in its results. In Lystra lived a young man called Timothy, who was destined to become one of the greatest workers of the early church, Paul's own companion and "son in the faith," and his successor after his death. In Derbe, little as we hear of the mission in that place, lived Gaius, who later became one of Paul's most constant and devoted disciples. And Iconium, from which the apostles were compelled to flee for their lives, became in time one of the most influential centers of Christian work in the whole of central Asia

Minor. Roads ran out from it in all directions. Thanks
to the abundant fertility of its neighborhood, and its
own location as a center of industry, travel and commerce, the city grew in size and importance. Under the
Emperor Hadrian it was granted the right of independent
civil jurisdiction. And for centuries it was one of the
great Christian cities of the eastern half of the empire.
But without the few weeks' visit of Paul and Barnabas,
in the year 47 A. D., there might never have been a
Christian church in this important, strategic center!

The apostles return to Syria.—From Derbe it was
a much shorter route home to follow the highway east
to Tyana, go south through the Cilician Gates and revisit Tarsus, then follow the road around the Gulf of
Issus and down to Antioch in Syria. Instead, Paul and
Barnabas determined to retrace their steps, braving all
the dangers such a plan involved, and visit once more
the disciples whom they had made thus far. They refused to desert the new and scattered converts in the
cities of Galatia. And so, as Luke says,

"They returned to Lystra and Iconium and Antioch (in Pisidia), confirming the souls of the disciples, exhorting them to continue in the faith, and
telling them that through many tribulations we
must enter into the kingdom of God. And when
they had appointed for them elders in every church,
and had prayed with fasting, they commended them
to the Lord in whom they had believed.

"And they passed through Pisidia and came to
Pamphylia. And when they had spoken the word in
Perga, they went down to Attalia; and thence they
sailed to Antioch, from whence they had been committed to the grace of God for the work which they
had accomplished. And when they arrived, they
gathered the church together and rehearsed all that

God had done with them, and how he had opened a door of faith unto the Gentiles. Then they tarried no little time with the disciples."—Acts 14: 21-28.

It was a year since they had set out for Cyprus. They had covered nearly fifteen hundred miles by ship or afoot, in all weathers, by day and night, in much hardship and tribulation. But "a door had been opened to the Gentiles"—a door of faith through which multitudes were to come into the kingdom of Christ and find life in his name. There is no false note in the words of our hymn:

> "The Son of God goes forth to war. . . .
> Who follows in his train?"

From the very beginning it has been true of his followers that

> "They climbed the steep ascent of heaven
> Through peril, toil, and pain."

We wonder, sometimes, if we ourselves are worthy to bear the name of Christian, for which these heroic pioneers "suffered the loss of all things, if only they might gain Christ!"

STUDY TOPICS

1. Sketch a map of Asia Minor and Syria, and show its political divisions about the time of Paul. Locate the chief cities and show the route followed by Paul and Barnabas on the first missionary journey.
2. What grounds can you imagine for the bitter opposition of the "unbelieving" Jews to the preaching of the gospel?
3. What significance did the healing of the lame man at Lystra have for the people? Explain this, and compare it with the effect of our Lord's miracles upon

the people of Galilee. Do you remember what Jesus said about the significance of his own miracles of healing? See Matthew 11: 2–6; 12: 28.

4. Read 2 Corinthians 11: 23–33. Do you know the lives of any other missionaries (for example, Paton or Livingstone) to compare with this? Are there any experiences described which remind you of the opposition to Jesus in his ministry?

5. Try to imagine the scene as the apostles returned to Antioch and reported to the church what had happened on their journey. Tradition says that Luke's home was at Antioch. Perhaps he now heard from Paul's own lips the account which he gives in Acts 13–14. Give in your own words a brief résumé of the first missionary journey.

6. We honor the patriots who lay down their lives to set their country free, or to liberate the oppressed. How ought we to feel toward those who, at fearful cost to themselves, have planted Christianity among the nations of the world?

7. Are we worthy of the sacrifices made to give us the true religion if we sit idly by and take no share in its further extension to all mankind? How may we share in this task to-day?

8. Would you be willing to endure what Saint Paul endured in order to spread the gospel? What were the motives which explain his courage and perseverance?

CHAPTER XIV

FOES WITHIN THE FOLD

NOT everyone in the church rejoiced at the "open door of faith" proclaimed to the Gentiles by Paul and Barnabas. There were some, like those who protested when Peter accepted the hospitality of the centurion Cornelius, who felt that there was a grave danger in this open welcoming of Gentiles into the church. They thought that heathen should become Jews first, and then advance to the perfect form of Judaism taught in the gospel.

THE "JUDAIZERS"

It is hard for us to understand such narrowness and bigotry, as it seems to us. But we must remember that for hundreds of years the preservation of the Jewish faith required the most strict exclusion of foreigners with their idolatry and heathen customs, often grossly immoral. Moreover, for twenty generations the Jews had been persecuted by foreign nations, either on account of their religion (as in the days of Antiochus Epiphanes), or on account of their wealth and the strategic importance of Palestine as a frontier state.

Jews and Gentiles.—In the first century of our era, there were great numbers of Jews who bitterly resented the Roman control of Palestine, and hated every mark of the "bondage" which it was felt their nation suffered. Although the Romans gave Palestine as good a government as any in the world at that time, and made an honest effort (at least under the early procurators) to deal justly with their subjects; although Jewish life and property were never more secure, this antagonism on the part of vast masses of the Jews only deepened from year to year. At last war broke out, and the Jewish nation endeavored to regain its freedom. After four years of unsuccessful revolution, 66–70 A. D., ending in a terrible siege of the capital city, Jerusalem was taken, the Temple destroyed, and its rebuilding forever forbidden.

Christianity versus Judaism.—Throughout his public ministry, Jesus set himself firmly against this tendency to exclusiveness and bigotry. "Many shall come from the east and the west and sit down with Abraham and Isaac and Jacob in the kingdom of heaven." The Temple was a "house of prayer for all peoples." The gospel was to be preached "to all the nations." Nevertheless, it took his followers a long time to understand the plain meaning of his message, and to realize that although it was addressed first of all to the Jews it was also meant for the Gentiles—was intended, in fact, for all mankind. So there were some, even within the Christian Church, who thought that in order to become Christians, Gentiles must first become Jews in religion; that is, they must become "members of the Covenant," accept its rites and observe the ceremonies prescribed by the Law, including the offering of sacrifices at the Temple in Jerusalem, the ceremonial washings of hands and household utensils, the observance of fasts and feasts, new moons and Sabbaths, and all the other requirements of the ancient code.

These men were no doubt sincerely alarmed over the admission of Gentiles into the church without the fulfilling of the sacred requirements. They were sure a curse would fall upon everyone who broke the Law, and therefore upon all who, while supposed—as members of the true Israel, the church—to be observing it, were ignoring its requirements. The preaching of Paul and Barnabas and others seemed to them the height of presumptuous folly and wickedness. All that Judaism had ever stood for in the world was being jeopardized by these irresponsible preachers among the Gentiles. They were making religion far too free and easy a matter! They were trifling with the souls of men, with the coming of the heavenly kingdom, with the justice and mercy of God!

THE COUNCIL AT JERUSALEM

So it came to pass, not long after Paul and Barnabas had returned from their missionary tour of Cyprus and Galatia, that certain of these extremely conservative Christian Jews came down from Jerusalem to Antioch and announced, "Unless you are circumcised, according to the Mosaic custom, you cannot be saved." No wonder this statement caused consternation! If these men, who claimed authority from the Jerusalem church, were right, then Paul's and Barnabas' work must all be done over; their converts must be converted to Judaism as well as to Christianity, and take upon them the "yoke of the Law" in its fullest details.

The delegation from Antioch.—The result was "no small dissension and questioning" in the church at Antioch. The further outcome was that Paul and Barnabas, who had led in this mission to the heathen, and along with them certain others of "the brethren," were delegated to go up to Jerusalem and consult the apostles and elders about the question. That the two missionaries had no doubt of the rightness of their course is shown by the fact that on their way to Jerusalem they told the Christians in Phœnicia and Samaria about the conversion of the Gentiles. "And they caused great joy to all the brethren."

The conference.—Arrived in Jerusalem, they were received by "the church and the apostles and elders," and rehearsed all that God had done through them, and how he had opened the way before them for the preaching of the gospel to non-Jews. No doubt they told how the members of their own race in Antioch and Iconium refused to hear the message, and how, on turning to the Gentiles, they heard the good news with joy; how the Spirit had been present with them in manifest proofs of his power, to heal and to inspire—even as in the earliest days of the church in Jerusalem and Judæa.

"But there rose up," Luke says, "certain of the sect of the Pharisees who believed (that is, who had become Christians), saying, 'It is necessary to circumcise them, and charge them to keep the Law of Moses'" (Acts 15: 5). The issue could not have been more squarely presented. Paul saw that his whole career, his calling as a missionary and apostle, his faith in Jesus as the Saviour of all mankind and his whole understanding of the Christian religion hung in the balance. It alarmed him to think that possibly he "was running, or had run, in vain" (Galatians 2: 2).

Peter's address.—After much discussion one way and another, Peter arose and made a brief but telling speech. His position from the very beginning as spokesman for the apostolic band, his record as a missionary in Palestine, his dignified bearing, all commanded respect for what he said. He began:

> "Brethren, you know how that from the first days God chose among you that by my mouth the Gentiles should hear the word of the gospel, and believe. And God, who knows the heart, bore witness

to them, giving them the Holy Spirit even as he did to us; and he made no distinction between us and them, cleansing their hearts (not by sacrifices or ceremonial washings but) by faith. Now, therefore, why do you put God to the test, laying a yoke upon the neck of the disciples which neither our fathers nor we have been able to bear? The simple truth is that we ourselves trust that we shall be saved through the grace of the Lord Jesus, in just the same manner as they."—Acts 15: 7-11.

The advice of James.—The next speaker was James, the brother of the Lord.[1] He was now a Christian and, perhaps on account of his relationship to Jesus, was admitted into the decimated ranks of the Twelve. Beginning with a long quotation from the prophet Amos (which was not quoted word for word, but gave the general sense of the passage, namely, that God should bless and save Gentiles as well as Jews), he continued:

"My judgment is that we do not trouble those who from among the Gentiles turn to God; but that we enjoin them to abstain from the pollutions of idols, and from fornication, and from what has been strangled (that is, meat not prepared in the Jewish manner), and from blood (which the Law forbade). For Moses from generations of old has in every city them that preach him, being read in the synagogues every Sabbath."—Acts 15: 19-21.

To this proposal the assembly agreed.

The result of the conference.—The result of the conference was a circular letter addressed by the council to the church in Syria and Cilicia, to be delivered by two

---

[1] He must not be confused with James the apostle, one of the Twelve, who was a martyr in the days of Herod Agrippa (Acts 12: 2).

men "chief among the brethren"—Judas, called Barsabbas, and Silas. The letter read as follows:

> "The apostles and elder brethren unto the brethren which are of the Gentiles in Antioch and Syria and Cilicia, Greeting.
>
> "Forasmuch as we have heard that certain which went out from us have troubled you with words, subverting your souls; to whom we gave no commandment; it seemed good to us, having come to one accord, to choose out men and send them unto you with our beloved Barnabas and Paul, men that have hazarded their lives for the name of our Lord Jesus Christ. We have sent therefore Judas and Silas, who themselves also shall tell you the same things by word of mouth. For it seemed good to the Holy Spirit, and to us, to lay upon you no greater burden than these necessary things: that you abstain from what has been sacrificed to idols, and from blood, and from things strangled, and from fornication—from which if you keep yourselves it shall be well with you. Fare ye well!"—Acts 15: 23-29.

Returning to Antioch, the delegates called together the church and read the epistle. At this, the "brethren" rejoiced, for it meant the full recognition of the rights of the Gentile Christians within the church, without accepting the burdensome yoke of the Law. Judas and Silas, being "prophets," exhorted the brethren with many words and strengthened their faith. They stayed in Antioch for some time before returning to Jerusalem —though some of the ancient manuscripts read (Acts 15: 34) that "it seemed good to Silas to remain there." Thus was settled the most crucial and difficult problem which the church at that time had to face. If the "judaizers" had triumphed, Christianity might have become but a vigorous and somewhat rebellious sect within Judaism. It might not have survived the destruction of Jerusalem and the overwhelming set-back which Jewish missionary effort throughout the world suffered immediately afterward. Instead, it was set free to run its course as the vital new world-religion, destined to spread forth to the ends of civilization—and beyond— and bring the blessings of spiritual enlightenment and salvation to whole ages and generations then unborn. Even to-day, we cannot read the record of that rejoicing of the "brethren" in Antioch without sharing in it. The question might arise again, and did. But the "apostles and elders" had gone on record. The church had spoken its mind. And in this particular, at least, its mind was "the mind of Christ," whose gospel ignored the lines of race and nationality in religion, and who was the Saviour not of Jews only but of all mankind.

STUDY TOPICS

1. Recall Peter's visit to the house of Cornelius in Cæsarea. How did he justify himself when he returned to Jerusalem, and what was the feeling of the church there? (Acts 11, especially verses 2–3, 9, 12, 15, 17–18.)
2. Explain the historical reasons for Jewish exclusiveness and intolerance of Gentiles.
3. Look up some of Jesus' sayings which show his broad and supernational view of religion. See Luke 4: 24–27, 5: 36–38, 7: 9, 13: 24–30, 16: 16, 31, 20: 9–16; Mark 11: 17, 13: 10, 14: 9; Matthew 28: 18–20.
4. In the second chapter of Galatians Paul gives some details of the Judaistic controversy not mentioned in Acts. Chapter 2: 1–10 may refer to Paul's visit to Jerusalem at the time of the famine, 46 A. D.,

but more probably to the present visit (48, 49 A. D.). Peter's vacillation (2: 11–16) took place either shortly before the council or shortly after; we cannot decide the question. Paul's account, written three or four years after this date (in 52), is to be preferred to that of Luke, written thirty-five or forty years after. It may be that Luke has confused two different conferences, though he did the best he could with the traditions at his disposal. Evidently, he did not have a copy of Galatians.

5. What were the tenets of the Pharisees? Why would they be inclined, even as Christians, to insist upon Gentiles becoming Jews if they wished to enter the church?

6. What is an "epistle"? How is it distinguished from a "letter"? Why was the message of the council called by the former name?

7. What gave the church in Jerusalem its prestige and authority over the churches in other cities?

8. Explain the importance of the decision reached by the conference, for the work of Paul and Barnabas, and for the future of Christianity. Was it a compromise or a victory?

CHAPTER XV

THE GOSPEL IN MACEDONIA

NOT long after their return to Antioch Paul proposed that he and Barnabas should return to Cyprus and Galatia, and visit the disciples they had made there a year or two before. Whether or not their first journey had been at Paul's suggestion we do not know. Certainly this one was, for Paul kept thinking of the few scattered believers in the far-off cities to the west, wondering how they fared, whether they were persecuted or not, or whether they had kept the faith. The plan pleased Barnabas, and so they arranged to go.

ONCE MORE IN ASIA MINOR

The plan, presumably, was to cover the same route as before, going first to Cyprus, which was Barnabas' old home, and then to Pamphylia, Galatia, and home again.

A new companion.—Barnabas, the kind and generous, was anxious to take with them his cousin Mark, who had now returned from Jerusalem. But Paul, remembering the young man's faint-heartedness at Perga, when they were just beginning the most arduous part of their former journey, refused to take him along. The refusal was perfectly natural. Such hardships as Paul and Barnabas had endured in Pisidian Antioch, in Iconium and Lystra, and the heroic courage of their followers in those cities, were foreign to John Mark's experience. Now that the battle was nearly won, he was not going to have a coward and weakling share the triumph! Or if dangers still awaited them, Mark was not the one to face them.

On the other hand, Barnabas saw in his young relative the promise of something better than he had yet displayed—a real devotion to Christ and a willingness to "minister." And Barnabas was right: John Mark later became one of that group of attendants to the apostles, helpers, and fellow workers in the missionary field to whom the early church owed an inestimable debt. One of our Gospels was written by him—or at least, is based upon narratives of Jesus' life and teaching which Mark wrote down.

Paul and Barnabas were each determined to have his way, and since neither would compromise an inch, they decided to part. Barnabas took Mark and sailed for Cyprus; Paul chose Silas, the "prophet" who had been sent down from Jerusalem to Antioch with the Epistle against the "judaizers," and set forth to revisit Asia Minor.

In Galatia again.—The route selected was the highway north and west through Syria and Cilicia, where Paul revisited the churches which he had founded in the years before his first missionary journey; then up from Tarsus through the Cilician Gates and west across the kingdom of Antiochus by the shortest road to Derbe and Lystra. Here they found the disciples and delivered the "decrees" of the council at Jerusalem. Why Paul should read them to his converts in Galatia, when the apostolic Epistle had been addressed only to the Gentile Christians in Syria and Cilicia, we do not know. Perhaps the reason is that he foresaw the same problem arising in Galatia which had recently troubled the Christians in Antioch—and in this he was not mistaken.

Three years later he was to write his impassioned *Epistle to the Galatians*, begging them not to yield to the "false brethren" who had come to spy out their liberty in Christ and enslave them once and for all in the fetters of the Law.

At Lystra, Paul found Timothy, a young man whose father was a Greek and his mother a Jewess who had been won to the gospel. He was now well known as a Christian in Iconium as well as Lystra, and Paul determined to take him along with himself and Silas as a teacher and "minister." The decision was a wise one, for Timothy became not only a constant friend and companion, but a faithful Christian leader, and when Paul was imprisoned and led away to die he took charge of the churches in Greece and Asia Minor as his successor. One tradition states that he was the first bishop of the church in Ephesus.

The journey to Troas.—Instead of returning to Antioch, now that the churches had been visited and "strengthened in the faith," and were seen to be increasing in numbers daily, Paul determined to press on still farther westward. Just as at the end of their tour of Cyprus, Paul and Barnabas crossed over to Pamphylia instead of returning home, so it was here. Paul saw before him, in imagination, the vast, populous, busy cities on the western coast. For hundreds of years, "Asia" (that is, the province so named) had been one of the most prosperous regions in the world. Cicero had said, in one of his speeches,

> "The revenues of other provinces, gentlemen, are so meager that we scarcely derive enough from them to meet the cost of their defense. But Asia is so rich and productive that the fertility of its soil, the variety of its fruits, the vastness of its pasture

lands, the multitude of its commodities for export far exceeds that of all other countries."—For the Manilian Law, 6.

Here were millions of people awaiting the message of the gospel. Paul wished at once to go down the long roads from the Galatian highlands and preach the good tidings in their cities.

But it was not so to be. Whether by vision or words heard in trance, or by some other strange premonition, the Spirit forbade their preaching in Asia. Westward they could not go. Eastward or southward they would not. Hence northward their journey lay. The course of this tour is difficult to follow. Paul, of course, traveled without a guide book, and Luke very likely wrote without a map. The Acts states that they traveled "through the region of Phrygia and Galatia," thus avoiding the province of Asia on their left. Planning to go into Bithynia, the province farther north, on the eastern shores of the Sea of Marmora, they were once more hindered by "the Spirit of Jesus." Passing by Mysia (the old Greek region south of the Sea of Marmora and east of the Hellespont), they came at last to Troas. We must assume that the route was somewhat as follows: Iconium to Antioch, Antioch north through Amorium or Pessinus to Dorylæum, or perhaps through Apameia (on the way to Asia) to Cotiæum or Dorylæum (on the way to Bithynia), then west over the rough, dangerous mountain roads of upper Phrygia to the highways of western or northern Mysia and down these to Alexandria Troas. At the very least, the journey from Pisidian Antioch to Troas covered between four and five hundred miles. And it ended within fifteen miles of Ilium, the Troy of Homer's epic. They were now almost a thousand miles from Syria. The missionaries had

crossed Asia Minor and stood before "the wide prospect"—Troas was only a stepping-stone to Europe!

PAUL AT PHILIPPI

At last it became clear why the Spirit had forbidden Paul and his two companions to preach in Asia
and Bithynia. One night at Troas, Paul saw a vision
—a Macedonian stood before him, beckoning him
and imploring, "Come over into Macedonia and help
us!"

Across the Ægean.—Paul lost no time in obeying
this word of command—for so he interpreted what he had
seen and heard. Taking passage on a vessel bound for the
harbor of Neapolis, they made the island of Samothrace,
thanks to a good wind, on the first day; the remainder
of the voyage was easily made on the day following.
Landing at Neapolis, the three hastened north twelve
miles to Philippi. This was the chief city of the district,
a Roman colony, inhabited mainly by Italians, the
wealthy owners and their employees in the nearby gold
and silver mines.

Before we go further let us note the striking change
in person of Luke's verbs. In Acts 16: 10 he says,
"When *he* (Paul) had seen the vision, at once *we* set
about going into Macedonia." Instead of "he" and
"they," the narrative now reads "we." Throughout the
remainder of the volume, there occur passages where
"we" is used instead of "they" (Acts 16: 10–17; 20: 5–
15; 21: 1–8; 27: 1 to 28: 16). It is thought that Luke is
here using excerpts taken from the account of someone
who actually accompanied Paul on the journeys described, possibly from his own diary written down at
the time. Certainly, these sections rank high as historical sources.

The conversion of Lydia.—Their first move in Philippi was to attend the synagogue on the Sabbath. But instead of a synagogue they found only a "place of prayer" outside the city wall, on the bank of a small stream. Here were several women gathered for worship— there were probably only a few Jews in Philippi—whom they addressed, following Paul's usual custom. Among them was a woman from Thyatira, in the province of Asia, a seller of purple cloth. She was probably unmarried and well to do, having her own "household" of slaves and workmen and managing the business herself. She listened intently to their message and "her heart was opened by the Lord"; she was baptized, and then invited the missionaries to accept the hospitality of her home.

The ventriloquist.—Another day, as Paul, Silas and Timothy (and Luke?) were going out to the *proseuchê*, or place of prayer, a slave girl who was a ventriloquist and fortune-teller saw them and began following them about. She was, people thought, possessed of a demon, a "python," and she brought her owners much gain from her "soothsaying." Whether in mockery or in earnest, she began shouting after the Christians, "These men are servants of God the Most High, and proclaim a way of salvation." This was repeated frequently, wherever, in fact, Paul or his friends met her on the streets. At last, one day, Paul turned and commanded the possessing spirit to leave her. At once she ceased to cry out, and evidently her soothsaying power was gone.

Her masters, angered at their loss, seized Paul and Silas and dragged them before the judges in the agora, accusing them of preaching a religion not recognized by the state. They described the apostles as Jews, and stirred up the anti-Jewish feeling of their Italian neighbors—a feeling common at the time, and probably strong in such a loyalist town as Philippi, for the Jews had just been expelled from Rome by order of the Emperor Claudius (Acts 18:2). A crowd gathered and sided with the girl's masters against the strangers; and the prætors, who should have been judges and heard both sides of the case, commanded them to be beaten with rods and thrown in jail.

Paul and Silas in prison.—All this was manifestly and brutally unjust. Paul and Silas had done no wrong. They were victims of that same superstition, fanaticism, and jealous intolerance which had already cast great obstacles in their way as missionaries, and which was later to arouse against the church the fiercest persecutions.

The next morning the prætors sent lictors to set the prisoners free. But Paul refused to go, on the ground that he and Silas were Roman citizens, and had been beaten publicly, condemned without a trial, and thrown in prison. "Let the prætors themselves come and lead us out!" So the lictors returned and reported what Paul had said. Much alarmed, that they had thus abused Roman citizens, the prætors came and begged them to come out of the prison and leave the city. Then Paul and Silas came out, and went to the house of Lydia. "And when they had seen the brethren, they exhorted them and departed."

Thus began the Christian mission on the continent of Europe. In response to a vision and a call, "Come over into Macedonia and help us," they had come—only to be beaten with rods, cast into jail, and ordered out of the city! Were the missionaries discouraged or downhearted? No; for they had a vision of God's plan, and they were fellow workers with him in carrying it out. And their Master was one who had never shunned suffering or self-sacrifice.

STUDY TOPICS

1. Trace on a sketch-map Paul's probable route from Antioch to Philippi, as described in this chapter. Where the route is uncertain, use dots rather than a continuous line. Samothrace had no harbor. The ship probably anchored overnight at the north end of the island. Study this route first on a large-scale map (for example, Murray's), and locate all the cities mentioned.

2. Explain why Paul and Barnabas disagreed over taking John Mark with them. What were their probable motives? Barnabas, like his Master, saw latent goodness and usefulness in one who really deserved no "second chance." How should this example affect our dealings with those who fail the first time? Does it suggest God's patience with us when we fall short and ask a "second chance"?

3. Why did Paul read the decrees of the Jerusalem council in Galatia?

4. What led Paul to Troas? Recall the visions he had seen (Acts 9: 3–6; 22: 17–21; Galatians 1: 16; 2: 2; compare 2 Corinthians 12: 1–4) and the activity of "prophets" in the early church (Acts 11: 27–28; 15: 32; 21: 10–11). Note also the direct guidance of the Holy Spirit which the early Christians obeyed (Acts 1: 24–26; 2: 4; 5: 32; 10: 44; 13: 2; 15: 28; 20: 22–23).

5. What is meant by the "we" sections? Look them up, and make a list of the journeys or parts of journeys described and the cities named.

6. Recall what you have already learned, or look up again, the significance of Roman citizenship and define the rights which Paul claimed at Philippi.

7. Look up Acts 16: 25–34, which recounts an old traditional story of an earthquake which occurred while Paul and Silas were in jail at Philippi. It is a beau-

tiful story, and not altogether improbable. But it evidently does not belong in the account here, for in verses 35–40 nothing is said of the earthquake; if it had occurred during the night, silence would have been impossible.

CHAPTER XVI

BEFORE THE AREOPAGUS

LEAVING Philippi, accompanied by Silas and Timothy, Paul journeyed southwestward along the fine military and commercial highway, called the *Via Egnatia*, which crossed from the Ægean to the Adriatic over the Balkan peninsula. Passing by Amphipolis, near the mouth of the Strymon River, thirty miles from Philippi, and going on through Apollonia, thirty miles beyond, they reached Thessalonica, nearly forty miles farther still. This city (modern Saloniki, famous in the recent European war) stood at the head of the Thermaic Gulf, and was at that time the residence of the governor and the seat of the government of the whole Macedonian province.

IN THESSALONICA AND BERŒA

Here Paul and Silas remained for a considerable time —Luke says for three weeks. A gift of money from the tiny church in Philippi made possible the continuation of this visit (Philippians 4: 15–16).

> "Now when they had passed through Amphipolis and Apollonia, they came to Thessalonica, where was a synagogue of Jews; and Paul, as his custom was, went in unto them, and for three Sabbath days reasoned with them from the Scriptures, opening and alleging that it behooved Christ to suffer, and to rise again from the dead; and that 'This Jesus, whom,' said he, 'I proclaim unto you, is the Christ.' And some of them were persuaded and consorted

146

THESSALONICA (MODERN SALONIKI)

with Paul and Silas; and of the devout Greeks a
great multitude, and of the chief women not a few.
But the Jews being moved with jealousy, took unto
them certain vile fellows of the rabble; and gathering a crowd, set the city in an uproar; and assaulting
the house of Jason, they sought to bring them forth
to the people. And when they found them not, they
dragged Jason and certain brethren before the rulers
of the city, crying, 'These that have turned the
world upside down are come hither also, whom Jason
has received; and these all act contrary to the decrees of Cæsar, saying that there is another king,
one Jesus.' And they troubled the multitude and
the rulers of the city when they heard these things.
And when they had taken security from Jason and
the rest, they let them go."—Acts 17: 1-9.

"Another king, one Jesus."—The charge that the
Christian missionaries were "acting contrary to the
decrees of Cæsar" means that they were refusing to pay
divine honors to the Emperor, not that they disclaimed
civil allegiance or refused to obey the laws on account
of their loyalty to Jesus. Divine honors were claimed in
the name of the Roman Emperor, at that time, because
he was looked upon as the incarnation of the "genius of
the empire." This worship was held to be a patriotic
duty. And among pagans, who worshiped "gods many
and lords many," there seemed nothing sacrilegious or
wicked in worshiping one more, even though he were a
human being like themselves. But for Christians such
an act was blasphemy. There was only one God, and
no imperial decree could justify the offering of worship
to any other. This was one of the great causes for the
persecution of the early Christians. We see it in its
earliest beginnings here at Thessalonica.

The letters to the Thessalonians.—Brief as was Paul's stay in Thessalonica, the seed was sown, and soon after we see a flourishing Christian church in that city. The earliest letters of Paul which have come down to us were the two which he addressed to these new converts, Jason and his friends. These letters are in our New Testament and were written from Corinth, shortly after Paul's departure from Thessalonica. He wrote to encourage them to continue steadfast in the faith, in the face of persecution (1 Thessalonians 1: 1-6; 2: 14-16). Some of them were so interested in the preaching of the coming of the kingdom of God and Christ's return that they gave up their work and became "busybodies" and got into trouble. To them Paul repeated his word of command, "If any will not work, let him not eat" (2 Thessalonians 3: 10). No doubt the letters contain other echoes of Paul's preaching, and we can imagine him saying (as well as writing) such admonitions as the following:

> "Brethren, we beg you to honor those who work among you, presiding over you in the Lord and maintaining discipline; hold them in special esteem and affection, for the sake of their work. Be at peace among yourselves. We beseech you to keep a check upon idlers; encourage the faint-hearted, sustain the weak, never lose your temper with any; see that none pays back evil for evil, but always follow what is kind to one another and to all the world; rejoice at all times; never give up prayer; thank God for everything—such is His will for you in Christ Jesus; never quench the fire of the Spirit; never disdain prophetic revelations, but test them all, retaining what is good and abstaining from whatever kind is evil."—1 Thessalonians 5: 12-22.

It was very hard for Paul to leave his new friends in

one city and press on to the next; but even when persecution did not force him to flee he felt compelled to do it, for he wanted to see Christianity planted throughout the civilized world before he died.

At Berœa.—Driven from Thessalonica, Paul and his companions journeyed to Berœa, a city lying forty miles to the southwest, at the foot of the Bermius Mountains, and near the northern end of the beautiful, rugged Haliacmon valley. Here also was a Jewish synagogue, where Paul, following his usual custom, began by preaching to his race. "These were more noble," says Luke, "than those in Thessalonica, in that they received the word with all readiness of mind, examining the Scriptures daily, whether these things were so" (Acts 17: 11). As a result, many believed, including a number of Greeks, both men and women. But, just as it had been at Lystra, so was it here: the Jews of Thessalonica, hearing that Paul was in Berœa, came and stirred up trouble among the "multitudes"—probably using the same dishonest charge as before. For Jews, if they were loyal to their religion, were just as guilty as Christians of refusing to pay divine honors to Cæsar. No worshiper of the one true God could dream of such a betrayal of his faith.

Foreseeing the trouble that was about to break out, Paul set out, with a few of the "brethren," to go down to the sea, leaving Silas and Timothy behind to carry on the work.

PAUL AT ATHENS

Instead of returning northward, Paul, still accompanied by the "brethren," took ship, probably at Chalastra (or perhaps further south at Heracleum) and sailed down along the coast. Passing Mount Olympus,

the ancient home of the Hellenic gods, and the Vale of
Tempe, and Mount Ossa; then out beyond Eubœa (the
tide in the inner straits of the Euripus was too dangerous), past the islands of Andros and Ceos; then rounding
westward past the Cape of Sunium with its glorious
temple of Poseidon shining in the sunlight against the
gray-green hills and blue skies of Attica, soon the island
of Salamis, then the Piræus, and at last Athens itself
came in view. Bidding the "brethren" farewell at the
pier, and sending a message to Silas and Timothy to
follow him at once, Paul set out for Athens, up the street
walled on both sides which connected it with the port.

The city of art and learning.—How was Paul impressed by his first sight of this ancient city, once the
world's capital of culture and civilization? As a Jew,
its glorious temples and statues, even the exquisite beauty
of its Parthenon with Phidias' colossal Athena standing
before it, its stadium and theaters, its halls of learning
and schools of philosophy would impress him less than
it would impress a modern man, either Jew or Gentile.
To the Jews of that time, who saw all about them the
darker side of polytheism, and who had suffered most
barbarous persecutions in the name of culture, Athens
itself might well seem only artistic and luxurious cam-
ouflage for the deepest and most degrading moral
corruption. Not all Jews felt that way. But Jews from
Palestine, sons of Pharisees, men trained in rabbinic
theology as Paul was, usually held such an attitude. To
Paul, it might easily seem that Athens was "wholly
given over to idolatry."

Among the philosophers.—Even its schools of philosophy might make little impression upon his mind.
All that their speculations did for men was to arouse—
but not really to satisfy—the hunger for God. One page

trom the prophets led men nearer God than all the
writings of Plato and the Stoics; and, for all its long-
continued efforts, philosophy had not succeeded in
giving men the intense love of right and hatred of wrong
which the Law of Moses had done. "The wisdom of this
world," said Paul, "is foolishness before God."

To-day, of course, we have more sympathy with those
old Greek and Roman teachers of philosophy, of morals,
of history and literature. We are still touched by the
words of the aged philosopher-slave, Epictetus, who
lived in Rome at the very time Paul was preaching the
gospel in Macedonia and Achaia:

> "Ought we not both in public and in private inces-
> santly to sing hymns and speak well of the Deity
> and rehearse his benefits? . . . What else can I, a
> lame old man, do but sing hymns to God? If I
> were a nightingale, I would act the part of a nightin-
> gale, if a swan the part of a swan; but since I am a
> reasonable creature it is my duty to praise God.
> This is my business. I do it, nor will I ever desert
> this post so long as it is permitted me; and I exhort
> you to join in the same song."—Discourses, 1:16.

Wandering teachers of philosophy, religion, and
morality were to be found at that time in almost every
city of the empire. It was as one of these traveling
teachers that Paul was invited to speak before the
Areopagus, the "university club" of the city. Lacking
now, under the Roman government, its ancient powers
and jurisdiction (it was the court which sentenced
Socrates), it had become little more than a lyceum or
debating society, a pleasant meeting place for congenial
academic spirits. "For all the Athenians and the
strangers there," as Luke says, "spent their time in
nothing else but either to tell or to hear some new

thing." Such rights as the Areopagus still possessed
probably did not exceed that of licensing new teachers
in the city, or approving their credentials.

A herald of "strange gods."—Paul preached in the
agora, or market place, each day. Here he met followers
and teachers of the Epicurean and Stoic schools of
philosophy. Some of them smiled haughtily over his
simple, unadorned preaching, and looked upon him as
an upstart (or "seed-gatherer," in the Athenian college
slang of the day), an ignorant man with a smattering of
learning on which he was trying to "bluff" his way as
a professor. Others said, "He seems to be one more of
these Oriental missionaries with two gods—his deities
he calls *Jesus* and *Anastasis*" (*anastasis* was the Greek
word for "resurrection"). So it came to pass that they
urged him to speak before them at the Areopagus—or,
as we would say, "the club."

Paul's address.—We do not know where they met.
"Mars Hill" is the traditional site; but the term is only
a translation of "Areopagus." Paul began in a tactful
way. He had recently observed, somewhere in the city,
an altar inscribed

TO AN UNKNOWN GOD

This had no doubt been erected by someone who had
seen a vision, or heard a strange and apparently supernatural voice, or been prospered in business or restored
to health by a God whom he felt to be in that particular
spot, but whose name he had never learned. Altars of
this kind, dedicated to "unknown gods," have been discovered elsewhere in the Greek world.

The inscription furnished Paul with his "point of
contact," and so he began a very polished, academic
address:

"Gentlemen of Athens, I note on every hand that you are a most religious people. As I passed along and viewed your sacred monuments, I found among them an altar with the inscription, TO AN UNKNOWN GOD. The One whom you thus worship in ignorance I have come to proclaim to you.

"God, who made the world and all that is therein, since he is Lord of heaven and earth, dwells not in sanctuaries erected by human hands; nor is he ministered to by the hands of men, as though he needed anything, he who is the Giver to all of life and breath and all things.

"Moreover, he created out of one every nation of mankind, to inhabit the whole face of the earth, having determined beforehand their periods and their boundaries, (and) to seek after God, if indeed in groping after him they might find him—He is really not far from any one of us. In fact, in him we live and move and have our being—a truth which certain of your own poets have expressed:
'For we also belong to his race.'
Since, then, we belong to his race, we ought not to imagine that the Deity resembles gold or silver or stone, a work of art and human design.

"The ages of ignorance (in the past) God has overlooked, but now he bids all men everywhere to repent, since he has appointed a day in which he is about to judge the world in righteousness through a man whom he has set apart, and has given proof of this to all men by raising him from the dead."—Acts 17: 22-31.

But when he reached this point in his address, the mention of the "resurrection of the dead," some mocked, and others said, politely, "We will hear you at some other time about this." They were either slightly amused or plainly bored. Academic men, teachers of philosophy in Athens, had no time for these Oriental superstitions! The fellow seemed harmless—no *Athenian* would take stock in such a religion. And so Paul was dismissed and went his way. Only one or two, Dionysius the Areopagite, and a woman named Damaris, impressed by the deep earnestness of Paul, followed him, heard more of the gospel, and believed. But as a whole, his effort in Athens was a failure. He went away determined more than ever to shun "philosophy and the wisdom of this world," to know nothing but "Jesus Christ, and him crucified," and to continue his preaching among the lowly and outcast—whose hearts were open and receptive enough to hear and believe the gospel.

It was just what Jesus had found in his ministry. These things were "hidden from the wise and understanding, but revealed unto babes." So it is still. God cannot make himself understood by the cynical, the proud, the self-satisfied, the patronizing. God is "the high and lofty One that inhabiteth eternity." But he "dwells with him that is humble in heart."

STUDY TOPICS

1. Trace on the map Paul's journeys described in this chapter. Study the roads and routes on Murray's map ("Graecia"), and find the places named.
2. Of what importance has Thessalonica (Saloniki) been in recent years?
3. Explain the accusation brought against Paul and his companions at Thessalonica. Look up *Emperor-worship* in the encyclopedia or in your ancient history.
4. Read the following passages from the letters of Paul to the Thessalonians: 1 Thessalonians 1: 1 to 2: 2; 2: 13–20; 3; 4: 9–12; 5: 1–11; 2 Thessalonians 1: 1–5;

2:13–17; 3:6–18. What are the main points in these passages? Jot them down in your notebook.

5. Make an analysis of Paul's address before the Areopagus. Why did his address fail? What was the character of his hearers?

6. Study the chronological table in this volume. Review it up to the present point, and see how well you can visualize the progress of the gospel thus far. Recall in detail the events there briefly indicated.

7. Would you say that Epictetus' words prove what Paul said at Athens about men "seeking after God"? What may this suggest to us about believers in other religions to-day? Is Christ the "fulfillment" of other hopes and prophecies, as well as those of the Old Testament?

8. Why does God require humility? Can you remember any words of our Lord upon the subject? Show how pride and self-satisfaction keep us from knowing and doing the will of our Father in heaven. Do you know any concrete examples?

CHAPTER XVII

PAUL AT CORINTH

FIFTY miles west of Athens, around the Saronic Gulf and across the narrow isthmus connecting northern and southern Greece, lay Corinth. It was at that time one of the most important commercial centers in the world. Julius Cæsar had begun a canal across the isthmus, which was not, however, finished until modern times. In Paul's day, a wooden railway transported freight, and even small vessels, from the Corinthian Gulf on the west to the Saronic on the east, and thus shortened by three hundred miles the sailing route east and west around the dangerous capes of Tænarus and Malea. This had been especially valuable in the old days when pirates roved the open Mediterranean and preyed upon the growing shipping of the world. As a result, Corinth had vastly increased in wealth and population. Probably between three hundred thousand and five hundred thousand persons, counting slaves, lived there in the first century. Sailors from every port in the world jostled elbows on the quays and sang their chanties as they strolled the streets. Rich merchants were here, agents and supercargoes and commission men from Spain and Gaul, Egypt, Persia, India, the Danube valley, Jewish traders and workmen, and, of course, Greeks and Italians in great numbers. Corinth was one of the key-cities of the empire. If Christianity could be planted here, its influence would reach far and wide—much farther and wider than from some provincial town like Derbe or Berœa.

For all its business and wealth, Corinth was a city famous for its luxury and vice. "To live as a Corinthian" was an epithet for self-indulgence and intemperance. Drunkenness was common and morals generally were lax. Religion was apparently honored, for there was a famous temple of Apollo, then several centuries old, which stood on the summit of Acro-corinthus, a towering mass of rock over eighteen hundred feet in height just south of the city, and could be seen for miles in every direction. But down in the town, religion, even the religion of Apollo, which had once been a noble and worthy faith, had little influence. Other worships had come in, like the immoral cult of Astarte, which had corrupted the ancient worship of the sailors' goddess, Aphrodite. The mass of the people were sunk deep in vice and sin. Hence Christianity, if it won followers in Corinth, was destined to have a hard struggle to hold its converts, and keep them from lapsing into the habits and customs of their neighbors.

THE HOUSE BESIDE THE SYNAGOGUE

Not waiting for Silas and Timothy, Paul moved on from Athens to Corinth. His unsuccessful effort to convince the members of the Areopagus, and the atmosphere of Athens as a whole, its complacent and artificial culture, showed him the uselessness of continuing his work there.

Aquila and Priscilla.—He had not been long in Corinth before he met a man and his wife, Aquila and Priscilla, who were to have a large share in Paul's life from then on. They were tentmakers, and belonged therefore to Paul's own craft; and although Aquila was a native of Pontus (on the south shore of the Black Sea), he and Priscilla had lived in Rome until lately, when all Jews had been expelled (49 A. D.) by edict of the Emperor Claudius. Perhaps they were Christians already. Six years later Paul addressed a letter to the Christians in Rome (Romans 1:7), so there may easily have been Christians there before the time of Claudius' edict. At least they extended hospitality to Paul at once, and he accepted it, toiling in the shop during the week and preaching on Sabbaths in the synagogue.

The house of Titus Justus.—A few weeks later Silas and Timothy arrived, and Paul began more active preaching of the gospel. This aroused the opposition of the orthodox Jews, just as it had done in other cities, and they refused to hear him any longer or permit him to preach in their synagogue. Then Paul "shook out his raiment," Luke says, and solemnly told them, "Your blood be upon your own heads; I am clean; from henceforth I will go unto the Gentiles."

One of the converts to Paul's message was a man with a Latin name, Titus Justus, whose house was next door to the synagogue. Leaving the synagogue, Paul began holding services in Titus' house, and this became the headquarters of the church from now on. It would not be surprising if such a situation, with the despised Christians holding services next door to the synagogue, aroused deep resentment among the narrow, orthodox Jews. Still more resentful were they when Crispus, the "ruler of the synagogue," was converted and became a Christian, together with his whole household. And besides him were many others, Jews and Greeks.

Freedom from persecution.—Whether the Jews were too few in numbers, or lacking in influence, or possessed of more generosity or discretion than those in other cities where Paul labored, or were still smarting from the blow given them by Claudius, we do not know.

But for some reason they made no attempt to persecute the missionaries or to start a riot among the people. Indeed, with one or two exceptions, Paul was from now on unmolested by members of his own race.

At this time he had another of his visions. One night in a dream he saw Jesus speaking to him and saying,

> "Be not afraid, but speak, and hold not thy peace. For I am with thee, and no man shall set on thee to harm thee. For I have much people in this city."— Acts 18: 9-10.

So Paul continued in Corinth, teaching and preaching in Titus' house beside the synagogue for a whole year and six months.

Paul's letters.—It was during this time that Paul wrote the Epistles to the Thessalonians. Before rejoining him in Corinth Timothy had returned to Thessalonica to see how the church was faring in that city; and when he came bringing the news of their stedfastness and loyalty Paul at once wrote the letter called First Thessalonians (see 3: 6-8 and 1: 2-5). A few months later he sent them a second letter, which we now read in our New Testament as Second Thessalonians.

It was perhaps about this same time, or shortly afterward, that he wrote his Epistle to the Galatians. It is one of the most impassioned letters ever written. News had reached Paul that the "judaizers" were resuming their work, not now in Syria or Cilicia, but in Galatia— the very churches where he and Barnabas had planted the gospel at the risk of their lives and amid terrible hardships and sufferings. He was told that some of the Christians were actually turning to this Jewish Christianity—or "Christian Judaism," as it ought to be called. Not only were the "judaizers" teaching that it was necessary for Christians to keep the whole Jewish Law, but they were attacking Paul's apostleship. They said that he received his gospel "from men," that is, from the original apostles in Jerusalem, and that he had never seen or known Jesus, and hence had no authority to represent him.

To this Paul replied in burning words. He was hurt to the quick. His heart ached for the simple, wayward, easily deceived believers in the remote upland cities of Galatia, some of whom were his friends, some of whom he had never seen, converted after his last visit. His just indignation against the underhanded tactics of his opponents was white-hot. Yet in not one word does he lose control of himself, or forget his true aim, to win back his converts, to defend the liberty of the gospel, to render harmless the attacks of his maligners.

It is easy to imagine Paul dictating this Epistle in his chamber in Titus' house, pacing up and down in anguished agitation. Timothy or Silas or some hired scribe would write down as rapidly as he could Paul's swiftly flowing sentences. At the end, he sits down and in his own coarse handwriting (it is said that his eyesight was poor) adds the conclusion:

"See with what large letters I write to you with my own hand.—As many as desire to make a display compel you to be circumcised and keep the Jewish Law. Far be it from them, though, to be persecuted on account of the cross of Christ! For those who receive the rite do not really keep the Law any better: they desire you to receive it only that they may glory in your flesh. But far be it from me to glory at all, save in the cross of our Lord Jesus Christ, through whom the world has been crucified to me and I unto the world. For neither is circum-

cision anything, nor uncircumcision; what counts is
a whole new creation—a fresh beginning, a new
life. As many as will be guided by this rule, peace
be upon them, and mercy, for they are the true
Israel of God.

"From now on, let no one trouble me (over keeping the Law); for I bear on my own body the slave-
brand of Jesus' ownership.

"The grace of our Lord Jesus Christ be with your
spirit, brethren. Amen."—Galatians 6: 11-18.

Thus was composed the letter which has been called
the "*magna charta* of Christian liberty." Its effect when
read in the churches of Galatia must have been what
Paul desired. For we hear of no further trouble from
the "judaizers"; and the churches addressed preserved
the letter—which they would not have done if they had
repudiated its author.

THE ARRIVAL OF GALLIO

Paul had now been in Corinth for eighteen months.
It was a time of peace and quiet. Day by day he labored
in Aquila's shop, and in his spare time and on Sabbaths
preached the gospel and conducted the Christian services
of worship in Justus' house.

A new proconsul.—Then came a change in the
political situation at Corinth. Gallio, a brother of the
Roman philosopher Seneca, was sent to the province of
Achaia as proconsul. The Jews took this opportunity to
bring charges against Paul. So they seized him and led
him into the prætorium on the excuse that "this man
persuades men to worship God contrary to the Law."
But before Paul had time to begin his defense, Gallio
had seen through the plot and said: "If it were some
crime with which you accuse this man, there would be

a reason for listening to you. But if it is only a technical question relating to your own religious law, see to that yourselves. I am not going to be a judge of such matters." With this he expelled them from the court.

The rabble, which had been stirred up by the Jews' seizure of Paul, was waiting just outside the court, eager for an opportunity to start a tumult. As the unsatisfied complainants came out, the crowd laid hold of their leader, Sosthenes, the new ruler of the synagogue (in Crispus' place), and gave him a terrible beating. Gallio, like many other Romans, was no friend of the Jews, and made no effort to stop this proceeding.

Paul's departure.—Gallio arrived in Corinth in the summer of the year 51. Later that summer or early in autumn, Paul left Corinth to return to Syria. Going down to Cenchreæ on the Saronic Gulf, accompanied by Silas, Priscilla, and Aquila, he crossed to Ephesus. There he remained over one Sabbath and visited the synagogue, then took ship again and sailed for the East. Priscilla and Aquila remained behind, and, as he left them, Paul promised to return.

It was three years since Paul and Silas left Antioch and set out across Asia Minor on the "second missionary journey." They had traveled more than two thousand miles when they returned, and had founded Christian churches far to the west of Cyprus and Galatia. Christianity was now a growing force in strategic centers of the old Greek world, on the north and west shores of the "Greek sea," the Ægean—Philippi, Thessalonica, Corinth. Only the eastern shores of the Ægean, the province of Asia with its great capital, Ephesus, remained to complete the circle. Paul was anxious to return and begin as soon as possible, if it were the will of God, his work in Ephesus.

STUDY TOPICS

1. Look up Corinth on a large-scale map showing elevations (for example, Murray's). Study Paul's route from Athens to Corinth; and from Corinth to Syria, via Cenchreæ and Ephesus. Where is the Isthmian Canal? the Acro-corinthus? On a map of the Mediterranean Sea, show the shipping routes that gave Corinth its importance.

2. Explain the importance of Corinth as a center for the spread of Christianity.

3. Read the following passages from the Epistle to the Galatians: 1: 1 to 2: 10; 3: 1–9; 23–29; 4: 12–20; 5: 16–26; 6: 11–18. What are their main points? How do they bear on Paul's purpose in writing the Epistle?

4. Look up the article "Gallio" in the Bible dictionary, and describe the stone found in four pieces at Delphi which dates his arrival in the province. If not in the Bible dictionary, see Deissmann, *St. Paul*, Appendix II; or Robinson, *Life of Paul*, p. 138ff.; or McNeile, *St. Paul*, p. xvff.

5. It seems never to have occurred to Paul that any people, whatever their condition, were "without the pale" of salvation. Corinth had a right to the gospel, as well as Jerusalem. Does the principle still hold good?

6. What do you think of Paul's self-restraint in writing Galatians? Can you think of any similar situations in which we ought to follow his example?

CHAPTER XVIII

THREE YEARS AT EPHESUS

It was toward the end of the year 51 that Paul had returned from Corinth to Syria. Luke's account of this journey is very brief; it is not found among the "we" sections, and hence we conclude that Luke was not with Paul at this time. "When he had landed at Cæsarea," says the *Acts*, "he went up and saluted the church [in Cæsarea? or in Jerusalem?], and went down to Antioch."

The third missionary journey.—How long he remained in Antioch is not known. Probably not very long; for after the heart-breaking news which drew forth from him the "Epistle to the Galatians," he would naturally be restless till he could actually visit the churches of that region and set in order personally the affairs upset by the "judaizers." Luke simply says, "And having spent some time there, he departed, and went through the region of Galatia and Phrygia in order, establishing all the disciples." This was the beginning of the so-called "third missionary journey," Paul's last and longest tour, including three years of preaching and teaching in Ephesus, the climax of his missionary labors.

THE GOSPEL IN EPHESUS

Ephesus was the capital and chief city of the vastly rich Province of Asia. For centuries the region had been famous for its wealth and culture. Its population was large, its fertile valleys afforded immense tillage and pasturage, while the travel and commerce of east and west passed through its western harbors and up its river roads. (Read again the words of Cicero, already given in Chapter XV.)

Paul's predecessors.—When Paul sailed for Syria the year before, he left Aquila and Priscilla in Ephesus, probably to arrange for his own coming and the beginning of the active Christian mission in that city. They found here a number of disciples of John the Baptist, and among them a famous preacher, Apollos, of Alexandria, who had been "taught by word of mouth the way of the Lord." He was a man "fervent in spirit," and he "spoke and taught carefully all he knew about Jesus," though his only baptism was that of John. He was preaching boldly in the synagogue when Aquila and Priscilla heard him; after the service they took him home with them, and expounded more fully the "way of God," that is, the life and teaching of Jesus, his resurrection, and the work of the Holy Spirit sent from him.

Soon after, Apollos made up his mind to cross over to Achaia—just as Paul and others traveled about preaching their message, so did Apollos. Upon this the "brethren" encouraged him, and wrote to the disciples in Corinth to receive him. The letter gave him a valuable introduction, and his work in Corinth was successful from the start. He engaged in public controversy with the Jews, and proved from the Scriptures that the Messiah was indeed Jesus of Nazareth.

Paul arrives.—At last Paul, having crossed Asia Minor by much the same route which he followed on his second journey, but not being "forbidden by the Holy Spirit" this time "to preach the word in Asia," arrived in Ephesus. Almost the first question he asked of John the Baptist's disciples was this, "Did you receive the Holy Spirit when you believed?" This was, as we have seen, a most conspicuous mark of the disciples of Jesus. Prophecy, speaking with tongues, gifts of healing were all marks of the possession of the Holy Spirit. John the Baptist had announced the coming of the Spirit as one of the marks of the coming age, the Messianic era or kingdom of God (Mark 1: 8). Jesus also had spoken of the Spirit, both as present in his own work (Matthew 12: 28; Luke 4: 18) and as the future possession of his disciples (Acts 1: 4–5). Hence Paul's question was a significant one.

They answered simply, "No; we have not even heard of the Holy Spirit." Paul then inquired, "What sort of baptism did you receive?" And they answered, "John's." Then Paul reminded them of John's own prophecy of the Coming One, which was fulfilled in Jesus, and they were baptized again, this time "into the name of the Lord Jesus." And when Paul had laid his hands upon them, as was the custom, the Holy Spirit "came upon them, and they spoke with tongues and prophesied." The number of these converts was twelve. They now formed, together with Priscilla and Aquila and certain "brethren" (who possibly like them came from elsewhere), the nucleus of the Christian church in Ephesus. Only twelve men—but it was a significant beginning. Jesus himself had begun his ministry with twelve.

IN THE SCHOOL OF TYRANNUS

A beautifully colonnaded street ran a straight mile from the immense open-air theater (whose ruins may still be seen) on the eastern side of the city to the harbor on the west. Down this street persons sitting in the theater could look, and see, beyond the shining marble gateway of the city, the ships lying at anchor in the harbor or sailing across the broad, blue, island-sheltered bay. Along this magnificent avenue were the libraries, the lecture halls, the shrines, the homes of the wealthier citizens. In one of these halls, most likely, was the lecture-room of Tyrannus. Paul had begun, as usual, by preaching in the synagogue. And, as usual, the Jews had listened at first with interest, but soon became incensed and angry. So Paul left them and began teaching daily in the school of Tyrannus.

Paul's success.—With such a prominent meeting-place, and almost recommended to the people of Ephesus by the owner of the school, Paul's preaching reached far and wide—until, in fact, as Luke says, "all who dwelt in Asia heard the word of the Lord, both Jews and Greeks." So great was the enthusiasm over Paul that simple-minded people treasured even such things as his handkerchiefs and working aprons, and took them to the sick, "and the diseases departed from them, and the evil spirits went out."

The sons of Sceva.—One story told of this time is almost humorous. Certain wandering charlatans, who professed to be able to cast out demons (no doubt "for a consideration"), seeing Paul's success and influence, undertook to exorcize in the name of the Lord Jesus. They would say, "I adjure you by the Jesus whom Paul preaches." There were seven brothers, who pretended to be sons of a Jewish priest and who undertook to exorcize in this manner. But the evil spirit (that is, the poor sick man suffering from this dementia or hallucination) answered, "Jesus I recognize, and Paul I recognize; but who are you?" And with that he leaped upon the exorcists with uncontrollable fury, wounding them and driving them out of the house. When the story became known, no doubt many smiled at it; but no doubt many more understood it as proof of the truth and power of the gospel. At least, even by this means "the name of the Lord Jesus was magnified."

Burning the books.—Seeing the success of Paul's message, and the healings which accompanied his preaching, many who had dabbled in this kind of "sorcery" came, confessed their deeds, and were baptized.

> "And not a few of those who practiced magical arts brought their books together, and burned them in public. And when their cost was figured up, it amounted to fifty thousand pieces of silver [$10,000]. So mightily grew the word of the Lord, and prevailed."—Acts 19: 19-20.

"GREAT IS ARTEMIS"

But not even in Ephesus was Paul to complete his ministry in peace. Opposition was rising against him, not from the exorcists, but from the makers of tiny statuettes of the goddess Artemis, whose shrine at Ephesus was world-famous and visited by multitudes of pilgrims every year. These statuettes were sold to the pilgrims for souvenirs (or perhaps as charms), and the business was very lucrative. The workmen engaged in this craft started a riot, which lasted for several hours and ended in the great theater on the eastern side of the city. It might have been very serious. But the city-clerk got the mob under control, thus probably saving the lives of Paul and several of the "brethren."

It began on the very eve of Paul's departure for Athens. He had been planning to visit the churches in Macedonia and Achaia once more, then return to Jerusalem and set forth on another westward journey, this time to Rome—and after that, to Spain. Timothy and

Erastus (a new friend and companion: see Acts 19: 22 and Romans 16: 23) had been sent on before into Macedonia. Paul remained behind for a few days before following them. It was then that the riot took place which so gravely endangered his life.

"A certain man named Demetrius, a silversmith who made shrines to Artemis, brought by this means considerable profit to his workmen. So he gathered them together, along with those who belonged to similar trades, and said: 'Men, you know we make our money by this trade. And you see and hear that not only here in Ephesus but almost all over Asia this fellow Paul has persuaded people into thinking that these are not gods which are made by hands. Now it is not only possible that our trade will fall off, but the temple of the great goddess Artemis will fall into contempt and the goddess be robbed of her glory, whom now not only Asia but the whole wide world adores.'

"At this, the men began to rage with anger and began shouting, 'Great is Artemis of the Ephesians!' Thus the city was filled with confusion. Then they rushed with one accord into the theater, having seized Gaius and Aristarchus, Macedonians who were traveling with Paul. (Paul himself was determined to go out among the people, but the disciples refused to let him go, and certain of the Asiarchs, who were his friends, sent word begging him not to enter the theater.) Some were crying one thing, some another; for the assembly was in confusion, and the majority had not the least idea why they were there.

"Just then the Jews undertook to present their case against Paul, and put forward a man named Alexander as their spokesman. Beckoning with his hand to command silence, he began an address to the people. But when they saw that he was a Jew, they shouted all the louder, for two whole hours, 'Great is Artemis of the Ephesians! Great is Artemis of the Ephesians!'

"At last the city-clerk succeeded in calming the mob and said to them: 'Men of Ephesus, who in the world is there who doesn't know that the city of Ephesus is Temple-warden of the great Artemis, and of her statue that fell from heaven? No one questions this. Therefore you ought to remain calm and do nothing rash. Instead, you have brought into the assembly men who are neither robbers of temples nor guilty of blasphemy against our goddess. If Demetrius and his fellow craftsmen have any grievance against anyone, the courts are regularly convened, and, moreover, there are the proconsuls. Other charges are settled in the assembly of the citizens. And the truth is, we are ourselves in danger of being charged with riot on account of this meeting; and there seems to be no reason which can be given for the gathering.' With these words he dismissed the assembly."—Acts 19: 23-41.

Thus ended three years of patient, self-sacrificing toil. Usually, Paul was not permitted to stay in one place so long. Here his work was ended, for the new church had been well founded and could now continue its growth independently; Paul could go on his way. The importance of Ephesus as a Christian center in the next generation and the next century, in the next five centuries of the church's history, proves the soundness of the foundations laid by Paul.

His work finished, Paul went on with his plans just as if no riot had occurred. He was a great enough man to be able to leave in such circumstances as those described and yet show no sign of defeat. Calling the disciples for a few words of counsel and farewell, he took his leave and set out for Macedonia.

STUDY TOPICS

1. Trace on the map the route of Paul from Antioch to Ephesus. What familiar cities did he pass through? Visualize the scene, and write down what was his probable purpose in visiting the churches of Galatia.

2. Recall from Chapter XVII Paul's friendship with Priscilla and Aquila. How did they come to be in Ephesus? What were some of the points on which they may have enlightened Apollos?

3. Look up "Ephesus" in the encyclopedia or in some volume describing its excavation to-day. Write a paragraph in description of the city.

4. Recall the appearance and preaching of John the Baptist from your study of the life of Christ. See Mark 1: 2–8; Luke 3: 1–20. What would be the beliefs and ideas of his followers?

5. Look up the article "Magic" or "Divination" in the encyclopedia or Bible dictionary. Find some examples of the contents of the "books" which were burned at Ephesus—for example, in Robinson's *Life of Paul*, p. 157f.

6. It may have been difficult for a learned and successful man like Apollos to have his views criticized and corrected by a tentmaker and his wife; but he accepted the correction and thus discovered "the way of God more perfectly." Don't you admire him the more for his humility and open-mindedness? How should we cultivate this virtue? Give an example.

7. Early Christianity set men free from superstition. Are there any superstitions observed by persons you know? Have you any, yourself? Are they consistent with faith in God as revealed in Christ?

CHAPTER XIX

TWO IMPORTANT LETTERS

How often we wish it were possible to visit one of the early Christian assemblies! How we should like to listen to the sermon and join in the worship! We should need, of course, to understand Greek. And we might need to be told what was meant by certain customs and manners of the early Christians, some of which they shared with their non-Christian neighbors. But such an experience would make real, once and for all, what now we can only imagine and try to visualize by the help of patient, careful study.

There is one way in which the lives of great men and important affairs of the past can sometimes be made real—by means of letters. The best biographies of prominent men usually give their "Life and Letters." As we read their correspondence we seem to be in the very time and place of the one who wrote it, to see the situation as he saw it at the moment, and to understand his motives and purposes better. It is fortunate that in addition to Luke's book of Acts we have a number of letters—chiefly by Paul—to illustrate and make vivid the actual life of the early church, to show us what the first Christians believed and thought, hoped and endeavored to do, how they conducted themselves in church and out of church, and what their leaders and missionaries taught them.

FIRST AND SECOND CORINTHIANS

In this chapter, we shall make a special study of Paul's First and Second Epistles to the Corinthians, trying to find out from them something about the church in Corinth to which they were addressed.

The occasion for the letters.—Like Paul's earlier epistles to the Thessalonians and the Galatians, these letters were written because of trouble which had broken out after Paul left Corinth. It was a danger involved in Paul's practice of founding a church, preaching a short while longer, and then pushing on to new fields: often the little group of Christians must have felt deserted and alone, and when difficulties arose there was no one at hand to straighten them out. Paul's method was necessary, if he was to preach to "all the Gentiles" in the remaining years of his lifetime. But it was a dangerous method.

We recall that before Paul arrived at Ephesus, Apollos had crossed to Corinth, where he was well received by "the brethren." So well was he received, indeed, that it was not long before certain members of that church professed a preference for his preaching over that of Paul. Greeks were always partisans, and they were also seekers after "wisdom." The brilliant discourse and the Alexandrian-trained Bible knowledge of Apollos appealed most strongly to them.

Problems of the Corinthian church.—But this was only a part of the trouble. Even earlier, several problems had arisen. One was occasioned by the gross immorality of one of the leaders of the church. Paul wrote at once counseling the church to exclude the offender from their company until he should repent. Other problems arose in regard to the eating of meat which had been offered to idols (that is, meat of animals slain as heathen sacrifices in the temples, and then sold in the markets as food). Certain of the new believers—especially those born Jews—felt this to be a defiling contact with the hated demons (so they viewed the Greek gods). Others—especially those born Gentiles—thought such an objection to be silly and overscrupulous: "An idol is nothing in the world," they said; "there is no God but one!" Other questions had to do with marriage, with the conduct of public worship, with "spiritual gifts," with the hope of the resurrection, with Paul's rights and authority as an apostle.

The preservation of the letters.—We know from several references in these letters that they do not represent the whole of Paul's correspondence with the Corinthian church. Some of the letters have been lost; or, at most, fragments of them have been copied into the second of the two which we find in our New Testament to-day. For the letters, naturally, were preserved first of all by the church to which they were addressed. If the one who had charge of them was a careful person, they would be carefully preserved. If not, some letters, or parts of letters, might easily be lost. Years afterward, when some Christian scholar or disciple of Paul tried to gather together the letters of his master, he would find at Corinth only those letters or parts of letters which had been preserved, handed down to that time. If the letters were poorly preserved, then there might be whole pages missing (that is, sections of papyrus, containing one or two columns of writing); edges and ends might be worn and ragged; loose pages glued together in the wrong order; and many words faded and become illegible. This is what happened to many of the early Christian writings, and to some much more than to others.

The original correspondence.—Modern scholars have carefully studied these epistles, and a great many of them have come to the conclusion that there were originally three or four—or even more—letters in this correspondence between Paul and the Corinthians. They were probably written in the following order:

1. A letter from Paul commanding the exclusion of the immoral member (now found, partly, in *2 Corinthians 6: 14 to 7: 1*), written from Ephesus about 53 or 54 A. D.

2. A letter from the Corinthians to Paul, asking about certain questions relating to marriage, food offered to idols, and so on. This was written about 54 or 55, and is *now lost*. At the same time news reached Paul of the factions in the church, some following Apollos, others Paul, still others Peter. Hence he replied to their letter and at the same time rebuked this party strife.

3. Paul's letter, our *First Corinthians*, written from Ephesus in the spring of 55. It may be that he made a short visit to Corinth after writing this letter. If so, his visit was a failure.

4. A severe letter of reproof, written in much sorrow and anguish of spirit, sent to Corinth by the hand of Titus, somewhat later in the spring of 55. This is now lost—unless *2 Corinthians 10–13* is a part of it. This letter had the desired effect. Titus returned with the news that the church had submitted to Paul, punished the offender, and wished to be reconciled to their absent friend.

5. A letter of reconciliation, sent by Paul from Macedonia in the summer of 55. This is our *Second Corinthians*—except the passages named in (1) and (4) above.

Read in this order, the correspondence becomes intelligible, and we are enabled to see not only the tiny church struggling for life in the midst of dark surroundings, heathenish, superstitious, immoral; but also we catch a glimpse of the moral and spiritual majesty of

Saint Paul. He could write in utter anguish of spirit, as he did once before in "Galatians," to those who were denying his apostleship, and crediting him with the motives of an impostor, and at the same time break forth into that glorious hymn in honor of unselfish love which we read in 1 Corinthians 13. He could be stern and uncomprising in reproof, because it was needed; at the same time he could be gentle and patient, writing only in hope of reconciling his alienated friends. This combination of sternness and tenderness, of severity and love, reminds us of Paul's—and our—divine Master. It is the very spirit of Jesus which Paul is describing in his enraptured lines:

"If I 'speak with tongues'—yes, tongues of men and of angels—and have no love, I am nothing more than a ringing gong or a clanging cymbal. If I have the gift of 'prophecy,' and know all mysteries and secret wisdom; and if I have such faith that I can remove mountains, but have no love, I am nothing. If I distribute all my goods to feed the poor, yes, and give my body to be burned, and have no love, it profits me nothing.

"Love is longsuffering, and kind; love does not envy; love does not try to display itself, show itself off; is never rude, nor self-seeking, nor irritable, nor resentful; love is never pleased when others do wrong, but rejoices in the truth; love is always forgiving, always believes the best of others, always hopes, always endures.

"Love never fails. As for 'prophesying,' it will disappear; 'tongues' will cease; 'knowledge' will pass away. For we know only in part, and we prophesy a little at a time; but when what is perfect arrives, what is partial shall pass away. When I was a child, I spoke and felt and thought as a

child; now that I am a man I have put away childish
things. At present we see only the dim reflections in
a mirror, but then it will be face to face; now I know
only in part, but then shall I understand perfectly
just as I have been understood perfectly all along
(by One who knows the secrets of man's heart).
Faith, hope, love remain; and the greatest of these
is love."—1 Corinthians 13.

THE FAITH AND WORKS OF THE CHURCH

When Paul spoke in this way of love, he meant something very practical. His solution of the problems of
his Corinthian friends shows this, for in every case he
applied the principle of charity. It was not a question
of *rights*, in most instances, so much as a question of
prudence, of the highest expediency, seen in the light of
brotherly love.

The question of meats.—As the Corinthian Christians went to market, they saw food for sale which had
been offered in the heathen temples. At dinners one
might be eating such food and not know it. If there
were any real defilement involved, the question was
serious, and one should always inquire whether or not
the supplies had come from the temples. Paul admits at
once the right of "the strong in faith" to eat, "asking
no questions as if the conscience were involved." But
at the same time they must bear in mind the difficulties
of "the weaker brethren."—The principle was also true
of those invited to banquet in the temples.

"But take heed lest by any means this liberty of
yours becomes a stumbling-block to the weak. For
if a man sees you who have 'knowledge' sitting to
dine in an idol's temple, will not his conscience, if
he is weak, be made bold to eat things sacrificed to

idols? Then through your 'knowledge' the weak one
is to perish, the brother for whose sake Christ went
the length of laying down his life? And thus, sin-
ning against the brethren, and wounding their weak
consciences, you are going to sin against Christ?—
I tell you, if meat is going to make my brother to
stumble, I will not touch it again forever, in order
not to cause my brother to stumble!"—1 Corinthians 8: 9-13.

The question about spiritual gifts.—The same principle held true of the "spiritual gifts," that is, the speaking with tongues, prophecy, and interpretation of
tongues. These apparently held a prominent place in
the public worship of the Corinthian church. But Paul
said: "Not what adds to one's own prestige, or seems
to impress strangers as extraordinary and marvelous,
but what is 'useful for edification' and builds up the
faith and strengthens the wills of the brethren—such
'speaking by the Spirit' is to be cultivated."

"Thank God, I speak with tongues more than any
of you! However, in the church I would rather
speak five words with my understanding, that I
might thereby instruct others, than ten thousand
words in a 'tongue.' "—1 Corinthians 14: 18-19.

The question about the Lord's Supper.—It seems
strange to us, but already certain abuses had actually
grown up around the Lord's Supper. This was celebrated
in the evening, or at night (see Acts 20: 11), just as
Jesus had observed the Passover the night before he
suffered. The Christians at Corinth could not come
during the day—they were busy workmen and slaves
and the evening was their only time for "church." But
they had made of the observance an occasion for feasting,
like that which took place in the heathen temples. And

some were hungry and others overfed. This roused Paul's feelings and he wrote them a sharp reproof:

> "What? Have you not houses to eat and drink in? Or do you despise the church of God, and put to shame those who are in poverty? . . . When you come together to eat, brethren, wait for one another. And if any man is hungry, let him eat at home (before he comes); in order that your assembly may not deserve the divine condemnation. And the rest I will set in order when I arrive."— 1 Corinthians 11 : 22, 33-34; see the whole passage.

It is evident enough that Paul was quite right when he said that the Christian "calling" (that is, the membership of the Corinthian church) included "not many wise after the flesh, not many mighty, not many noble; but God chose the foolish things of the world that he might put to shame the wise; and the weak, to shame the strong; and the base and despised—that no flesh should glory before God!" (1 Corinthians 2 : 26–29; the statement was true of many another early Christian congregation).

Such was the beginning of the Christian Church. Among peasants and fishermen of Galilee, despised by the learned priests and scribes from Jerusalem, Jesus had wrought out his work and planted the seed. Among the lowly, the ignorant and superstitious and poor—and morally weak—Saint Paul and the other missionaries of the gospel now spread the good news of Jesus and eternal life, planted the church, and started Christianity on its long and expanding course of development.

STUDY TOPICS

1. Recall the letters which Paul addressed to the Thessalonians and Galatians. What were their subjects?

2. Recall what was said in Chapter XVIII about Apollos. How did he become a Christian? How did he come to be in Corinth?

3. Explain how the letters of Paul were preserved, and show their value for our study of the early church. What happened when letters were not carefully preserved?

4. Read the following passages from Paul's correspondence with the Corinthians, and note the main subject in each passage:

(1) 2 Corinthians 6: 14 to 7: 1; (2) 1 Corinthians 1: 1-25; 2: 1-5; 3: 1 to 4: 5; 6: 1-8; 10: 23 to 11: 1; 14: 26-33; 39-40; (3) 2 Corinthians 7: 5-16.

5. Memorize 1 Corinthians 13, in the version of the Authorized or Revised Bible, after studying its meaning by help of the translation given above in the text. Can you think of any teachings of Jesus which it echoes? See Matthew 5: 43-48, for example.

6. Luke does not mention the trouble which arose in Corinth, as it was not sufficiently important; it had occurred long ago, when he wrote, had been soon settled, and was now almost forgotten. If Paul's letters had been lost, we should never have heard about it. But note how Paul's letters and the narrative of Acts fit together. See 1 Corinthians 16: 5-9, which was written just before the riot in Ephesus (Acts 19: 21-23); and 2 Corinthians 1: 8-11, which was written just afterward.

7. Paul's principle was to avoid occasions of offense (or of "stumbling") on the part of the weaker brethren. Does this reflect the teaching of his Master? How does it apply to us? Are tactfulness and courtesy and forbearance part of a Christian character? Give an example, if you can, which you personally know.

CHAPTER XX

IN JERUSALEM AGAIN

PAUL had planned, even before the riot caused by Demetrius, to leave Ephesus and visit once more his churches in Macedonia and Achaia. After that he intended going to Jerusalem, and then on to Rome. One reason for desiring to revisit Jerusalem was no doubt to see the church there, and at Antioch, where he had many friends. But the chief reason was that he intended to take up an offering from the Gentile churches and give it to "the poor among the saints in Jerusalem." There were many poor in that city, as we have already seen. The apostles had long before requested Paul to remember them (Galatians 2:10), "which very thing," he says, he "was also zealous to do."

Nothing could possibly cement more closely the Jewish and Gentile groups in the church than such an expression of sympathy and charity. And it shows what a great man Paul was, who planned this act of generosity. For we recall that it was from Jerusalem that the "false brethren" went out and tried to undo his work in Galatia, as they had done in Antioch and Cilicia. Lately they had even appeared at Corinth, starting a faction and calling themselves either "the party of Cephas" (that is, Peter), or "of Christ" (that is, in contrast to Paul). But Paul was too big a man to give way to motives of meanness and a desire to "get even." He would welcome such an opportunity to do good, he would not make the poor brethren in Jerusalem suffer for the sins of their misguided fellows. There shines forth the true Christian spirit, the spirit of Jesus, just as really in Paul's act of kindness and generosity as it does in the sublime language of the thirteenth chapter of First Corinthians.

It was with undisguised eagerness and enthusiasm that Paul wrote, at the end of the letter we now call First Corinthians, about his plans for this relief fund:

> "Now concerning the collection for the saints, as I gave order to the churches of Galatia, so also do ye. Upon the first day of the week let each one of you lay by him in store, as he may prosper, that no collections be made when I come. And when I arrive, whomsoever ye shall approve by letters, them will I send to carry your bounty to Jerusalem; and if it be necessary for me to go also, they shall go with me."—1 Corinthians 16: 1-4; see also 2 Corinthians 9.

A WINTER IN CORINTH

Immediately following these words about the collection, Paul adds (addressing the disciples in Corinth), "I am coming to you, when I have passed through Macedonia, . . . and perhaps I may spend the winter with you, that you may help me on my way (in the spring) whithersoever I go."

Through Macedonia.—Immediately after the riot in Ephesus, Paul set out to fulfill these plans. Passing up along the coast to Troas (2 Corinthians 2: 12), he found here a door of opportunity opened for preaching the gospel. But he remained only a short while. Timothy and Erastus (and Titus?) had gone on before into Macedonia, and he was trying to overtake them. Not finding Titus at Troas, he says, "I had no relief for my spirit"; and so he hastened across to Macedonia, probably following the same route as on the second missionary journey. Here he no doubt visited the Christians in Philippi, Thessalonica and Berœa. Luke hastens over this journey with the words, "When he had gone through those parts and given them much exhortation, he came into Greece." It may be that it was on this journey that he traveled "even unto Illyricum," as he writes shortly afterward (Romans 15: 19), spending the summer and early autumn in this tour of Macedonia and northern Greece.

In the house of Gaius.—At last, as winter approached, he arrived at Corinth, and was heartily welcomed by his now reconciled friends. Gaius, whom he described as "my host, and of the whole church" (Romans 16: 23), took him into his home, and entertained him during his stay. Here he remained for three months, until spring arrived and travel was safe once more both by sea and by land. It must have been a happy winter. All the anguish and bitter feeling of the year before was now gone. Generous-spirited Paul, we can be sure, would not even mention those old troubles and disloyalties. The collection grew larger week by week, and many new disciples were added to the church.

The Epistle to the Romans.—Here it was that he wrote the most formal and theological of his letters, the Epistle to the Romans. Christianity had already, by some means, reached the Imperial City. Christians traveling to Rome, or going there to reside, or "prophets and teachers" like those at Antioch, had brought with them the message and started the church in that city. Paul had planned for some time to "see Rome" and preach the gospel there—and then in Spain. Now, instead of traveling westward down the Gulf of Corinth to the western sea and thence to Italy, he was going eastward to Jerusalem. It might be that he should never reach Rome at all, if opposition broke out in the East. It might be also, that the "judaizers" would outrun him, and corrupt with their false teachings the faith of the Christians in Rome before Paul could get to them. Hence he wrote the letter called *To the Romans*. It is almost a theological treatise, dealing with the Mosaic Law and God's purpose in establishing it, the relation of sin and its consequences to the commandment given by God, the freedom of Christians from the condemnation upon those who failed to keep this Law, and the final salvation of the Jewish people in spite of their rejection of Christ and the gospel. Such subjects were very important both to the Jewish and Gentile Christians in Rome, whom Paul was anxious to visit; and he wanted to reach them at once, not waiting until he returned from Jerusalem.

At the end of the Epistle to the Romans (Chapter 16) has been added a small letter, or a page from a larger one, which Paul wrote about the same time to the church in Ephesus. It abounded in salutations and greetings, and shows us what a much-loved and loving man Paul was, how wide his circle of friends, how deep and intense his affection.

ON THE WAY TO JERUSALEM

Paul was now about ready to start for Palestine. He intended to take ship at Cenchreæ, as before, and either cross to Ephesus, if the ship followed that route, or sail directly for Syria. He was anxious to reach Jerusalem if possible before Pentecost, when he should present the gift from the Gentile churches. But this plan was thwarted by the discovery of a plot among the Jews, who were determined to get rid of Paul. Instead of sailing across the Ægean, he returned by land as he had come, through Macedonia, then across by sea to Troas, and thence southward.

Paul's companions.—In this way, several men went with him from Macedonia, commissioned to present the gift of their churches to the poor in Jerusalem (like those Paul expected from Corinth: see 1 Corinthians 16: 3–4). There were Sopater from Berœa, Aristarchus and Secundus from Thessalonica, Luke himself from Philippi (Acts 20: 5–6), Gaius of Derbe, and Timothy. All except Luke had gone before to Troas when he and Paul set sail just after Passover. Finding them there, Paul went on alone by foot to Assos, which lay thirty miles southeast on the Gulf of Adramyttium. His reason for this was doubtless the fact that sailing ships were sometimes unable, for days at a time, on account of adverse winds, to round the point of Lectum and pass the straits north of Lesbos. And he was hastening on to reach Jerusalem before Pentecost, now barely a month away. He even planned to sail past Ephesus and sent word to the elders of the church to meet him for a few hours when the ship stopped at Miletus—a sixty-mile journey for the Ephesians.

Paul's charge to the elders of Ephesus.—Taking ship again at Assos, they touched at Mitylene on the east coast of the island of Lesbos. The next day they stood off Chios, the following touched at Samos—they were coasting southward inside the fringe of islands— and the next day reached Miletus. Here the elders of the church at Ephesus met him, and Paul addressed them in words of tender farewell. The address is given, of course, in the words of Luke; but the thought is sufficiently like that of Paul's epistles to guarantee its authenticity. If we had nothing else that Paul ever said, this address would be enough to mark him out as a noble, generous, and heroic Christian soul.

"You yourselves know, from the first day that I set foot in Asia, after what manner I lived with you all the time, serving the Lord with all lowliness of mind, and with tears, and with trials which befell me by the plots of the Jews; how that I shrank not from declaring unto you anything that was profitable, and teaching you publicly, and from house to house, testifying both to Jews and Greeks repentance toward God and faith toward our Lord Jesus Christ.

"And now, behold, I go bound in the Spirit unto Jerusalem, not knowing the things that shall befall me there: save that the Holy Spirit testifies unto me in every city, saying that bonds and affliction await me. But I hold not my life of any account, as dear unto myself, in comparison with accomplishing my course and the ministry which I received from the Lord Jesus, to witness to the gospel of the grace of God.

"And now, behold, I know that you all, among whom I went about preaching the kingdom, shall see my face no more. Wherefore I testify unto you this day that I am pure from the blood of all men. For I never shrank from declaring to you the whole counsel of God. Take heed to yourselves and to all the flock, of which the Holy Spirit has made you guardians, to feed the church of the Lord which he purchased with his own blood. I know that after I am gone savage wolves will enter in among you, not sparing the flock; and from among yourselves will come men speaking perverse things in order to lead away the disciples after them. Therefore, keep watch! Remember that for three whole years I ceased not to admonish every one night and day with tears!

"And now I commend you to God, and to the
word of his grace, which is able to build you up and
to give you the inheritance among all the sanctified.
I coveted no man's silver or gold or apparel. You
yourselves know that these hands ministered to my
necessities and to those who were with me. In
everything I set you an example, how to toil and
help the needy, and to remember the words of the
Lord Jesus, who said, 'It is more blessed to give
than to receive.'"—Acts 20: 18-35.

When he had finished speaking they knelt down and
joined in prayer. Then with many tears and loving
farewells they saw him to his ship. Weighing anchor,
the vessel bore southward down the coast until it was
out of sight on an almost straight course toward the
island of Cos. Paul's words were destined to be fulfilled:
his Ephesian friends were never to see his face again.

Eastward bound.—By short daily stages, their vessel
first reached Rhodes, the great naval station off the
southwest corner of Asia Minor, then Patara, a harbor
on the mainland. Here they took passage on a vessel
bound for Phœnicia, a straight voyage of four hundred
miles. The first stop was Tyre, where the ship tied up
for a week and unloaded its freight. Here Paul and his
companions visited "the disciples," who warned Paul
not to venture near Jerusalem. The danger he faced
was greater than he realized. Undaunted, however, they
passed on, and sailed to Ptolemais, the port of Galilee,
and then to Cæsarea, where they were entertained by
Philip the evangelist, one of the Seven, who had four
daughters who were prophetesses. Here again Paul was
warned, this time by the old prophet Agabus, who took
Paul's girdle and bound it about his own hands and
feet and said, "Thus saith the Holy Spirit, 'So shall the

Jews of Jerusalem bind the man who owns this girdle,
and shall deliver him over to the Gentiles.' "

> "And when we heard these things," Luke says,
> "both we and they of that place begged him not to go
> to Jerusalem. Then Paul answered, 'What are you
> doing, weeping and breaking my heart?—for I am
> ready not only to be bound but also to die at Jeru-
> salem for the name of the Lord Jesus.' And when
> he would not be persuaded, we ceased, saying, 'The
> will of the Lord be done.' "—Acts 21 : 13-14.

In the Holy City.—Soon after, Paul set out for
Jerusalem, accompanied by his companions from the
west and now also by certain disciples from Cæsarea.
Among them was Mnason, an early disciple, with whom
they spent the night somewhere on the way, and early
next day they caught sight of the city, gleaming in the
splendor of the spring sunshine, the goal of Paul's long
journey, and soon to be the scene of a last great adven-
ture which still awaited him.

He had completed the longest of his journeys. It was
four years since he last saw Syria and Palestine. He
could now look back upon his missionary career as a
whole, as he had written to the Christians in Rome:

> "From Jerusalem, and round about unto Illyricum,
> I have fully preached the gospel of Christ; making
> it my aim so to preach the gospel, not where Christ
> was already named, that I might not build upon
> another man's foundation."—Romans 15 : 19-20.

Cilicia, Cyprus, Galatia, Macedonia, Achaia, Asia—
six provinces, the heart of the eastern half of the empire
—were the field of his labors for Christ. It was the work
of a lifetime which Paul had crowded into eighteen busy
years, from the year 38, when he began preaching in

Cilicia, to the year 56, when he arrived for the last time at Jerusalem. Of these the busiest had been the last nine, since he and Barnabas set out (in 47) on the first missionary journey from Antioch to Cyprus. What a wonderful nine years these had been! Through what dangers had Paul passed, what sufferings, discouragements, difficulties! Yet he triumphed over all, and accomplished so much, as a simple, loyal, devoted soldier of Christ. He was "ready," as he said, "not to be bound only, but even to die for the name of the Lord Jesus," if that was God's will. He had been "ready" all along to do whatever came next in his life of service. Such unconquerable faith and loyalty and obedience were the secret of Paul's immense and successful work.

STUDY TOPICS

1. On a sketch or outline map show Paul's course from Ephesus to Corinth, then to Jerusalem, as described in this chapter. How were his plans altered at Corinth?
2. Describe the "collection for the poor saints" and show how it proves Paul's greatness and generosity of spirit. What does the word "saints" mean in such a connection?
3. Read the following passages in the Epistle to the Romans, and note their main subjects in your notebook: 1: 1–17; 3: 1–3; 5: 1–11; 6: 12–14; 7: 7 to 8: 18; 10: 1–3; 15: 14–33.
4. Read the little epistle to the church in Ephesus appended to the Epistle to the Romans (Romans 16). How many friends does he mention in his greetings? Does this indicate in any way the size of the church at that time?
5. What were the main points of Paul's charge to the elders of Ephesus?

6. Review the events of Paul's life during his nine years of intense missionary activity. Study the chronological chart and go over your maps of his journeys.

7. Paul's "collection" was intended, partly, to allay the suspicion of his opponents in Jerusalem. That was a novel way to meet underhandedness! Does it ever work? Have you seen anyone try conquering suspicion by generosity? Name a few instances where it might at least be tried. Then ask yourself if you would care to try it!

CHAPTER XXI

PAUL'S ARREST

ARRIVED in Jerusalem, Paul went at once to "the brethren," who, so Luke writes in the book of Acts, "received us gladly." The following day Paul and his companions presented themselves to James (who was head of the church in Jerusalem) and all the elders, who were present, apparently, to welcome Paul. After saluting them in the formal manner of the Jews and early Christians, he went over one by one the full details of his work in Asia Minor and Greece, "the things which God had wrought among the Gentiles by his ministry." When they heard the wonderful stories he told, of the conversion of men like Timothy and Gaius and Aristarchus and Luke, of Apollos and the twelve men at Ephesus, of the burning of the books of magic, of riots and persecutions, of his shipwreck and beatings and stonings, of the triumphant progress of the gospel in spite of all hindrances and opposition, of the manifest guidance of the Holy Spirit, and the visions of Jesus which he had seen—Jesus still the leader and helper of his followers—they marveled and "glorified God." It was truly a wonderful story, when they first heard it from the lips of Paul himself, even as it is to-day when we read it in the book of Acts.

AN ATTEMPT AT CONCILIATION

Then in turn the apostles and elders related to Paul the growth of the church in Jerusalem and Palestine, "how many thousands there are among the Jews who have believed." They were all, even as Christians, still just as zealous in keeping the Law of Moses as were their non-Christian Jewish neighbors. And they had heard of Paul, for his fame had spread throughout the whole Jewish world; but they were distressed when informed that he taught the Jews of the Dispersion to give up the Law, to ignore its rites and neglect its customs. This of course was untrue. What Paul actually did teach was that *Gentiles* might become Christians without taking upon them the burden of the Law. To orthodox Jews, on the other hand, this meant that Gentiles were being admitted to all the privileges of the Jewish religion without having to accept any of its obligations, such as circumcision, sacrifices, the tithes, the annual Temple-tax, and the pilgrimages to the Temple. And so in their jealousy, and aroused by a vague and exaggerated rumor, they spread the report that Paul was teaching Jews to forsake the Law. This report, reaching Jerusalem, greatly pained the Christian Jews; for it seemed to justify the complaint of their orthodox neighbors, that the followers of Jesus were lax in observing the duties of the old religion.

The four men under vows.—"So," said the elders, "they will certainly hear that you are in Jerusalem. Now, do as we tell you, in order to disarm suspicion and prove that the rumors are unfounded. There are four men here, disciples, who have been keeping a vow, and, according to the custom, not cutting their hair while the vow lasted. The vow is fulfilled, and they must cut their hair and offer the sacrifices for purification in the Temple. But they are very poor, and cannot afford the cost of their offerings. You yourself have just fulfilled a vow (see Acts 18: 18), but have not yet offered your sacrifice. Take these men with you, go to the Temple, pay for them as well as yourself, accomplish your purification, and thus prove these rumors false. You will show beyond doubt that you yourself walk orderly, keeping the Law and aiding others in keeping it."

In the Temple.—Now, it is true Paul's main concern was the freedom of the gospel (from the burden of the Old-Testament Law) *among Gentiles*. With the Christians among the Jews he was not so much concerned— out in the Dispersion they were not able to observe its requirements punctually, anyway, on account of their distance from Jerusalem. He had stated his principle in the letter to the Galatians: "Neither circumcision availeth anything, nor uncircumcision; but a new life" (Galatians 6: 15). But he was intensely anxious that the church, both Jewish and Gentile, should remain united and not split up into warring factions. This was one of his purposes in taking up the collection of money for the poor members of the Jerusalem church. And so in order to keep the peace, and to overcome the prejudices of the brethren in Jerusalem, he agreed to the plan and went next day to the Temple. The rites of purification were performed, and the offering was presented for each one in the group, Paul and the four poor Jewish brethren.

The riot.—Each day for seven days Paul was to go to the Temple before his purification was complete. One day toward the end of the week, as he was in the outer court, some Jews from Asia who had seen him preaching in Ephesus—and had perhaps shared in the riot started by Demetrius—recognized him and shouted out: "Men of Israel, help! This is the one who teaches all men everywhere to hate us and our religion and Temple. Here he is! And he has brought heathen Greeks inside the inner court, thus defiling it!" For there was an inscription just outside the inner court, on the terrace which led up to it, reading as follows:

> NO GENTILE SHALL
> ENTER THIS SANCTUARY.
> WHOEVER DOES SO
> WILL BE RESPONSIBLE
> FOR HIS OWN DEATH
> WHICH WILL FOLLOW.

The fanatical Jews from Asia, having seen Trophimus, one of Paul's friends from Ephesus (see Acts 20: 4), with him in the city, supposed that he was one of the four men Paul had brought into the sanctuary.

A tumult began at once. Everyone heard it said that this dastardly heretic and apostate, not content with undermining the faith of his fellow Jews outside Palestine, had actually come to the city, and defiled the Sacred Place with his heathen followers! The rumor spread like fire. The whole city was stirred. People were running through the streets. An angry crowd seized Paul and dragged him out of the Temple. The Temple gates were swung shut, for fear he should enter again. Down the Temple hill and into the city they dragged him, probably planning to take him outside the city wall and there stone him to death. Hearing the riot, the Roman officer in command of the Castle of Antonia, the garrison at the northwest corner of the Temple, rushed down with several companies of soldiers. When the Jews saw the soldiers coming they ceased beating Paul. Then the officer commanded his men to bind Paul with two chains, manacling either wrist to the wrist of a soldier, and demanded information as to who he was and what his crime. The crowd answered, some one thing, others another. The officer could not make out the cause of the disturbance and so ordered Paul led into the castle.

PAUL IN CUSTODY

Even as they ascended the stairs to the castle, the crowd became so violent Paul literally had to be carried along by the soldiers. The mob was howling, "Away with him! Away with him!"—just as it had howled nearly thirty years before when Pilate tried to rescue Jesus from their fury.

Paul's address.—Nearing the castle, on the platform at the head of the stairs, Paul spoke to the officer and requested permission to address him. The officer, Claudius Lysias, supposed Paul to be some mad fanatic, perhaps the Egyptian seditionist who had recently started an uprising among the Zealots; and when Paul spoke to him in Greek and asked permission to continue, the officer was greatly astonished. Then Paul continued, "I am a Jew, a citizen of Tarsus in Cilicia (no mean city!), and I request you to let me speak to the people." The permission granted, Paul turned and standing at the head of the stairs lifted his manacled hand to ask for silence. When the mob quieted down he began as follows, speaking now in Aramaic, "Brethren and fathers, hear the defense I am about to make." At this, hearing him speak in their own Aramaic tongue, they became still more quiet.

His defense consisted of a straightforward, manly account of his own past history, his early zeal for the Law, his persecution of the Christians, his conversion, his baptism and the vision which sent him forth as an apostle to the Gentiles. Thus far the audience remained silent. But at the hated word "Gentiles" they broke out again, screaming and shouting and crying out:

"Away with him, away with him! He is not fit to live!"
Tearing off their garments and throwing dust in the
air, the frenzied mob seemed to be getting beyond
control. Claudius, not knowing Aramaic, understood
this second outbreak as little as the first, and ordered
Paul scourged and examined. As they were about to
tie him up to the whipping-post, Paul turned to him
and asked, "Is it lawful to scourge a Roman, uncon-
demned?" This was the chief surprise of all to the
officer. This man whom he had rescued from a fanatical
mob was not only an educated man, but a Roman
citizen! He would have to exercise great care in handling
such a prisoner!

Before the Sanhedrin.—The next day, the officer
invited the Sanhedrin to meet and try Paul, since his
case seemed to involve some technicality of Jewish
religious custom with which the Roman government
made it a practice not to interfere. Here Paul accomplished a feat which saved his life, one which was worthy
a practiced lawyer, and showed his shrewd understanding of the minds of men. That the court would be
"packed against him" he knew from the start. But
the trial had barely begun when Paul exclaimed,
"Brethren, I am a Pharisee, a son of Pharisees; the
charge against me concerns the hope of the resurrection
of the dead!"

The significance of these words is to be seen in the
fact that the Sanhedrin was made up partly of Sadducees
and partly of Pharisees. Paul's words precipitated once
more the bitter and violent controversy which held these
two schools wide apart. So great became the clamor
that the officer, fearing for his prisoner's life, commanded
his men to lead Paul once more into the Castle of
Antonia.

That night in his cell the apostle had a vision. He saw Jesus standing beside him and saying, "Be of good cheer; for as thou hast testified concerning me at Jerusalem, so must thou also bear witness at Rome" (Acts 23: 11).

Paul sent to Cæsarea.—The next day a conspiracy was formed among the Jews. Over forty of them pledged neither to eat nor drink until they had killed Paul. News of the plot reached Paul's nephew, a young man living in the city, and he at once went to Paul with the news, who in turn sent him to the commandant of the garrison. Seeing the hopelessness of a fair trial in Jerusalem, and the increasing danger his prisoner was in, Claudius Lysias called two centurions and gave orders to take Paul to the governor, Felix, in Cæsarea. Seventy cavalry, two hundred infantry, two hundred spearmen were to accompany him as a guard—the regulation heavy guard of a high Roman military officer. Setting off at once, they marched that night as far as Antipatris. Since they were now out of the chief zone of danger, the infantry and spearmen returned to Jerusalem while the cavalry pushed on rapidly the next day to Cæsarea. Here they handed over their prisoner to the governor, who ordered him confined in the Herodian palace until his accusers arrived for the trial.

Less than two weeks before, Paul had landed in Cæsarea a free man, accompanied by his friends from the west, and set out for Jerusalem, eager to present the gift he had gathered for the poor of his nation! Now he was a prisoner under heavy guard, bound with chains to his captors whenever he left his cell, unable to reach his friends, awaiting the coming of his enemies and accusers, face to face, it might be, with death. As for his gift, the collection upon which he had spent such

pains, over which he had felt such enthusiasm, so far
as we know not one word of appreciation or gratitude
was uttered by the "poor saints" or their leaders in Jerusalem. Jesus had known the ingratitude of his people.
Now Paul too was learning it.

And yet, like a ray of light streaming into the dark-
ness of his prison, there were the words of the vision,
"Be of good cheer, Paul; thou hast testified to me at
Jerusalem, and so shalt thou bear witness at Rome!"

STUDY TOPICS

1. Look up, on the diagrams of Jerusalem and the Temple
   (*The Life and Times of Jesus*, facing pp. 183, 193),
   the places mentioned in this chapter, the Court of
   the Gentiles, the Court of the Men of Israel, the
   Castle of Antonia, the Council Chamber of the
   Sanhedrin. Draw a diagram and locate these in
   your notebook.
2. Explain the plan of James and the elders for Paul to
   conciliate the Law-observing Christians in Jerusalem. Why was the plan a dangerous one?
3. Explain the truth or untruth of the Jewish account of
   Paul's preaching and work among the Gentiles.
4. Look up the rites of purification (Numbers 6: 13–21;
   these were appointed for "Nazirites," but were
   modified for those who had fulfilled ordinary vows);
   and see the article "Purification" in the Bible dictionary.
5. Read Paul's defense, Acts 22: 1–21. What were its
   chief points? How and why was it cut short?
6. Read the account of the conspiracy in Acts 23: 12–22.
   Paul's nephew is never mentioned again. He may
   have been a Christian, but probably was not—as
   Christians he and his mother would not have learned
   of the plot. But he was a brave lad, and possessed
   some of the courageous spirit of his heroic uncle. It

CÆSAREA: THE RUINS OF SAINT PAUL'S PRISON

took real grit to go to the captain and inform against
his own people, the priests, and the men vowed to
commit murder.

7. Read Lysias' letter to the governor in dispatching the
prisoner to him, Acts 23: 26–30. Find Antipatris on
the map. Trace Paul's journey under guard to
Cæsarea.

8. Was Paul's generosity wasted? Is it worth while
being kind even to those who do not appreciate it?

CHAPTER XXII

THE APPEAL TO CÆSAR

For two years Paul was to remain a prisoner in Cæsarea. Instead of an immediate trial, which might reasonably have been expected, ending either with conviction or acquittal, he was kept in prison during the entire remaining term in office of the governor of the province. No doubt the governor thought this the easiest way to insure the peace: if Paul were released, the authorities might have more trouble on their hands!

TWO YEARS IN CÆSAREA

Five days after Paul's hasty transference from the Castle of Antonia in Jerusalem to the Palace of Herod in Cæsarea, his accusers appeared before Felix and brought their charges. Not only were members of the Sanhedrin in the delegation, but even the high priest, Ananias—men who, according to their own views, should have been ashamed to appear as litigants in a Gentile court. In addition, they had engaged a professional Roman lawyer, Tertullus, to plead their case. No pains were being spared to procure Paul's conviction.

The first trial.—Tertullus began his speech as soon as Paul was called by offering Felix the most abject and unjustifiable flattery. "Seeing that under you we enjoy much peace"—which was untrue—"and that by your wisdom evils are being corrected in this nation"—evils were flourishing, the country was overrun with bandits, and the nation was on the verge of insurrection!—"we accept your administration, Your Excellency, with gratitude on every hand." Having now won the favor of the governor by this conscienceless adulation, he proceeded, with a flourish: "But, in order not to be tedious to you"—we may imagine how tedious his words were to Felix!—"I entreat you of your clemency to hear us in a few words. We found this fellow a general trouble-maker, a mover of insurrections among the Jews all over the world, and a ringleader of the sect of the Nazarenes. Moreover, he even attempted to profane the Temple, but we seized him. If you will only examine him for yourself, he will, we are sure, convict himself of his guilt."

Paul's defense.—It was a difficult position that Paul was in. This scheming, crafty group opposing him, with a wily, unscrupulous lawyer as their spokesman, were not going to stop at half-measures. The punishment for insurrection was death. And by his flatteries, Tertullus had already won Felix over to his side.

Paul's answer was a dignified, honest statement of facts. He began with a tactful compliment, but there was no flattery in his words.

> "As I know that you have administered justice for this nation through a long course of years, I take courage in making my defense, especially since you can easily ascertain that it was only twelve days ago that I went up to Jerusalem to worship. Neither in the Temple nor in the synagogues nor in the city was I found arguing with anyone or stirring up a crowd. Nor can they prove the charges they bring against me.
>
> "I acknowledge that it is after the way they call a heresy that I worship the God of our fathers, believing nevertheless all that is contained in the Law or written in the prophets, trusting in God that, as

they foretell, there shall be a resurrection of the just and the unjust. And I constantly endeavor for this reason to keep a clear conscience both toward God and toward man.

"It was after an interval of several years that I came to bring alms to my people, and to present offerings; in the course of which I was found in the Temple, not unpurified, nor with any crowd, nor starting a tumult. The trouble was caused by certain Jews from Asia—who should be here now to bring charges before you, if there is anything to be said against me. Failing their appearance, let these men themselves say what crime they found, when I stood before the Sanhedrin—unless it was simply the statement I made that 'On account of the resurrection of the dead I have been called in question to-day.' "—Acts 24: 10-21.

In an impartial and unprejudiced court, Paul's case would have been continued until his real accusers arrived, or dismissed when the charges already made were not substantiated. For he simply challenged his opponents, or the governor, to examine his record and find of what wrongdoing, or insurrection, he was guilty. Of course none would have been found; and, as a matter of fact, no further investigation was made. His real accusers, as he said, had failed to appear. And they did not appear later.

A corrupt governor.—But instead of freeing Paul, Felix, who was avaricious and what we to-day call a "grafter," a taker of bribes, had caught eagerly at Paul's words, "I came to bring alms to my people." Perhaps he could hold Paul until his friends were willing to buy his freedom! So he made an excuse and said, "When Lysias, the commandant, comes down I will settle the case." At the same time he ordered that Paul should be given a certain amount of freedom and his friends allowed to visit him.

In this way Paul was kept in custody for two whole years. Occasionally Felix sent for him and asked him to preach—it was a novelty to have an educated preacher of a new religion among his prisoners. Each time he hoped Paul would offer him money in exchange for liberty. But the bribe was not forthcoming, and Paul returned each time to his quarters in the guardhouse under the command of a centurion. And often, no doubt, he walked out on the high parapets of the old prætorium, looking westward toward the gray-blue Mediterranean, toward the sunset, toward Rome! Ships were putting out from the great harbor every day, beyond Herod's breakwater, northward and westward toward Cilicia, Asia, Galatia, Greece—and Rome. Would he ever see Rome, after all?

ON THE WAY TO ROME

At the end of two years a change of governors took place in Palestine. In the spring of the year 59, Porcius Festus was appointed by the Emperor Nero to be pro-curator of Judæa and Samaria. He arrived, no doubt, in early summer. He was a typical Roman, strict, businesslike, quick to act, and not changing his mind once it was made up. Three days after his arrival in Cæsarea, he set out to see Jerusalem, the chief city of his province. While there the chief priests and leading citizens informed him against Paul, and asked him to hold the trial at once in Jerusalem—they planned to have Paul assassinated on the way. Festus' answer was brusque: "Paul is a prisoner at Cæsarea, where I myself am returning shortly. Send down your counsel and make a regular accusation against him."

The second trial.—The trial before Festus was no more satisfactory than the one before Felix. The charges were serious, but not proved. Finally Festus asked the prisoner, "Are you willing to go to Jerusalem and there stand trial?"—he hoped in this way to please the Jewish authorities, his new subjects. But Paul, perhaps aware of the plot to assassinate him, or at least knowing the danger and uselessness of such a course, replied: "I am standing before Cæsar's judgment seat, where I ought to be judged, as a Roman citizen; I have not wronged the Jews, as you know quite well. If I am a criminal and worthy of death, I do not refuse to die. But if none of their charges is true, it is against the law to hand me over to them for trial. *I appeal to Cæsar.*"

The fateful words were uttered. This was his right, as a Roman citizen, to appeal from all lower and provincial courts to the judgment of the Emperor himself. No doubt he had thought it over many times—this was the only way in which he saw any hope of reaching Rome, or even of release from tedious imprisonment under governors more interested in peace and their own prosperity than in justice.

Festus answered after conferring briefly with his legal staff, "You have appealed to Cæsar; to Cæsar you shall go." Festus undoubtedly thought this the best possible riddance of a troublesome and vexatious case!

Before Agrippa.—In sending a prisoner to the Emperor it was necessary to state the charges against him. Festus was somewhat perplexed to define the charge, inasmuch as the Jewish accusations were not proved, and no technical point at law was involved which a provincial governor could not decide. Likely as not, the Emperor would think Festus a weak administrator if he sent Paul to him without clear charges. So when King Agrippa II (who was king of all that part of Palestine not under the Roman procurator) came down to Cæsarea to pay his respects to the new governor, Festus conferred with him about the case. Paul was led before them and permitted to offer his defense for the third time—or perhaps the twentieth. It consisted of a clear narrative of his early life as a student in Jerusalem, his Pharisaic education, his persecution of the Christians, his conversion, and his obedience to the heavenly vision. Though he did not persuade Agrippa or his host, they agreed that he had done nothing worthy of death or even of bonds—"and might have been set at liberty if he had not appealed to Cæsar!"

Julius the centurion.—At last the day came when Paul and certain other prisoners set sail for Rome, in the care of the centurion Julius of the *cohors augusta*. With Paul were Luke and Aristarchus of Thessalonica. Their ship was from Adramyttium (near Assos, on the northwest coast of Asia Minor) and was probably homeward bound at the time. It was to make several stops along the southern coast of Asia Minor and Julius there could transfer his prisoners to some ship sailing for Italy.

The storm.—Their first day's voyage brought them to Sidon, fifty-five miles north of Cæsarea. Here Julius gave Paul permission to go ashore and visit his friends.[1] From Sidon they headed for Myra, on the coast of Lycia in southwestern Asia Minor, but had to go out of their way to the east and north of Cyprus as "the wind was contrary." It was already September, and after October 1 navigation was closed on the open Mediter-

---

[1] The Romans were usually lenient with prisoners, since it was impossible for them to escape far and the penalties were serious. "Wherever you are," wrote Cicero to an exiled friend, "you are equally under the power of the conqueror."

ranean. The delay caused by going around the lee of
Cyprus was a loss of precious time. Reaching Myra,
Julius found an Alexandrian grain-freighter sailing for
Italy, and boarded it with his prisoners and their guard.
They sailed slowly westward for several days, with an
adverse wind, until they stood off Cnidus—at the end
of the peninsula jutting out from the southwest corner
of the province of Asia. Here, instead of trying further
to tack against the wind and pass to the north of Crete,
they headed south-southwest to get under the lee of the
island, which with its high mountains and cape (Salmone)
would break the force of the wind. This was dangerous
—for they were now on the open side of Crete, and if
the wind shifted suddenly their heavy freighter would
be hard to manage in the wide, open sea to the south
and east of the island.

And this is exactly what happened. Enticed from
Fair Havens, where they first stopped, in the hope of
reaching the good harbor at Phœnix where they had
decided to winter, they set out much against Paul's
counsel and advice. At first the wind blew gently from
the south. Suddenly, a strong northeast wind—*eura-
quilo*, the sailors called it—broke upon them, and before
they could swing-to and head north or east and tack,
or directly northeast and ride out the gale, it was too
late. To turn meant rolling in the trough of the waves
and foundering. There was nothing to do but steer
into the lee of Cauda, an island southwest of Crete, and
there take in the pinnace (which was used in rowing
ashore and as a lifeboat), undergird the vessel with
cables, and trim the sails. At least they could make a
stiff fight to beat away from the quicksands of north
Africa (Syrtis). "Lowering the gear" is probably
equivalent to our "reefing the sails"—they were pre-

paring to run before the wind and head west rather than southwest, if possible.

Shipwrecked.—This they succeeded in doing, though the storm increased in violence and continued, like some of our "equinoctials," for two weeks. The next day after leaving Cauda—where they found no refuge—they began throwing overboard the freight; the third day they threw over the spare ship-tackle and private baggage of those on board. Darkness came on and continued for days. They ate nothing. Everyone despaired of reaching safety. No one knew where they were, whether near Syrtis, or Sicily, or the coast of Carthage; stars and sun had been hid for days. Only Paul remained courageous, for he knew that the words of his vision would be fulfilled and he would yet see Rome! Even during the raging tempest he had a vision in which an angel said to him, "Fear not, Paul, thou must stand before Cæsar. And lo! God hath granted thee all them that sail with thee!"

About midnight on the fourteenth night of the tempest they seemed to be nearing land. Dropping the lead they found it to be true; and casting four anchors astern, they dragged until morning. At dawn they saw before them a small bay with a sandy beach, and let go the anchors and tried to make it. Instead, the ship struck a reef and was wrecked. But all on board reached land safely, and they found themselves on the island of Malta —only fifty miles south of Sicily, on the very road to Rome!

Rome at last.—Here they spent the winter, receiving kindly treatment from the islanders, and in the early spring Julius and his prisoners set out for Rome. Taking passage on another Alexandrian vessel, The Twin Brothers, they touched at Syracuse, Rhegium, and

Puteoli—where Paul remained with "the brethren" for a week. From Puteoli to Rome was one hundred and thirty miles. Christians from Rome, having heard that Paul was on the way, came as far as the Market of Appius and the Three Taverns to meet him. They felt they already knew him through his epistle addressed to them three years before; they had heard of his work in Asia Minor and Greece, and were anxious to minister to him while he awaited his trial before Nero.

Another day and he was in the imperial city, the goal of his dreams for years, won at last through what hardships, dangers, disasters! It was a long way from Cæsarea to Rome. It was a still longer way from Tarsus, where he was born; from Jerusalem, where he went to school; from Damascus, where he was converted—especially by the far-ranging route Paul had followed, over land and sea, wandering through many countries and cities and strange peoples in order "to preach Christ to the nations." At last he was in the capital of the whole civilized world, and stood before the throne of the world-emperor, Nero Cæsar. Here also he was to preach, and "bear witness before kings."

STUDY TOPICS

1. Analyze Paul's defense at his first trial. What were his arguments in reply to Tertullus?
2. Read Paul's defense before Agrippa, Acts 26: 2–23. What were his main points?
3. Read Luke's account of the voyage and shipwreck (Acts 27). Trace the course of the voyage on an outline map, and be able to explain why it was not a direct course from Cæsarea to Rome, and why changes were made in the route as planned.
4. During Paul's stay on Malta (Acts 28: 1–10) he healed

many sick persons, and no doubt preached the gospel during his three months there. Read the account in Acts, and note how even Paul's adversities "turned out to the advantage of the gospel."

5. Trace Paul's route from Malta to Rome.

6. Do you think that simple, honest words are preferable to flattery? Do people usually take seriously what is told them by known flatterers? What is involved in accepting or offering undeserved compliments?

7. What was the secret of Paul's courage?—A vision, or faith in God who sent the vision? Do you remember a similar incident in the life of Jesus? Can faith give us courage, to-day, in facing dangers? Give an example.

CHAPTER XXIII

PAUL IN ROME

When they reached Rome, Paul was permitted to rent quarters outside the prison and there await the calling of his trial before Nero. The trial could not take place until his accusers arrived. Meanwhile, he was still a prisoner, chained to his guard, who was responsible with his own life for his prisoner's safety and security.

PAUL PREACHING AGAIN

Almost his first act after reaching the city and engaging his quarters was to call together the leading members of the Jewish synagogue and state his case to them. He hoped not only to give them a more favorable and fairer opinion of himself but to win at least some of them to the faith and obedience of Christ. What wonderful hope and courage he possessed, after all he had suffered at the hands of his countrymen, actually to attempt to win those who were in a position to do him much harm, never despairing of his own people—trusting always that in the end "Israel should be saved"!

Paul and the Jewish leaders.—When the Jewish leaders came, he addressed them as follows:

> "Brethren, although I had done nothing against the people or the customs of our fathers, yet I was delivered a prisoner from Jerusalem into the hands of the Romans; who, when they had examined me, desired to set me at liberty since I was not guilty of any crime. But when the Jews spoke against it, I was constrained to appeal unto Cæsar; not that I

had anything to accuse my nation of. For this
cause therefore I have asked you to come and speak
with me; it is on account of the hope of Israel that
I am bound with this chain."—Acts 28: 17-20.

Their reply was friendly and courteous.

"We neither received letters from Judæa concerning you, nor did any of the brethren come hither and
report or speak any harm of you. But we desire to
hear what you think; for as concerning this sect,
it is known to us that everywhere it is spoken
against."—Acts 28: 21-22.

Then they set a day to hear Paul expound his faith, his
interpretation of the "hope of Israel" (that is, the hope
of the Messiah and the kingdom of God).

On the day appointed a large number of Jews gathered
at Paul's lodging, and Paul spoke to them all day long,
from morning to evening, "testifying the kingdom of
God, and persuading them concerning Jesus, both from
the Law of Moses and from the prophets."

Paul's unfailing optimism was once more justified.
Among those who listened to him that day there were
some who believed and became members of the growing
church in the city of the Emperor. But, just as everywhere else, some refused to believe and departed, disputing among themselves.

Preaching to Gentiles.—But Paul's conscience was
now free. He had spoken his message, as usual, "to the
Jews first." He was now at liberty to turn to the Gentiles
—and he told his hearers so before they left him. "Be
it known therefore unto you that this salvation of God
is sent to the Gentiles; they will also hear."

"And he abode two whole years in his own hired
dwelling, and received all that called upon him,

> **preaching the kingdom of God, and teaching the things concerning the Lord Jesus Christ with all boldness, none forbidding him."—Acts 28: 30-31.**

With these words, the book of Acts concludes. Paul continued teaching and preaching to all who would come and listen. In one of his later letters he sends the greetings of some of the Roman Christians to the church he is addressing, and says, "They of Cæsar's household salute you" (Philippians 4: 22): even slaves of the Emperor's own palace were numbered among the Christians. In another letter he names some of his Gentile friends in Rome—Eubulus, Pudens, Linus, Claudia (2 Timothy 4: 21). A little later we find a large and powerful church in Rome, with numerous bishops and deacons and teachers. Before the century was over, the Epistle of Clement to the Corinthians, and perhaps also the Epistle to the Hebrews and the Gospel of Mark, had been written in this city. In later times the Roman Church became the leading church in western Europe, and all through the Dark Ages it stood like a lighthouse in the blackness of the night. Though we know nothing of its origin—it had been founded before Paul arrived in the year 59—there is little doubt that the preaching of Paul in his "own rented house" on one of the side streets near the prison greatly aided its early growth and partly explains its later expansion and importance. Imprisonment did not discourage Paul; a prisoner's chain could not prevent his preaching the gospel. "The word of God is not bound," as he said.

THE IMPRISONMENT LETTERS

Nor did his imprisonment prevent his communication with the churches which he had founded. Luke, Aris-

tarchus, Timothy, Tychicus, and others were with him
in Rome. Messengers came and went between Paul and
his friends in Asia and Macedonia and Greece. Letters
were exchanged. Gifts were sent Paul to pay his expenses
and provide some comforts while he awaited his trial.

The Epistle to the Philippians.—Some of the letters
have survived and come down to us in the New Testament. One of them is the Epistle to the Christians in
Philippi. It was written to thank his friends for a gift
of money—their fourth gift of this sort—which had been
sent by the hand of Epaphroditus. He had intended to
stay in Rome and be of what service he could to Paul,
but fell sick and had to go home. With him he took
Paul's letter as an expression of the apostle's appreciation and thanks for their generosity. It is one of the
tenderest messages we find among Paul's letters, and
reveals that gentleness and humility which, for all the
sternness and severity of his preaching, won the deep,
lasting affection of his friends.

> "I thank my God whenever I think of you, always
> making my supplication with joy, for your fellowship
> in the furtherance of the gospel from the first day
> until now; being confident of this very thing, that he
> who began a good work in you will perfect it until
> the day of Jesus Christ: even as it is right for me
> to be thus minded on behalf of you all, because I
> have you in my heart; inasmuch as, both in my
> bonds and in the defense and confirmation of the
> gospel, you all are partakers with me of grace. For
> God is my witness, how I long after you all in the
> tender mercies of Christ Jesus. And this I pray,
> that your love may abound yet more and more in
> knowledge and all discernment; so that you may
> approve the things that are excellent; that ye may
> be sincere and void of offense unto the day of Christ;

being filled with the fruits of righteousness, which are through Jesus Christ, unto the glory and praise of God. . . .

"For to me to live is Christ, and to die is gain. But if to live in the flesh—if this is the fruit of my work, then what I shall choose I know not. But I am in a strait betwixt the two, having the desire to depart and be with Christ—which is very far better: yet to abide in the flesh is more needful for your sake." —Philippians 1: 3-11; 21-24.

"Have this mind in you which was also in Christ Jesus, who being in the form of God counted it not a prize to be on an equality with God, but emptied himself, taking the form of a servant, being made in the likeness of men; and being found in fashion as a man, he humbled himself, becoming obedient even unto death—the death of the cross. Wherefore also God highly exalted him and gave unto him the name which is above every name; that in the name of Jesus every knee should bow, of things in heaven and things on earth and things under the earth, and that every tongue should confess that Jesus Christ is Lord, to the glory of God the Father." —Philippians 2: 5-11.

"Finally, brethren, whatsoever things are true, whatsoever things are honorable, whatsoever things are just, whatsoever things are pure, whatsoever things are lovely, whatsoever things are of good report; if there be any virtue, and if there be any praise, think of these things. The things which you learned and received and heard and saw in me, these things do; and the God of peace shall be with you."—Philippians 4: 8-9.

No other letter of Paul's, except the brief note addressed to Philemon, conveys so much of its author's inner feeling, personal faith, profound conviction.

The letter to Philemon.—Philemon was a wealthy man living in Colossæ, a hundred miles east of Ephesus on the main highway. He was a Christian. The church had recently been founded in Colossæ by some of Paul's fellow workers during the three years he spent at Ephesus, and was still meeting in Philemon's own house. Philemon had a slave, Onesimus, who had run away and gone to Rome. Strange as it may seem, he had come in contact with Paul, heard his preaching, and been converted. Paul was now sending him back to his master. It would be Philemon's right to punish Onesimus severely for running away. But Paul writes to urge him to deal gently with the lad, whom he calls "my child, born in my imprisonment."

> "Although I have no hesitancy, in Christ, to enjoin you to do what is right, yet because of my affection for you I rather beseech it, being such a one as Paul the aged, and now also a prisoner of Christ Jesus: I beseech you for my child, whom I have begotten in my bonds, Onesimus, who was heretofore unprofitable to you, but now is profitable not only to you but to me. I have sent him back to you in his own person, that is, my very heart. For I would much rather have kept him here with me, that as your slave he might be doing service to me, your friend. But, of course, I could not do that without consulting you, in order that such a kindness might be voluntary and not forced from you."— Philemon 8-14.

We may be sure that Philemon, receiving such a message, welcomed back his young slave and indeed treated him "as a brother." It is to be noticed that Paul expects (verse 22) soon to be released, after which he will visit Philemon at his home in Colossæ.

The Epistles to the Colossians and Ephesians.—
At the same time Paul took the opportunity of Onesimus'
return to send letters to the churches in Colossæ and
Ephesus—through which the young man would pass on
his way home. Epaphras, "a faithful minister" in the
church at Colossæ, had come to Rome bringing Paul
news of a dangerous kind of speculation which had
sprung up among the Christians there, beliefs which
made much of honoring angels and observing Jewish
festivals, and which looked upon Christ as only one
among several "manifestations" of God. Paul writes to
correct these false beliefs, and sends the letter by
Tychicus, who probably took Onesimus along with him
and was also, like Epaphras, "a faithful minister and
fellow servant in the Lord," and had authority to speak
for Paul to the Colossian Christians.

The Epistle to the Ephesians is very similar to that
to the Colossians, as is quite natural if they were written
at the same time and about similar subjects. It deals
with deep theological questions and with the profound
"mysteries" of the faith—the "incarnation," or appearance of the Son of God in human flesh, the gift of the
Holy Spirit, the "sealing" of those who are saved, the
church as Christ's "Body" on earth, the "reconciliation"
effected by Christ upon the cross, the unity of the
church made up of both Jewish and non-Jewish Christians.

And it contains very practical directions as well,
such as the following:

> "Wherefore, putting away falsehood, let everyone
> speak the truth with his neighbor; for we are mem-
> bers one of another. . . . Let him that stole steal
> no more, but rather let him labor, working with his
> hands at some good task, that he may have some-

thing to give the needy. Let no corrupt speech proceed out of your mouth, but such as is good for edifying those in need of it, that it may bring grace to the hearers. And grieve not the Holy Spirit of God, by whom you were sealed unto the day of redemption. Let all bitterness and wrath and angry temper and petulance and bitter speaking be put away from you, with all malice: and be kind one to another, tender-hearted, forgiving each other, even as God in Christ forgave you."—Ephesians 4: 25-32.

Other Epistles.—If Paul wrote any other epistles at this time, they have perished—they were either not saved by those who read them or were lost later on in the course of time. The two letters to Timothy and one to Titus are supposed to have been written by Paul after his "release," and before he was imprisoned in Rome for the second time. But the tradition regarding Paul's "release" is very vague, and the style and language of these epistles, in the form in which we have them to-day, are not quite the style and language of his earlier letters.

"I HAVE FOUGHT THE GOOD FIGHT"

How long Paul was kept waiting for his trial before Nero we do not know. Luke's statement that he remained "two whole years in his own hired dwelling" brings us to the year 61. The traditional view which represents him as released in 61 (on account of the failure of his enemies to appear and accuse him?) assumes that he afterward visited Spain, as he planned, and also the east—Asia, Macedonia, Greece—and was arrested finally at Nicopolis (for what reason the tradition is silent), taken to Rome, and beheaded during

Nero's persecution of the Christians in 64.[1] We do not know whether or not this tradition is true.

Paul's spirit.—But at least we are sure that Paul must have died as he had lived—ever ready, if need arose, to offer his last testimony to his Lord, and offer the "supreme sacrifice" of loyalty and obedience. The words of the Second Epistle to Timothy are perfectly true of Paul's spirit:

> **"I have fought the good fight, I have finished the course, I have kept the faith. Henceforth there is laid up for me the crown of righteousness which the Lord, the righteous judge, shall give to me at that day; and not only to me, but also to all them that have loved his appearing."**—2 Timothy 4: 7-8.

If there was any man in the world at that time who could honestly say those words, it was Paul of Tarsus, chained to a guard in his house at Rome.

Paul's achievement.—Next to our Lord, Paul is the greatest figure in the history of Christianity. His writings and his achievements fill half of the New Testament. He was the greatest Christian missionary. Almost unaided he led the fight for the freedom of the gospel, and released Christianity to become the world-religion rather than a Jewish sect. His clear insight into the fundamental principles of Jesus' teaching, his courage of conviction, his utterly unselfish sacrifice of his own comfort, ambitions, and earthly happiness, his "obedience to the heavenly vision" and to the voice of Jesus speaking to him through the Spirit often and again in his career, through disappointments and defeats, successes and triumphs, in persecution and in

---

[1] The apostle Peter is said to have been martyred at the same time, crucified head downward, as he was unworthy, he said, to die in the same posture as his Lord.

peace—this is what led him finally to victory. All European history, from the end of the first century to the present day, has been different because Paul of Tarsus was born and became a Christian.

He was a man of prodigious energy and zeal, an indefatigable worker, stern and uncompromising in facing wrong, a hater of lies and half-truths, a powerful opponent of sins of the flesh and of those of the heart and mind as well; yet tender and generous, loving and gentle toward those, to win whom for Christ he gave up everything in the world. He was a man in whose life the spirit of Jesus was manifest, in spite of all hindrances and limitations and the defects of a thoroughly human character. He is one of whom we cannot read without admiration and gratitude for his lifework in spreading the Christian religion among the Gentiles.

STUDY TOPICS

1. Read Colossians 1: 1–23; 2: 1–23; 4: 7–18; and Ephesians 1: 1–14; 3: 1–21; 4: 1–7; 6: 10–24. Summarize the main points in your notebook.
2. Read the whole Epistle to the Philippians and the Epistle to Philemon. Make a list, from these epistles, of Paul's companions in Rome. Write a brief description of Paul's character as revealed in these two letters.
3. Review Paul's life and missionary career. Write a sketch of five hundred words briefly summarizing it.
4. Draw a map showing the expansion of early Christianity up to the death of Paul, as far as we know it from the New Testament. Color in red the cities and regions noted on the earlier map (Chapter XI) and in blue those evangelized later. Paul's journeys may be shown by dotted lines.
5. Paul was an unfailing optimist—not with the "chronic

optimism," however, of mere good spirits (for once there was a time when he had been full of despair, that is, before his conversion). His hopefulness was a part of his religion. Do you think this ought to be a part of every Christian's religion? Why?

6. Write in your notebook a sketch of Paul's character, telling what interests or impresses you most about him. Are these characteristics which you would like to imitate in your own life?

7. Choose the passage you like best in Paul's Epistles, and memorize it.

PART THREE

THE CHURCH AFTER PAUL

CHAPTER XXIV

CHRISTIANITY IN THE DAYS OF NERO

THE persecution of the Christians in Rome under Nero was a signal for persecution elsewhere. Heretofore, as we have seen, the government more than once, through the provincial officials, shielded the Christians from the onslaughts of their Jewish opponents or the violence of popular fanaticism. The early Christians were among the most loyal subjects of the empire. Their attitude is well expressed in the epistle, written probably some time later, known as *First Peter:*

> "Be subject to every constituted authority for the Lord's sake; whether it be to the emperor, as supreme, or to governors, as appointed by him for the punishment of evildoers and the honoring of them that do well. . . . Honor all men. Love the brotherhood. Fear God. Honor the king."—1 Peter 2: 13-17.

Prayers were offered in Christian worship for the emperor's safety and the security of the empire. But all of a sudden, the "powers that be" were turned against the church, and henceforth the disciples of Christ are made to realize that every one of them may at any time be called upon to bear witness "even unto blood."

We have no account of the persecution in the New Testament, for Luke's second volume, the book of Acts, closes with the year 61. Nevertheless, it contains some letters and an old Christian prophecy which in an interesting way throw light upon Christian thought and feeling at the time. These we shall examine in this chapter.

AFFAIRS AT ROME UNDER NERO

Nero was made emperor in the year 54, thanks to the intrigue of his mother Agrippina. For five years more he remained under the influence of his old teacher, the philosopher Seneca, and ruled wisely and well. But when Seneca was innocently banished in 59, Nero cast aside all restraints and flung himself into a career of cruelty and vice.

Nero's crimes.—Throughout later history, Nero's name has been associated with the worst tyranny, brutality, and sensuality in a sovereign. Forsaking his duties as head of the empire, he toured the cities of Greece as a musical composer, dancer, and charioteer, competing for prizes on the stage and in the arena. Naturally, the court at home soon split into factions, each endeavoring to rule by intrigue and threats. Nero, growing more and more suspicious and autocratic, ordered the assassination of one after another of the prominent and influential citizens of the imperial city. This included his old master, Seneca; his stepbrother, the son of the Emperor Claudius; his wife, and even, finally, his own mother, Agrippina. As a result of these and other of his crimes, the city seethed with secret rebellion, destined to lead in 68 to his own death.

The great fire in Rome.—Meanwhile, in 64, a vast fire broke out in Rome, lasting for more than a week and not dying down until it had consumed a large part of the city. The palace of Augustus on the Palatine hill in the heart of the city, the old-fashioned wooden buildings around the *circus maximus,* and thousands of citizens' homes were burned. So bitterly was Nero hated that at once rumor described the Emperor himself starting the fire and watching the city burn while a musical performance of his own depicted the conflagration of Troy. The story of "Nero fiddling while Rome burned" may be untrue to fact, but it shows how intensely he was disliked. The Romans at least believed him capable of such a crime.

The Christians accused.—Anxious to clear himself of blame, Nero helped to circulate another rumor which charged the Christians with starting the fire. There must have been a great many Christians in the city by that time for such a story to spread and gain credence— the populace at least knew that some such strange and suspected sect existed! The fanatical and now homeless mob demanded vengeance upon those guilty of firing the city, and so Nero ordered large numbers of the Christians put to death with horrible tortures. The Roman historian Tacitus describes (Annals 15:44) in gruesome detail the torments of the martyrs, who were dressed in the skins of wild animals and attacked by wild and hungry dogs, or dipped in tar and nailed to crosses where they were lighted as torches at night. It was at this time, perhaps, that the apostles Peter and Paul were put to death—Paul beheaded and Peter crucified head downward.

THE PERSECUTION IN ASIA MINOR

The signal had been given at Rome. It was evidently safe now to put Christians to death. The old fires of jealousy, suspicion, fanatical hatred flamed forth, and in widely sundered regions Christians paid the penalty for believing in Christ and looking for the coming of his kingdom. Adherents of the Jewish and other rival religious systems, political enemies, the superstitious and bigoted rabble who opposed any innovation and disliked "foreigners" and "foreign gods" on principle, selfish artisans, like Demetrius, who found that Christianity interfered with their trade—all these were waiting their chance to attack the followers of Christ. At last their time had come! Though the persecution was not authorized by the imperial government, and was not directed against the Christians as such (that is, because they were believers in Christ), yet its results were almost as serious in some places as if it had begun with an edict from the Emperor.

The Book of Revelation.—Naturally, the persecution was most severe in places where Christianity had been recently established, where the Christians were not very well known or their religion generally understood. Such were some of the cities in the province of Asia. Paul had spent three years at Ephesus, from 52 to 55, and from this headquarters his assistants had gone out to establish the church in nearby cities. Perhaps some of the country towns had been evangelized by persons who had gone up to Ephesus, heard Paul and been won to Christ, and then returned to spread the message and share the new life in Christ with their old neighbors and friends. Such a man, perhaps, was Philemon of Colossæ. It was in these small, new, but growing churches of western Asia Minor that the persecution now raged.

There is a book in the New Testament, called the *Apocalypse*, or Revelation, *of John*, which contains some letters addressed about this time to Christians in the chief cities of this region; and there are also other references in the volume to the persecution under Nero. The form in which we have the book to-day is later in date, for it was probably edited, with the addition of

THE LAST PRAYER

J. L. Gerome

much new material, toward the end of the reign of Domitian (81–96) when still another persecution had broken out. But these older sections of the book are useful as showing us what the Christians felt and thought when they found themselves threatened with death on account of their faith.

A vision of the Son of Man.—The original work was written by a Christian called John—some say the apostle John. The author had been banished to the rocky, desolate island of Patmos, one of the Cyclades, forty miles southwest of the harbor of Miletus. There on a Lord's day (the Christian Sunday, not the Jewish Sabbath) he was "in the Spirit" and saw a wondrous vision which he was commanded to "write in a book" and send it to the seven churches of Asia—at Ephesus, Smyrna, Pergamum, Thyatira, Sardis, Philadelphia, and Laodicea.

The account of his vision is as follows:

"And I turned to see the voice which spake with me. And having turned, I saw seven golden lampstands; and in the midst of the lampstands the 'One like unto a Son of man,' clothed with a garment down to the foot, and girt about the breast with a golden girdle. His head and his hair were white as white wool, like snow; and his eyes were as a flame of fire; and his feet like unto burnished brass, as if it had been refined in a furnace; and his voice was as the voice of many waters. And he had in his right hand seven stars; out of his mouth proceeded a sharp, two-edged sword; and his countenance was like the sun shining in full strength.

"When I saw him I fell at his feet as one dead. But he laid his right hand upon me and said: 'Fear not. I am the First and the Last, and the Living One. I became dead, and behold, I am alive unto

the ages of ages, and I hold the keys of Death and of Hades. Write therefore the things you have seen, and the things that are now, and shall be hereafter: the mystery of the seven stars that you saw in my right hand, and the seven golden lampstands. The seven stars are the angels of the seven churches, and the seven lampstands are the seven churches.' "
—Revelation 1: 12-20.

The "One like unto a Son of man" is of course Jesus, whom the Christians expected to return in glory at any moment (see Acts 1: 11; 1 Thessalonians 4: 16; 2 Thessalonians 2: 8). The term had been used in the Old Testament (Daniel 7: 13), and was now understood to mean the Messiah; indeed, Jesus himself had so used it (Mark 14: 62). For John, the coming of Jesus as the Son of man in glory, that is, as the heavenly Messiah, was the only hope of salvation and rescue from persecution for himself and his fellow Christians.

"Behold, he comes with the clouds;
And every eye shall see him,
Even they that pierced him,
And all the tribes of earth shall mourn because of him.
Even so. Amen." —Revelation 1: 7.

But the greatest significance of his vision was that Jesus, himself, even now "in glory," stands in the midst of his persecuted churches, the Son of Man amid the golden lampstands, and holds in the hollow of his mighty hand his suffering but faithful followers.

The seven letters.—Now follow the epistles to the seven churches, as messages from their divine Lord, to accompany the narrative of the vision. The churches were located in cities lying roughly in a circle north and east of Ephesus, on the main highways of the province,

important centers from which the messages would be
read and repeated to the scattered believers in the
surrounding villages and towns further inland. A messenger could make the circuit, reading the appropriate
letter in each church.

The first is addressed to Ephesus, naturally, for it was
the capital of the province. "I know thy toil and
patience . . . but I have this against thee, that thou
didst leave thy first love. Remember from whence thou
art fallen, and repent, and do the first works! . . . To
him that overcometh will I give to eat of the tree of life
which is in the Garden of God" (Revelation 2: 1–7).
Likewise to each of the others was a message addressed,
full of comfort and warning, consolation and reproof,
ending always with encouragement and the promise of
some special blessing in the coming kingdom—the
"morning star," the "white stone," the "name of the
city of God." To one, Laodicea, were addressed the
wonderful words which have inspired so many sermons,
hymns, and works of art:

"Behold, I stand at the door and knock;
  If any man hear my voice and open the door,
  I will come in to him, and will sup with him,
    And he with me.
  He that overcometh, I will give to him
  To sit down with me in my throne,
  Even as I also overcame, and sat down with my
    Father
  In His throne."   —Revelation 3: 20-21.

The mark of the beast.—But along with this message of consolation and encouragement for the persecuted
Christians of the rich senatorial province of Asia, addressed to them by their divine and glorified Lord,
Revelation contains the strange prophecy found in

chapter 13. It describes the great "beast coming up out of the sea," as in the book of Daniel (chapter 7), only here the reference is to the Roman Empire. Like all the heathen empires which had ruled the world in earlier days, and more cruel than them all—with the clawed feet of the "bear," the mouth of the "lion," and many-colored like the "leopard" (13: 2)—this empire has received from the "dragon" (Satan) all its power and authority. This is indeed a bitter picture of the Roman Empire—and must have been written by some Jewish rebel, who was also a Christian, between 60 and 70 A. D.

> "And it was given unto him to make war with the saints, and to overcome them. And there was given unto him authority over every tribe and people and tongue and nation. And all that dwell on the earth shall worship him, every one whose name hath not been written in the Lamb's book of life. . . . If any man hath an ear, let him hear. If any man is destined for captivity, into captivity he goes; if any man kills with the sword, with the sword must he be killed. Here is the patience and the faith of the saints."—Revelation 13: 7-10.

"The saints" are the persecuted Christians, suffering captivity and the sword under Nero. Then the vision continues:

> "And I saw another beast coming up out of the earth; and he had two horns like a lamb, and he spake as a dragon. And he exercises all the authority of the first beast in his sight. And he causes the world and them that dwell therein to worship the first beast, whose death-stroke was healed. And he does great signs, even making fire to come down out of heaven upon the earth in the sight of men. And he deceives them that dwell on the earth by

means of the signs . . . saying to them that they should make an image to the beast. . . . And it was given unto him to give breath to it, even the image of the beast, that the image should speak, and cause as many as should not worship the image to be killed. And he causeth all, the small and the great, the rich and the poor, the free and the slave, to receive a mark on their right hand or upon their forehead; and no man is able to buy or to sell, save he that hast the mark, even the name of the beast or the number of his name. Here is wisdom! He that has understanding, let him count the number of the beast; for it is the number of a man; his number is six hundred and sixty and six."—Revelation 13: 11-18.

In this passage the "beast" is no longer the empire; it is "a man," whose "number" is 666; and the "second beast" is the imperial priesthood which enforces his worship. Who is this man, this beast-man that other men are compelled to worship under penalty of death? Many interpretations have been offered, but the most probable is to translate the name into Hebrew, the language of the original author, and sum up the letters after the ancient fashion.

$$
\begin{array}{ll}
N = 50 & \\
R = 200 & Q = 100 \\
W = 6 & S = 60 \\
N = 50 & R = 200 \\
\hline
306 & \text{plus} \quad 360 = 666
\end{array}
$$

NRWN–QSR (Nerôn Qasar) is the Hebrew for the Emperor Nero—"Nero Cæsar"! The cryptogram is solved. It would have been dangerous to refer in so many words to the worship of the Emperor. Hence this

cryptic, oracular style of writing, which was common
in all the apocalyptic literature of Judaism and early
Christianity (see Daniel 9 : 27 and Mark 13 : 14).

The coming judgment.—There were other documents, Jewish or Jewish-Christian in authorship, of
which the author of John's Apocalypse made use. In
one of these occurs the solemn chant of exultation over
the coming fall of Rome:

> "Fallen, fallen is Babylon [Rome] the great;
> It has become the habitation of demons
> And the abiding-place of unclean spirits. . . .
> Rejoice over her, thou heaven,
> And ye saints, ye apostles, ye prophets;
> For God hath judged your cause against her!"
> —Revelation 18 : 2, 20.

The victory of the saints.—But this is not the final
message of the book. Strange and weird as are its
visions, confused as seems their order and obscure their
meaning, the Apocalypse of John is a wonderful book of
consolations and promises. The oppressed and persecuted Christians may indeed be annihilated upon
earth—John seems to expect they will all be put to
death as martyrs; nevertheless, they shall be raised
from the dead to reign with Christ upon a renewed
earth, and at last from heaven shall descend "the New
Jerusalem, coming down out of heaven from God, made
ready as a bride adorned for her husband."

> "And I heard a great voice out of the throne saying,
> 'Behold, the tabernacle of God is with men,
> And he shall dwell with them
> And they shall be his peoples,
> And God himself shall be with them,
> And be their God.

> And he shall wipe away every tear from their
> eyes;
> And death shall be no more;
> Neither shall there be mourning,
> Nor crying, nor pain, any more;
> The first things are passed away.'
> And he that sitteth on the throne said,
> 'Behold, I make all things new.' "
> —Revelation 21: 3-5.

This promise is the climax of the book. What consolation, encouragement, spiritual strength it must have given those brave and faithful men and women—yes, and boys and girls—who followed Christ and "bore his name in their foreheads" and gave their witness in those far-off days when "witness" and "martyr" were interchangeable terms! As we read over its strangely beautiful pages we can see those first readers, secretly gathering by night for their services of worship and meetings of fellowship in darkened houses on narrow, little-known streets in the obscure quarters of the ancient cities of "Asia." The pages are old and worn; there are spots on them where tears once fell, and there are stains which once were red with blood. It meant something to be a Christian in those days!

STUDY TOPICS

1. Look up, in *The Life and Times of Jesus*, pp. 48–51, the significance of the title, "the Son of Man." Look up also the references to the Bible given in the chapter above.
2. Try to name some of the reasons which might have been given by an educated Roman to excuse the outbreak against the Christians. Remember that many of them were Jews; many were hated by their fellow

Jews for giving up the ancestral religion; and pagans, especially the ignorant rabble, were opposed to "new gods"—as were the Boxers in China.

3. Read Revelation 18, the chant over fallen Babylon, and note the references to its wealth and commercial prestige.   What is the correct interpretation of "Babylon"?   (See also Revelation 17: 9, 18.)

4. Explain the "number of the beast" in Revelation 13: 18.

5. Read some of the songs of rejoicing over the future victory of Christ and his saints—Revelation 5: 9–14; 7: 10–12; 11: 15–18; 12: 10–11.   What would these songs mean to those who first read them?

6. The book of Revelation is sometimes explained as referring to still-future events, to take place at the end of the world.   Would promises of such far-off events, thousands of years in the future, have had much meaning for persecuted Christians in the days of Nero and Domitian?

7. Evidently, most of the language of Revelation is figurative and symbolic.   But no such picture of heaven and the life to come is to be found elsewhere in the Bible.   Mention two or three facts about that life which are taken for granted in what you have read in the book.   Is there any unhappiness in that life?   Are Christ's servants in his presence or not?   Will sin and disobedience to God continue?

CHAPTER XXV

THE CHURCH IN PALESTINE

THE reign of Nero was one of the darkest periods in the world's history. His persecution of the Christians was only one, if one of the worst, of his many misdeeds. We must not, of course, take Nero as a fair example of the Roman emperors, for some of them were brave and honorable men and good administrators. Nor must we suppose that the Christians were persecuted *as Christians.* The day was soon to come when angry mobs roared out the cry, "Christians to the lions," and riot filled the streets of Rome and other capitals until their thirst for blood was satisfied. But that evil time was not yet. Christians were not the only ones who suffered under Nero. He was universally hated for his injustice —and particularly in Palestine.

CHRISTIANITY AMONG THE JEWS

We have read some of the older sources of which the author of the Revelation of John made use, which date from the days of Nero and were written, in all likelihood, by Jews. They may have been written in Palestine. All the provinces suffered under the reign of "the beast." But in Palestine revolutionary feeling ran especially high. Two years before Nero's death (that is, in 66 A. D.), a serious war broke out, which ended only with the fall of Jerusalem and the destruction of the Temple in 70 A. D. Involved in this tragedy and in the events which led up to it were the Christians who lived in Jerusalem and throughout Palestine. How fared the church in that region during those sad and troubled years?

Zealous for the Law.—It will be remembered that when Paul arrived in Jerusalem in the year 56, just before his arrest, he found the Christians in that city carefully observing the Jewish Law. This was only natural, for they had been born Jews, and continued to observe the ancestral rites and customs even after they became Christians. They believed that the Messiah was none other than Jesus; that he was in heaven, soon to come in glory, hold the Last Judgment, and set up his reign upon earth. And meantime they were doing all they could to hasten his coming (on Jewish principles) by observing the Law with care and strictness. Hence James and the elders could say to Paul, "You see, brother, how many thousands there are among the Jews who have believed [in Christ]; and they are, all of them, zealous for the Law" (Acts 21: 20).

As Paul had already pointed out more than once to his Gentile friends, this observance of the Law by Christians really reduced Christianity to nothing more than a sect of Judaism, a sect that believed just as all other Jews believed, save that they identified the Messiah with their Master, Jesus. In time such a sect was bound to disappear, as, indeed, Jewish Christianity did disappear in later centuries, its last vestiges being engulfed by the rising tide of Mohammedanism in the eighth century.

Nevertheless, in the first century, this Jewish Christianity lost none of its original power. The Christian Jews were respected, feared, and sometimes hated by their orthodox neighbors. It may be that their careful observance of the Law helped to win over many of their neighbors to the new faith, and thus served a missionary purpose. One or two quaint and interesting anecdotes have been handed down in popular tradition from those days, showing how orthodox Jews and "Nazarenes" lived side by side, if not in entire harmony at least not in open conflict.

One such apocryphal story is told of James, the brother of the Lord who was "bishop" or head of the Jerusalem church in the fifties and sixties. He was highly respected by his Pharisaic neighbors for his piety, and was accordingly surnamed "the just." So frequent were his visits to the Temple to pray for the forgiveness of his people that his knees, it was said, became calloused like a camel's. When the scribes and Pharisees saw the growing danger that the whole Jewish people would "expect Jesus as the Messiah," they went to James and said: "We beg of you, restrain the people, who are being led astray after Jesus as if he were the Christ. At the approaching feast of the Passover go up on the wing of the Temple and speak to the assembled crowd and tell them the truth about Jesus." But James answered with a loud voice, "Why do you ask me about Jesus the Son of man? He is now sitting in the heavens, on the right hand of the Great Power, and is about to come on the clouds of heaven!" Whereupon they cast him down from the wing of the Temple, and beat him to death with clubs (see Eusebius, *Ecclesiastical History*, 2: 23).

Opposition from the Jews.—But it must not be supposed that no further opposition or persecution took place. Orthodox Jews could not tolerate some of the doctrines of the Christians; and the existence of a rival synagogue, calling itself the *Ecclesia*, or *Qahal*, the congregation of the "true Israel," was more than most conservative Jews could endure. The open enmity of the early days had passed, but the persecution was none the less real even when it took a different course. For example, it might appear in the treatment of Christian workmen by their orthodox employers. The heartlessness of rich landowners in withholding the wages of their laborers (probably Christians) is denounced in the *Epistle of James*.

> "Go to now, ye rich, weep and howl for your miseries that are coming upon you! Your riches are corrupted, and your garments are moth-eaten. Your gold and your silver is rusted; and their rust shall be for a testimony against you, and shall eat your flesh as fire. You have laid up your treasure in the last days. Behold, the hire of the laborers who mowed your fields, which is kept back by you through fraud, crieth out; and the cries of them that have reaped have entered into the ears of the Lord of Hosts. You have lived delicately on the earth, and taken your pleasure. You have nourished your hearts in a day of slaughter. You have condemned and killed the righteous; he doth not resist you."—James 5: 1-6.

So far as the author of these words can see, there is no hope of redress save in the coming of the Messiah (Jesus) to hold the Judgment. And he adds, "Behold, the judge stands before the doors!" (5: 9.)

Scattered over Palestine, from Galilee and the region of Cæsarea Philippi on the north to the fringes of the desert on the south, in the little villages as well as in the larger centers of population, were to be found the Christians, or "Nazarenes," Jews who added to their faith this one principle, that they believed the Messiah to be none other than Jesus; and believing, they undertook to live as he commanded, observing the Law in the spirit which he exemplified and taught, and looking day by day for his coming on the clouds of heaven "with power and great glory." It is not unlikely that the Gospel of Matthew was written (somewhat later) in Palestine or Syria. It is noteworthy that this expecta-

tion of Jesus' coming in glory as the Messiah is greatly
emphasized and elaborated in this Gospel. The traditions of earlier Palestinian Christianity made much of
this hope; and the fact is perfectly natural, considering
the constant unrest and oppression and danger in which
the Jewish Christians lived.

THE FALL OF JERUSALEM

All through the years leading up to the "middle
sixties," when Nero had sunk to the deepest depths of
vice and crime, and all the world seethed with unrest,
little Palestine was steadily preparing all unconsciously
for its fate. No one dreamed—save a few seers, most of
whom echoed the prophetic words of our Lord—of what
lay in store for the Holy City and the Holy Land in the
next few years.

The insurrection of the zealots.—For decades—in
fact, ever since the Roman occupation began—there had
been Jews who bitterly opposed the payment of tribute
to Cæsar. Any recognition of "the wicked kingdom" was
sinful disloyalty to God and his sacred covenant with
Israel. Some of these, called *zealots*, were ready to seize
the sword and throw off forever the hated Roman yoke.
As things went from bad to worse, under Nero; as
procurators were sent out to Jerusalem by the Emperor,
one after another, ignorant of Jewish customs and
arbitrary in the use of their authority; as, finally, the
smoldering wrath of the nation could be restrained no
longer, it burst forth in the year 66 in a flame of insurrection.

Gessius Florus was the last of the procurators of
Judæa, and he was probably the worst. Brigandage
flourished on every hand, the procurator himself sharing
the spoils. Private and public murder, systematic

terrorization, organized cruelty covered the land. When the storm of revolt broke out, in the spring of 66, Florus was driven from Jerusalem, the Emperor's offerings were thrown out of the Temple and the Roman garrison killed after its surrender. Cestius Gallus, the legate of Syria, marched into Palestine with a force of twenty thousand, burned the "New City" on the north side of Jerusalem, retreated, and was routed at Beth-horon. Nero now sent out an army of sixty thousand men, under the able general Vespasian. The summer of the year 67 was spent in subduing Galilee, where the Jews under Josephus (later the historian of the war) offered stout resistance. With the loss of Galilee, the Jews in Jerusalem were driven to more desperate measures. The zealots now took the lead and, like the Russian Bolshevists, massacred their opponents and all who were suspected of lacking sympathy with the revolution.

Vespasian learned of the internecine strife within the city and took his time, knowing its capture would be the easier the longer he delayed. In 68 he conquered the country east of the Jordan and Judæa. Then came the news of Nero's death, and for a year the invasion was at a standstill. On July 1 in the year 69 Vespasian was himself hailed emperor by his troops and left Palestine for Rome, leaving his son Titus to besiege and take Jerusalem. Divided now into bitter, murdering factions, weakened by famine and reduced by pestilence, the most terrible scenes were enacted within the beleaguered city. Wall after wall gave way before the assaulting troops of Titus. At last, in the month of August of the year 70 the very citadel of Judaism, the sacred Temple, was stormed and set on fire. A month later the Upper City was taken, where a few defenders had gathered to fight to the bitter end, and Jerusalem had fallen! The prophecy of Jesus had come true; her enemies had come, and cast up a mound about her, and dashed her even with the ground, and left not one stone upon another— and all because she "knew not the time of her visitation" (see Luke 19: 41-44).

The flight of the Christians.—Through this tremendous political and social upheaval passed the Jewish Christians. There is an old tradition that just before the final siege of the city an oracle was discovered which bade them flee. Leaving the doomed capital they gathered at a village called Pella, in northeastern Palestine, east of the Jordan and just south of the Lake of Galilee. We do not know what this "oracle" was; in the confusion of the siege many stories of signs and portents and mysterious voices spread abroad. But it may be that the oracle was nothing more nor less than the words of our Lord as reported in the document sometimes called the "Little Apocalypse" (Mark 13, Matthew 24, Luke 21).

> "But when ye see the abomination of desolation standing where he ought not (let him that readeth understand!), then let them that are in Judæa flee unto the mountains; and let him that is on the housetop not go down, nor enter in, to take anything out of his house. . . . For in those days shall be tribulation, such as there hath not been the like from the beginning of the creation until now, and never shall be. And except the Lord had shortened the days, no flesh would have been saved; but for the sake of the elect, whom he chose, he shortened the days."—Mark 13: 14-15, 19-20.

It is noteworthy that Luke, instead of the "abomination of desolation," has the words, "When ye see Jerusalem compassed with armies, then know that her desolation is at hand" (Luke 21: 20).

After the war, many Christians remained in Palestine, though great numbers had fled to other countries, especially to Egypt and Asia Minor, where there were already large colonies of Jews. There was now no Temple in Jerusalem, at which to offer the sacrifices required by the Law.

Decline of Christianity in Palestine.—More and more, from the end of the first century onward, Christianity in Palestine sank into insignificance. Orthodox Pharisaic Judaism triumphed, codified its rules, its interpretation of the Torah, and as far as possible ignored every mention of Jesus and his followers. In the Talmud, the final codification of its traditions, Jesus is described as "a magician who deceived and led Israel astray."

The position of the Jewish Christians in Palestine is suggested in a story told by the second-century Christian writer, Hegesippus. He relates that Domitian, having heard that the Christians worshiped another king than Cæsar, whom they expected to come and reign, commanded all the family of David to be sought out, in order to destroy the representatives of the Jewish royal line. Among those arrested were two grandsons of Judas, the brother of our Lord. When questioned as to their property, they answered that it amounted to only nine thousand *denarii* (about $1,700)—and this was not in money but simply the value of a poor forty-acre farm on which they toiled to raise their annual taxes. Then they showed their calloused hands in proof of their statement. And when asked about Christ and his kingdom, they replied that it was "not a temporal or an earthly kingdom, but celestial and angelic; that it would appear at the end of the age, when coming in glory he would judge the living and the dead and give to everyone according to his works." Domitian was disgusted with what seemed to him their foolish superstition, and called off the hunt for treason. (See Eusebius, *Ecclesiastical History*, 3: 19-20.)

Though there were always some Christians in Palestine, down to the days of Mohammed, their number seems to have been small and uninfluential.

The significance of Judaism for Christianity.— It was in "the fullness of the time" that Jesus came. The world was ready for the gospel. Roman government and roads, Greek language, Jewish faith in one God and the religion of the Old Testament, with synagogues in every notable city of the empire and a persistent missionary propaganda—these prepared the world for Christ. But if Christ's coming was none too early, it was also none too late. Christianity spread, the church was organized and grew, Jesus himself had appeared, while Judaism still flourished and spread abroad, just before it received the blow which destroyed its prestige and ended its usefulness as a messenger preparing the way for the Messiah.

It is impossible not to see "the hand of God at work in history," in such a situation as this. Judaism did not perish—it is very much alive even to-day—but it lost something infinitely precious in the eyes of every Jew when the Temple was laid in ruins. Nevertheless, before this catastrophe took place, Jesus appeared and announced a kingdom higher than that of any one race or nation, a religion superior to all political and social divisions among men, and destined not only to survive the shock of Jewish intolerance and Roman persecution and the destruction of the central shrine of Jewish faith, but to outlive all other governments, religions, worships.

STUDY TOPICS

1. Turn back to Chapters XI and XIV and describe the state of the church in Palestine when last we considered it. Was it at peace, or suffering persecution? See Acts 9: 31; 12: 1–3, 24.

2. What was the chief difference between orthodox Jews and Christians in Palestine in the first century? Remember that both orthodox (Pharisaic) Jews and Christian Jews looked for the coming of the Messiah.

3. What religious and economic conditions are reflected in the Epistle of James? Read the epistle and note its main teachings, briefly summarizing them in your notebook.

4. The following passages have been taken to indicate a Palestinian (or at least Jewish Christian) origin for the Gospel of Matthew: 1: 1; 5: 17–20; 8: 10–12; 13: 37–43, 52; 16: 11, 17–19; 19: 28; 28: 15. See if you can explain their significance in this sense.

5. What was the meaning of the Christian "oracle" received before the fall of Jerusalem?

6. What was the attitude of later orthodox Judaism to Christianity, and its view of our Lord, as recorded in the Talmud? How could such a view arise?

7. Show how Christianity arrived "in the fullness of time," and how a few years later might have been just too late—so far as we can see—for the purposes of God.

8. Is the "social teaching" of Saint James (and other New Testament writers) of importance to-day? Does Christianity imply "social justice"—in industry, business, trade? What would this world be like if the teachings of Christ and the apostles were fully applied?

CHAPTER XXVI

THE MAKING OF THE NEW TESTAMENT

THE early Christians had no New Testament, such as we have to-day; at least, they had none until it began to be gathered together toward the middle of the second century. Instead, they had the Old Testament, which was the Bible of Judaism. All Christians, Jewish and Gentile, used this Bible. The Jewish Christians in Palestine read it either in the original Hebrew (though this was now a purely "literary" and not a spoken language) or in the common dialect known as Aramaic, into which the Lessons were sometimes translated in the synagogue by an interpreter, called the *methurgeman*. Christians outside Palestine in the Greek-speaking Mediterranean world, whether Jewish or Gentile by birth, read it in the Greek version known as the Septuagint. This translation was used in the services of both the Jewish synagogue and the Christian ecclesia. It is an interesting translation, in many parts quite literal, in others freely paraphrased, and yet preserving a dignified style and a religious tone quite suited to the translation of sacred writings. The influence of this translation is to be seen in many later writers, and even in the New Testament. For example, Saint Luke proves upon almost every page of his Gospel and the book of Acts his years of familiarity with the Septuagint.

THE EARLIEST CHRISTIAN WRITINGS

Quite naturally, the earliest Christian writings, which form the bulk of our New Testament, were written from time to time as need and occasion arose. The writers did not set out to provide a Christian Bible, or to supplement the Bible they already possessed. The production of the New Testament was thus unconscious, though it was surely a process guided by the Holy Spirit and took place in the providence of God.

Christianity among the lowly.—There are several reasons to explain why the early Christians did not write a complete record of the spread of their faith, or even a full and detailed account of the earthly life of their Lord. One of these is the fact that, as Saint Paul said—in words we need to recall again and again—"Not many wise, not many mighty, not many noble" were called (1 Corinthians 1: 26). The great majority were poor and ignorant. As Jesus foresaw, the truths of the gospel were "hid from the wise and understanding, and revealed unto babes" (Matthew 11: 25). Our religion first spread, both in Palestine and in the world outside, among peasants and fishermen, workingmen and artisans, the poor and uneducated of the ancient world. The picture of "Christ Among the Lowly" is most true in its symbolism. For it was they only, for the most part, who welcomed the message of deliverance and the promise of the kingdom to come; the "wise and understanding" were too well satisfied with the world as it was, with themselves its leaders and guides. As in Galilee "the common people heard him gladly," so in the whole Græco-Roman world, "the lowly" responded to Christ's teaching and the teaching concerning him which was spread abroad through the work of the early missionaries and apostles. Of course there were exceptions; Paul himself, and Mark and Luke and Apollos, and others besides, were learned men; and it was not long before there were Christian believers within the very "household of Cæsar"—close, that is, to "the noble." But the great majority of Christ's first followers were not men and women who would either produce or preserve detailed records of the rise of their religion. The very language of the New Testament indicates its lowly origin. Its Greek is not the Greek of historians and philosophers, but of the common people, the *koinê*, or "common" Greek of the masses. And most of the early Christians were so poor that it is not until the fourth century that their sacred books were copied upon permanent material (*vellum*), instead of the fragile papyrus commonly used; our oldest manuscripts of the New Testament belong to the century of Constantine and the church's triumph.

A Book of Martyrs.—Another reason for the scanty remains of early Christianity is the persecutions. Such records as survived were saved from the fires and destructions of those recurrent outbursts of bigotry and fanaticism. When Christianity came to be persecuted as a proscribed and outlawed religion, then every sacred writing or article of church furniture or ornament or picture used in its worship was also proscribed, in the effort to destroy the new faith root and branch. But even earlier still its effects are to be seen: not only the book of Acts and the letters of Paul, with their records and echoes of opposition, and the Apocalypse of John, called forth in successive parts or "editions" by the persecutions under Nero and Domitian; not only the Epistle to the Hebrews, and the other New-Testament Epistles, with their reflections upon "the fiery trial" or their anticipations of trial about to come, but even the Gospels bear those marks. They were written in days when to be a Christian was to invite insolence and oppression, and they were written for those who had to count the full cost of discipleship.

Many of the sayings of our Lord, therefore, and the incidents of his life, were selected and written down in the Gospels because they referred to the persecution of his followers after his death. Such sayings as those about "forsaking father and mother," "putting the hand to the plow" and not looking back, being "cast out of the synagogues," "turning the other cheek" to one's smiters, the man building a tower, "confessing Christ before men"—these and many other words of Jesus were burned into the memories of the Christians and were written down in the Gospels because they assured the disciples that their Master had foreseen all that they were to endure, had foreseen what lay beyond the transient "sufferings of this present time," and had himself suffered with and for them to bring in that glorious kingdom of his Father which was promised "to him that endureth to the end."

The whole New Testament is thus in a sense a "Book of Martyrs"—at least it was a martyrs' book. It is all that survived the terrible persecutions of the early days.

The coming kingdom.—There is a third reason, and one which shows itself in almost every part of the New Testament, to explain why so few detailed records have come down from the first century. The early Christians expected the speedy coming, or *Parousia*, of the Lord from heaven. Jesus was soon to return as Messiah and Judge, hold the Last Judgment, and pass sentence on all mankind, raise his martyred followers from their graves, and set up the kingdom of God. Persons who expected Jesus to do this at once, who thought each morning as they arose that this day might be the last of "the present evil age" and to-morrow see the dawn of the endless Reign of Christ—such persons did not sit down and write annals of their own times or chronicles of the recent past. Their minds and hearts were full of the coming of their Lord; their duty was to watch and pray—"for in an hour that ye think not the Son of man shall come." They lacked the motive for composing historical records.

The first collected writings.—Nevertheless, some writings appeared, not as historical records, but, as we have seen, drawn forth by the occasion. These were the first, as far as we know, of the Christian writings to be preserved for future use and copied for wider reading: the letters of Paul to his scattered groups of friends and churches in Asia, Macedonia, Galatia, Corinth, and Rome. According to his own direction, in one or two instances, his letters were read in other churches than the one addressed (see Colossians 4: 16). This no doubt led to copying, as the church addressed would wish to preserve the original bearing Paul's own greeting or signature at the end. In time copies were probably circulated even more widely; the Asiatic Christians would exchange copies of his letters to them for copies of other letters, addressed to the Corinthians, the Galatians, and so on.

In this way an extensive and fairly complete set of Paul's letters would be compiled—and this was the beginning of the collection of the early Christian writings known as the New Testament. Reading these letters at the services and meetings of the church, reading them just as the Jews of the synagogue read the appointed selections from the Old Testament, was a step in the direction of making them "canonical" or authoritative. They were already beginning to be looked upon as sacred books. It was only a question of time until other books were added to the collection, and the whole group looked upon as of equal value to the Greek Old Testament, the sacred collection taken over by the Christians from the Jews. But the beginning, we must remember, was probably made when Paul's friends and devoted followers gathered together, perhaps even before his death, such of his letters as they came across or could discover in the churches to which the great apostle wrote.

THE GROWTH OF THE GOSPELS

In some such way, without intending to write or to collect a Bible ("Bible" is from *biblia*, which means "books"), the other Epistles of the New Testament were produced and preserved, some without even the names of their authors (for example, the Epistle to the Hebrews).

Other epistles were written, like those of Clement, Ignatius, and Polycarp; but these were omitted from our New Testament for the reason that they were later in date and not written by apostles—and, in fact, do not as a rule stand on so high a plane as the letters of the first century. What we should remember, though, is that for the most part the early Christian literature was "epistolary" in form. Letters were the chief and almost the only way in which the early churches could keep in touch with one another. Even when messengers were sent from church to church, they usually carried written messages of encouragement, exhortation, and friendly greeting.

The earliest Gospels.—But the time came when the "eyewitnesses and ministers of the word" (Luke 1: 2) fell asleep—the early Christian word for "death"—or laid down their lives as martyrs. It therefore became necessary to commit to writing their accounts of the life of Jesus and the early days of the church in Palestine. Farther and farther across the empire spread the message of the gospel. Men who had never heard of Jesus save from the Christian missionaries—men like Theophilus, the friend of Luke, to whom he dedicated his

Gospel and Acts (Luke 1: 1–4, Acts 1: 1–2)—were anxious to know more about the Lord than they could learn from the missionaries.

Moreover, the return of Christ was delayed longer than the first believers anticipated, and there was need to commit to writing the oral accounts of his earthly life and teaching lest these should perish and be forgotten with the death of the first generation of his followers. This need was first felt some time just before or after the fall of Jerusalem. So it came to pass that written accounts were prepared, in more and more complete form, of "all things that Jesus began both to do and to teach, until the day he was received up."

"The Sayings of Jesus."—The earliest of these documents, so far as we know, is one which to-day is found only in the Gospels of Matthew and Luke, as one of their "sources." It was a collection of Jesus' *sayings*, mainly, sayings like those of the Sermon on the Mount, the parables, the admonitions and commands given to the disciples, the public and private teaching of the Master.

The way in which this document may be discovered in the pages of our first and third Gospels is interesting. Matthew and Luke, as we know to-day, used the Gospel of Mark as their basic narrative, rearranging it, "editing" and revising it, inserting into it other material for the sake of completeness. If this other material, which they added to Mark, be studied by itself very carefully, it will be seen that much of it is found almost word for word in identical form in both these later Gospels. And if the methods of composition, style and diction, interests and aims of Matthew and Luke are examined, it will be seen that the differences in their treatment of this material are practically the same as their differences in treating Mark. Discount these differences, and we find a unified and homogeneous document which was their chief source, in addition to Mark, for the teaching and sayings of our Lord. This document is commonly known to-day as "The Sayings of Jesus," though scholars usually prefer to use an algebraic symbol for it, "Q" (which stands for *Quelle*, the German word for "source").

This document, our earliest written "Gospel," was composed some time, perhaps, in the fifties or sixties of the first century, probably in Palestine, and perhaps even in Jerusalem. Most probably it was for the use of missionaries and teachers of the gospel, for it was written in Greek, and was meant for those who had no adequate oral account of the words and teachings of Christ.

Mark's Gospel.—The next Gospel, in order of composition, was the Gospel of Mark, which gives more of the narrative of Jesus' life, an outline of his ministry, and an account of the trial and passion and resurrection. Tradition says that Mark wrote it in Rome after Peter's death, remembering as carefully as he could all that Peter had related of the Master's life—Mark had been Peter's "interpreter" and companion, as he had once been for a short time the companion of Paul and Barnabas. His object was to show that our Lord was Messiah even in his earthly life, just as truly as he was after the ascension. Therefore he gives the accounts of the miracles, as proofs of divine power, and the cries of the demons who recognized him as the Son of God. The last page of Mark (or column, on a scroll) has been lost, our oldest manuscripts breaking off with a preposition in verse 8 of chapter 16. The present conclusion was added later, and is merely a summary of what was found in the other Gospels.

The Gospels of Matthew and Luke.—Matthew and Luke are in a sense revisions of Mark, with which each has combined in his own fashion the material found in the "Sayings" and elsewhere. "Matthew's" object was to group about several great topics the teaching of Jesus and the narrative of his life, such as the exposition of the Law in the Sermon on the Mount, and the discourse of our Lord at the sending out of the Twelve; he had in mind as he wrote the needs of the church at his own time, the questions and problems which arose before it, and he was intensely interested in the coming of the Kingdom, which he pictured in very literal fashion. He was a Jew, and wrote for Jews, both Christian and non-Christian, frequently quoting the Old Testament, and proving from its predictions that Jesus was indeed the promised Messiah.

Luke aimed at the instruction and confirmation in his faith, through historical investigation, of the friend to whom he addressed his two writings. Luke's method was to search out the best traditions and documents and arrange these in the most probable order. It is to his diligent and loving research that we owe the beautiful and precious account of the infancy and early years of Jesus given in his first two chapters, and also some of the most important incidents and greatest parables in the life of Christ.

The Fourth Gospel.—The Gospel of John, as it has been known for centuries, is the last of our New-Testament Gospels. It is not so much a narrative of Jesus' life and teaching as an interpretation and defense of Christianity, of Christ, of Christ's meaning for all mankind. It was intended to offset the attacks of Jewish critics about the end of the first century and to show that Jesus was the Word, or "Logos," of God: the one who was with God from all eternity and at last manifested him to men by becoming incarnate and taking human flesh. This is a great mystical and theological concept, and it is illustrated from traditions of the life of Christ which were accessible to the author but not found, for the most part, in the three "synoptic" Gospels. He treats the miracles as "signs," as seven great symbolic manifestations of divine, supernatural power and love. It is not a Gospel in the same sense as the other three; it does not make so much of historical narration; it aims to prove the truth of a majestic, sublime idea, which was already a part of the church's faith; it was written "that ye may believe that Jesus is the Christ, the Son of God, and that believing ye may have life in his name" (John 20:31)—and so it is a *Gospel* in an even higher sense than the other three.

The New Testament's permanent value.—Thus came into existence, in the course of fifty years or more of persecution, opposition, and triumphant advance in the face of all attacks, a book, or collection of books, which is almost the only Christian record we possess of those precious years, and of the still more precious years of the life and ministry of Jesus, his passion and resurrection, the founding of the church in Palestine, and its spread throughout the eastern half of the Roman world until it entered the gates of the eternal city itself. We see it at the very beginning of its long task of "leavening, till the whole lump be leavened," the customs, manners, institutions, ideals, motives, hearts, and minds of men. No age has seen a purer form of Christianity than that first faith of the early apostles, martyrs, and evangelists. As we read their writings, and learn through them to know and worship and obey the Master whom they loved and followed, the prayer rises to our lips,

> "O God, to us may grace be given
> To follow in their train!"

We discover the permanent value of the New Testament when we learn to use it, and to find in it God's Word to each of us in our own lives, and to his church, still waging the warfare of faith in his name.

STUDY TOPICS

1. Which were the earliest writings of the New Testament, and why?
2. Explain why the records of the rise of the Christian religion are scanty and fragmentary. Give three reasons.
3. Look up some of the papyrus letters, bills, etc., which illustrate the "common" Greek spoken by the mass of the people in the first century. See Deissmann, *Light from the Ancient East*, or Milligan, *Selections from the Papyri*.
4. What first led to the collection of the New Testament writings? What part had Paul's Epistles in this process?
5. Describe the growth of the Gospels, and explain how one of their earlier sources is found.
6. Read some of the following passages from the document called "Q": Luke 9: 57–60; 10: 2–16; 11: 9–13; 12: 22–31; 13: 18–21; 14: 16–23. Are any of these passages found in Mark? (What is the significance of this question?)
7. Read over Mark 1: 16 to 3: 19 and mark the passages which you think most like reminiscences which Peter would relate. What bearing has this upon the traditional origin of our second Gospel?
8. How does the fourth Gospel differ from the other three?
9. If the New Testament is almost our only record of the beginnings of Christianity, how ought Christians to regard it? Have you a plan for regular Bible reading?

CHAPTER XXVII

THE BLOOD OF THE MARTYRS

AFTER the close of the first century the next record of the spread of Christianity is found not in any Christian writing but in the letters of a Roman governor addressed to the Emperor Trajan. Like many that have gone before, it also is a record of persecution. Pliny the Younger, as he is called (to distinguish him from the Elder Pliny, who was a writer of natural history), was sent in the year 111 or 112 to administer the fertile and populous province of Bithynia. This province lay in northwestern Asia Minor, on the shores of Propontis (Marmora) and the Black Sea, and had suffered much from the lax and extravagant mismanagement of earlier proconsuls. Pliny was given the powers of imperial legate, and his first duty was to bring a bankrupt province back to prosperity, and incidentally to tighten the reins of Roman control over its affairs through the better administration of justice and the suppression of disloyal secret societies.

CHRISTIANITY IN BITHYNIA

Here Pliny found a large number of guilds or clubs (*collegia*)—we might call them "lodges" to-day—which existed to advance the interests of their members. Some of them were like modern trade-unions; each member was assessed a certain amount, meetings were held once a month, the poorer members or those out of work were given benefits or relief, and their funeral expenses were paid from the common fund. Such guilds were to be found throughout the empire, although they had been severely restricted by a decree of the Senate in the time of Augustus, requiring them to hold their meetings in public, not oftener than once a month, and then only after they had received a special license from the authorities. The danger of such associations was that they easily became centers of political unrest.

The church as a trade-guild.—One of the first acts of Pliny, following instructions from the Emperor, was to issue an order for the suppression of all guilds and clubs. At once this brought up the problem of dealing with the Christian Church, which resembled in some ways the prohibited *collegia*. The problem was complicated by certain industrial conditions of the province which Pliny had undertaken to remedy and which had been seriously affected by the spread of the new religion. As he traveled about Bithynia he had been astonished to find the temples almost deserted, the old-fashioned worship nearly abandoned, and the trade in animals for sacrifice waning. The reason was, he learned, that the province swarmed with Christians! Here was new and unexpected trouble on his hands.

At what date Christianity spread into Bithynia, we do not know.[1] Perhaps it was a result of the active missionary work of the church in the province of Asia, or possibly it had come up along the trade-route from Galatia, or even crossed from Philippi or Thessalonica in the west. Whenever and however founded, by the year 112 there were Christians enough in the province to imperil the ancient trade in sacrificial animals, and rouse the opposition of those who depended upon it for their livelihood. Just as Christianity had been opposed in Ephesus by those whose trade it affected, so here also its influence had become apparent in a striking and public manner, and was opposed for its injury to business.

---

[1] The Christians there were addressed in the Epistle known as First Peter.

The governor's perplexity.—At this juncture informers (*delatores*) came forward with accusations against the Christians. Pliny summoned the accused to appear before him and questioned them about their membership in an illicit organization. Some denied this; others confessed. Those who confessed he questioned a second and even a third time with threats of punishment. "Those who persisted," he says in one of his letters, "I sent to execution; for I had no doubt that, whatever it was they admitted, contumacy and stubborn obstinacy ought not to go unpunished."

This was plain tyranny, though Trajan might—and did—approve; but the matter did not end here. Shortly afterward an unsigned paper was posted in a public place containing a long list of persons alleged to be Christians. Instead of ignoring this list, Pliny took the illegal step of searching out those thus anonymously accused and brought them to trial. By this time he knew more about Christianity and realized that it was a religion, not a trade-guild, with which he was confronted. He adopted three severe tests of their loyalty to the Roman religion and state; they were to repeat after him a prayer addressed to the gods, to burn incense in sacrifice, and make a libation; they were to adore, with sacrificial incense and wine, the statue of the Emperor; and they were finally to pronounce a curse upon Christ. Refusal of the first branded one an atheist, in pagan eyes; refusal of the second was treason; refusal of the third proclaimed the atheist and traitor as a Christian. Some of those accused asserted that they had never been, or had long ceased to be, followers of this faith. Others refused firmly to recant.

It now occurred to Pliny to inquire what this religion amounted to, which could inspire such ardent and heroic loyalty, and what were the crimes it led to and justified. To his surprise, as he wrote in a letter to Trajan, there was no crime at all—

> "They maintained that the extent of their crime is this, that on a fixed day they meet before daylight and sing by turns a hymn to Christ as God (carmen Christo quasi Deo); and bind themselves with an oath (sacramentum)—not for the commission of a crime, but—not to commit theft or robbery or adultery, not to break their word, nor to deny a deposit when claimed. After this it is their custom to depart and meet again for the purpose of taking food— common and innocent food (not human flesh, as has been alleged); and even this they ceased doing after my edict was issued forbidding clubs, according to your instructions."—Pliny, Epistle 97.

Trajan's rescript.—In order to find out if this testimony were really true, Pliny ordered two Christian slave-women tortured; but they only affirmed what had already been said, and so the governor concluded that Christianity was nothing more than "a baneful and absurd superstition." He could not very well go on trying Christians for their belief, since it seemed politically harmless, and especially as the Christians included a large part of the population of the province. So he wrote to the Emperor for directions, in the letter just quoted, and received in reply Trajan's answer, or *rescript:*

> "You have adopted, my dear Secundus, exactly the right course in examining the cases of those denounced to you as Christians. For, indeed, no general rule can be laid down as a fixed form of procedure. They must not be sought out; but if

they are denounced and convicted, they must be
punished, unless anyone who denies he is a Christian proves it by adoring the gods; however suspicious his conduct may have been, he shall earn
pardon by repentance. But anonymous posters
ought not to be regarded in the case of any crime;
for that would set a very bad example, unworthy of
our times."—Pliny, Epistle 98.

It is evident that Trajan was anxious to suppress the
activities of anonymous and irresponsible informers.
This was a measure of safety for the persecuted Christians. But it is also evident that the Roman authorities
had no intention of compromising with a faith which
denied the gods and refused a simple and complacent
rite of loyalty to the imperial authority. It was only a
step from this to the persecution of Christianity *as a
religion.*

IGNATIUS OF ANTIOCH

About this time, or perhaps a little later, an attack
was made upon the church in Antioch in Syria. Christianity had been established there for sixty years or
more—two generations—so that many of the faithful
had been followers of Christ all their lives long. And
the church was, of course, large in numbers to provoke
the opposition that arose.

Condemned to the lions.—It is not said what occasioned the persecution. It may have been the disastrous
earthquake which destroyed part of the city in 115 (if
the date of the persecution is that late); such calamities
were often attributed to the wrath of the gods against
believers in alien religions, who were robbing the local
deity of his lawful worship and offerings. Antioch was
a city of polyglot population, divided by factions and

CHRIST OR ARTEMIS

Edwin Long

parties, and alarmed at that time by the threatened approach of the Parthians. However the persecution began, it led to the arrest and condemnation of the bishop, Ignatius, before the Roman legate. He was sentenced to be conducted to Rome and there thrown to the beasts in the arena.

On the way to Rome.—Soon began his long, slow journey overland to Troas, guarded by military escorts and accompanied, like Saint Paul on his way to Rome, by friends and companions. At Philadelphia, Smyrna, Troas, delegations from the nearby churches visited him, fondly kissing his chains in token of their homage; and he wrote to the congregations they represented the brief letters of greeting and exhortation and counsel which still survive. One of these is his epistle to the Ephesians, whose bishop, Onesimus, had come to Smyrna to visit him.[1] It begins as follows:

> **"Ignatius, who is also called Theophorus, to the church which is at Ephesus in Asia, most deservedly happy, being blessed through the greatness and fullness of God the Father, and predestinated before the world began to an enduring and unchangeable glory, being united and chosen through his true passion, according to the will of the Father and Jesus Christ our God: All happiness, by Jesus Christ, and his undefiled grace!"—Ignatius, Ephesians 1: 1.**

No sad and melancholy greeting, this, for a man on his way to the lions! An exuberant joy and intense devotion has obliterated, for Ignatius, all thought of his own fate. The spirit of the martyr comes out toward the end of this letter, where he wishes that his life may be laid

---

[1] Was this the Onesimus for whom Paul wrote the note to Philemon?

down for his readers—"my soul be for yours"—and in the passage where he writes,

> "Pray also without ceasing for other men; for there is hope of their repentance and attaining unto God. Let them therefore at least be instructed by your works, if they will be no other way (i. e., by words). Be mild at their anger, humble at their boasting; to their blasphemies, return your prayers; to their error, your firmness of faith; when they are cruel, be gentle, not endeavoring to imitate their ways. Let us be their brethren in all kindness and moderation, but let us be followers of the Lord: for who was ever more unjustly used? more destitute? more despised?—so that no root of wickedness may be found in you, but that ye may remain in all holiness and sobriety of body and spirit, in Christ Jesus."
> —Ignatius, Ephesians 10.

Is not this the very spirit of the Sermon on the Mount, and of the Master "who, when he was reviled, reviled not again"?

From Troas, the guard took passage across to Neapolis, thence conducting their prisoner to Philippi on the Via Egnatia across the Balkans. Here two other martyrs, Zosimus and Rufus, were handed over to the escort, and the Christians of the city displayed to Ignatius and his companions the same love and generosity which they had shown in the old days to Saint Paul, regarding the chains of the martyrs as "the very 'diadems of the elect.'" At Ignatius' request, they wrote to Polycarp, Bishop of Smyrna, begging him to forward their letter to the church in Antioch; thay also asked him to send them copies of such letters of Ignatius as he possessed.

His death.—After this we hear no more of the martyr. He doubtless perished in the arena at Rome, the church commemorating his martyrdom on February 1, though his death was perhaps in October. We see him for only a brief interval, as he makes his way across the strongly Christian province of Asia, chained to his guard, exulting in spirit, forgiving his persecutors, glad to die for Christ and in the place of his fellow Christians, a truly heroic and Christ-inspired man.

POLYCARP OF SMYRNA

Forty years later, on the 23d of February, 155 A. D., Polycarp, Bishop of Smyrna, Ignatius' friend and visitor during his stay in that city, laid down his life also as a martyr.

"Away with the atheists."—It was during a popular spectacle and celebration at Smyrna, when dignitaries were gathered from all parts of the province for worship, business, and amusement, the latter including *venationes*, or wild-beast shows. The origin of the disturbance is not known, though it reached at least as far as Philadelphia, and eleven victims had already given their lives in Smyrna before Polycarp was taken. It is said that they were severely tortured in order to force them to recant— a new method of persecution, and one which the imperial rescripts, so far as we know them, did not authorize.

As these eleven brave witnesses sealed their testimony to Christ in their own blood, the fury and madness of the mob rose to high pitch. The arena rang with cries: "Away with the atheists! Bring Polycarp here, their bishop and leader!" The proconsul, Quadratus, totally ignoring the principles and rules of procedure laid down by the emperors, sent his captain of police to arrest the bishop. Polycarp, who was now an old man, had already been hidden by his friends in a farmhouse outside the city, and might have remained in safety had not one of his slaves been seized and tortured till he revealed his master's hiding-place. Polycarp refused to attempt further flight, and yielded, saying, "God's will be done."

Though the hour was late, he was hurried back to the city and led into the stadium. Soon the mob gathered, and Quadratus hastened to hold the trial. "Swear by the genius of Cæsar," ordered the proconsul, "repent, and say, 'Away with the atheists [that is, the Christians].'" Lifting his hand solemnly, as if to swear, the aged bishop replied, "Away with the atheists [that is, the real atheists, not the Christians]." "Swear," said Quadratus, "and I will let you go. Curse Christ!" But Polycarp replied, "Eighty and six years have I served him, and he never did me wrong; how can I blaspheme my King who saved me?"

Polycarp's death.—Hereupon the mob cried out to cast Polycarp to the lions. But this the Asiarch forbade, since the days of the *venationes* were now past. Then the mob demanded that Polycarp should be burned alive. Without waiting for permission, men hastened to gather wood for fuel, the helpless old man was tied to a stake, the fire lighted, and—the flames being too slow in reaching him—the executioner was called to slay him with a sword.

Thus perished one of the noblest Christians of the second century, one whose witness for Christ and whose teaching were impressed upon a large body of friends and disciples; one of whom the Christian history of that century is full, and whose "testimony" at the stake was the crown of a long life of witnessing for his Lord. His death was not the result of legal process but of the blind fanaticism of an infuriated mob. His "trial" was as infamous and unjust as that at which our Lord was condemned; it was only semilegalized murder.

Yet neither martyrdom nor the base perversions of

justice nor the outbursts of ignorant fanaticism were enough to daunt the courage of the Christians or stay the victorious onward march of their faith. Since the days of "Antipas, the faithful witness," at Pergamum (Revelation 2:13), the first martyr of the church in Asia, it had been true that "the blood of the martyrs was the seed of the church." It was still to be true for many years to come. And it has been true ever since, in every country where the gospel has been preached and in every age of the church's long life.

STUDY TOPICS

1. Look up the province of Bithynia on a map of Asia Minor or the Roman Empire. What were its chief cities? Look up the reference to First Peter.

2. Who was Pliny the Younger? Look him up in your ancient history or the encyclopedia.

3. What was the opposition to Christianity in Ephesus, referred to above? See Chapter 18, or Acts 19. Explain how the opposition arose in Bithynia.

4. When was Christianity founded in Antioch? See Chapter 11, or Acts 11. What great names were already connected with the history of its church?

5. Who was Onesimus, for whose sake Paul wrote a letter?

6. Trace on the map that part of Ignatius' journey to Rome which his letters reveal to us. What was its probable continuation?

7. Compare the procedure of Pliny in trying Christians with that of Quadratus in Smyrna at the trial of Polycarp. Note what seem to you injustices in the process, and find out if you can whether or not these were in accordance with Roman law.

8. How do you account for the bitter hatred of the Christians by their persecutors?

9. How did Ignatius manifest the spirit of Christ? Can you recall words or deeds of Jesus which may have inspired Ignatius?

CHAPTER XXVIII

TWO CENTURIES OF GROWTH

WE enter now what has been called the "subterranean period" in the church's history. The records become even more scanty, though writings of other than historical purpose, especially apologies, epistles, theological works, continued to be produced in increasing number. It was the age of the great persecutions. It was the age of the catacombs. It was the period of slow, silent, secret growth in which the hidden force of Christianity gradually undermined the prejudice and fanaticism of the pagan world. When it emerged, in the time of Constantine, its victory was sudden and almost complete, so effectively had its work been accomplished during the two preceding centuries, so widely had it succeeded in leavening the thoughts and feelings of men.

Gradual expansion of the church.—Very largely the growth of the church in this period has to be inferred from its extent at the end of the third century. It began as a sect or cult outside the pale of legal toleration, numerically a minority, subject to the attacks of self-interested informers, and liable to the penalties of the law against secret organizations. It continued as a suspected and defamed society; successive efforts were made to stamp it out, more than once with the full force of imperial approval; and yet it continued to grow, like the seed in the parable, "night and day, of its own accord, no one knows how." Even by the middle of the second century, Tertullian, the African lawyer and advocate of Christianity, could say,

"We are but of yesterday, and we have filled your cities, your islands, your stations, your country towns and settlements, your council chambers, your very camp, your palace, your Senate, your bar. We have left you only your temples. We can count your armies: the Christians of a single province exceed them in number."—Tertullian, Apology 37.

The day was coming, inside a very few generations, when Christianity would be either sufficiently in the majority, or at least a strong enough minority, not only to free itself from persecution but to become the established religion of the empire. Surely this was a marvelous growth for two hundred years!

CHRISTIANITY FROM HADRIAN TO DIOCLETIAN

Brief and fragmentary as are the sources for this period, their variety and interest is very great. We have more and more frequent notices of Christianity from now on in the works of pagan writers. Lucian the satirist, Celsus the teacher of philosophy, Galen the medical writer combat it in their various ways, by satire, by serious argument, by polite tolerance and explanation of its strange beliefs. Christian writers appeared, who undertook both to refute the charges brought against their religion and to expound its tenets in a way suited to convince or at least win the toleration of the responsible and educated classes in the empire. Letters were written, like the one from the churches in Vienne and Lyons (in Gaul) recounting the persecution there in the year 177. All these supply us with information, scanty as it is, for our period.

The catacombs.—And all along, through these dark decades, as a background which makes vivid even to-day our reading of the short and simple annals of the persecuted, there are the inscriptions in the Roman catacombs—the chilly, stone corridors under the city where the Christians held their forbidden services, baptized their children, partook of the Eucharist, and buried their dead. The faith which shines in the darkness of those rock-hewn chambers is brighter than anything in the world outside. No pagans ever wrote on their tombs such epitaphs as these:

ARETUSA IN DEO

—"Arethusa rests in God"; or

ALEXANDER SUPER ASTRAS

—"Alexander has ascended beyond the stars"; or the tenderly beautiful one,

EIRENE IN PACE

—"Irene is in peace"; Irene, whose very name means "peace," has found it at last, freed from the terrors of the tyrant and persecutor.

Hadrian's rescript.—Trajan's successor was likewise a soldier, Hadrian, one of the best emperors Rome ever enjoyed. He was a great statesman and succeeded in improving the methods of taxation—there were arrears of over $40,000,000 when he ascended the throne. He was determined, moreover, to improve the administration of justice and do away with some of the barbarities still permitted by the law. In religion he was one who dabbled in various cults, and therefore might be expected to tolerate new and suspected faiths, including Christianity. We are not surprised to read, then, in a work by Eusebius, the early church historian, that "this was especially a time in which the doctrine of salvation attained its full power and spread among all men" (*The Preparation for the Gospel* 4: 17).

Under Trajan individual Christians had been accused by informers; and the charge, apparently, referred simply to membership in a secret and therefore illegal society. But now we hear of popular outbreaks, like the one in which Polycarp was to suffer, when the mere name of Christian was enough to excite a mob and rouse the utmost fury of popular hatred and violence. The chief trouble took place in Asia, the old missionary field of Paul and Apollos, and now thickly populated with Christians. The proconsul Granianus wrote to Hadrian, as Pliny had written to Trajan, asking for directions in dealing with the victims of the outbreak. Hadrian replied, after a time, addressing Fundanus, who was now proconsul, with his famous rescript in which he directed that

> "If the people of the province are able to maintain their charge against the Christians so far as to answer in open court, they must adopt this simple method, and not use demands and mere clamor. . . . If then, anyone accuses them and proves that they act in any way contrary to the law, you must give decision by the legal method, in accordance with the gravity of the offense. On the other hand, if anyone accuses them simply as an informer (for purposes of extortion), see that you punish him with due regard to the seriousness of the case."— Eusebius, Ecclesiastical History 4: 9.

Copies of the rescript were sent to other governors, and it supplied a rule of procedure for many years, even under later emperors. Though there were a few martyrdoms in the reign of Hadrian, the persecution was not so violent as it had hitherto been and was to become later on.

The Antonines.—Hadrian died in 138 and was succeeded by Antoninus Pius, and he in turn, in 161, by his adopted son, Marcus Aurelius Antoninus. "The Antonines," as they are known to history, were good emperors in many ways, faced with an impossible task, however, on account of the economic and political conditions within their empire and the growing barbarian power threatening its frontiers. Marcus found a refuge from despair in the study of Stoic philosophy and left the world his famous meditations entitled "To Himself." It seems strange that the Christians were persecuted under these wise and gentle rulers. The reason is doubtless that in their view the empire and its interests came first, and any movement which suggested a divided loyalty, or set men's minds upon another world than this, or required allegiance to some unknown spiritual potentate, naturally appeared to be dangerous and to deserve stamping out at all costs.

The Thundering Legion.—There is a story of one of the legions in Marcus' time, the Twelfth, known as the "Thundering Legion," which legend has made into a wonderful miracle. In a battle with the savage Germans and Sarmatians the soldiers were nearly overcome with thirst. The Christians in the army prayed to Christ in their extremity and a heavy storm broke. The soldiers caught the water in their upturned shields, drank, and sprang forward to pursue their foes, already in flight from the violent lightning and thunder. A relief on the Antonine column still shows the scene, though the rainfall is credited to Jupiter *Pluvius*, the Rain-giver. Pagan historians, on the other hand, assert that an Egyptian soothsayer produced the storm by magic. But the

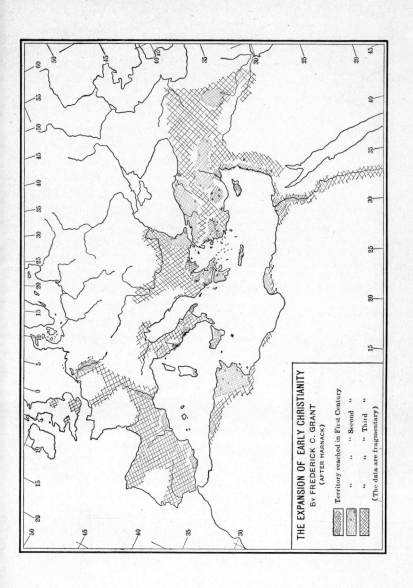

THE EXPANSION OF EARLY CHRISTIANITY
By FREDERICK C. GRANT
(AFTER HARNACK)

Territory reached in First Century
"   "   "   Second   "
"   "   "   Third   "
(The data are fragmentary)

Christians believed, for many centuries, that it was the divine response to the prayers of Christians in the legion, which it may indeed have been; and the story is known as the "Legend of the Thundering Legion." At the very least it indicates that Christianity had spread into the army, even into the Twelfth Legion, usually stationed in Cappadocia, but then engaged on the Danube or Rhine. Tertullian's words, "We have filled . . . your very camp," were true. The Roman army became first one of the widest fields and then one of the most effective agencies for the spread of Christianity.

Later emperors.—There were worse emperors after the Antonines; yet for twenty years after Marcus the Christians enjoyed peace. No fresh persecutions were begun, and the old animosity was in the way of dying out. Then followed under Septimius Severus a renewed effort to crush out the unauthorized guilds, and along with them the Christian Church. Propagation of the faith was forbidden and many martyrs gave up their lives in Egypt and North Africa, among them the noble woman, Perpetua. Thus it went on, through decade after decade, an era of persecution alternating with one of toleration. Christianity, even in peaceful days, had not yet received public and official recognition. The fires of persecution might break out at any moment, as they did again and again. The Emperor Decius, though he reigned for only two years (249–251), issued an edict against the Christians which resulted in numberless martyrdoms. "Some fled, some were captured. The deserts and the mountains were filled with fugitives who perished by famine and cold and wild beasts and robbers. And not a few maidens and soldiers gloried in the witness of a triumphant death which they were allowed to render to Christ."

After the persecution under Decius and the unsuccessful attempt of Valerian to force the Christians into conformity with the state religion, the church enjoyed forty-five years of peace, thanks to the Emperor Gallienus. In 261 he issued an edict which virtually acknowledged Christianity as a *religio licita*. But the long peace of almost half a century only prepared for the last and worst of the persecutions, that under Diocletian (303).

WHY WERE THE CHRISTIANS PERSECUTED?

It is strange that the educated civilization of the Roman Empire, in many ways the highest the world had ever known up to that time; that enlightened and humane emperors and civil officials, disciples, for the most part, of Zeno and Epictetus; that urbane and tolerant and cosmopolitan people like the inhabitants of Alexandria and Ephesus, Carthage and Rome, should permit, or themselves engage in, the persecution of innocent and devout men and women, helpless children, poor and humble folk who could not by any stretch of imagination be accused of political designs. What is the explanation of this strange anomaly?

Reasons for the persecutions.—In the first place the Christians were undoubtedly technically guilty of breaking a Roman law: their society was one not authorized by the Senate. It is, of course, extremely doubtful if it ever could have been so authorized, even had application been made for a license. The emperors, and their legates and proconsuls, were exceedingly suspicious of all secret societies—and not without reason, as we learn from the history of the times. Too often the trade-guilds and mutual-benefit societies became hotbeds of revolution. As Trajan wrote to Pliny, "Whatever the name we give these societies, and whatever their excuse for existing, they soon turn out to be guilds" (Pliny, *Epistle* 34).

Added to this was the refusal of the Christians to pay homage to the genius of the empire through sacrifice or libation to the gods, or through reverencing the statue of the emperor. To pagans, polytheists, worshipers of "gods many and lords many," such reverence and prayer was mere matter of course, a patriotic form or ritual, against observing which no reasonable man or loyal citizen could object. But to the Christian it was idolatry and worse, the worship of a man in place of God—in a word, it was the adoration of Antichrist.

Moreover, the church administered its own finances and discipline without regard to the state. This was politically harmless; but the very existence of such powers increased the suspicion of the authorities and lent a semblance of truth to exaggerated rumors and the malicious tales of informers. Then the mutual charity of the Christians, their secret signs and greetings, their meetings held at night or just before dawn, the sacraments and sacred compacts,[1] not only still further aroused the suspicion of the authorities and the animosity of their neighbors but brought down upon the Christians the full force of the law.

Like our so-called "blue laws," there were Roman statutes, some of considerable antiquity, against each one of these features of early Christianity. These were as a rule ignored; but in times of popular disturbance, when the mob was roused and demanded its victims, the authorities had no recourse but to enforce the law in all its rigor. The worst tragedy of the persecutions is that they were, in so many instances, stupid and

---

[1] These were understood by non-Christians as oaths like the military *sacramentum*—see Pliny's letter.

blind and unnecessary even from a sane pagan point of view. The best blood in the empire was being poured out in the arena, in the mines, at the stake, and no one had the intelligence or ability to understand and conciliate and secure fair play. The truth seems to be that the imperial authorities simply did not know what to do with Christianity. They had never experienced a religion of this kind before. It was technically illegal; but it was manifestly a harmless and even an inspiring faith —and they solved their problem by trying to stamp it out!

Popular fanaticism.—Aside from official permission or instigation, there was, of course, a widespread popular misunderstanding which made the official persecution possible. The Christians were supposed to be atheists who had deserted the religion of their forefathers, since they did not worship the gods; and they were even said to be cannibals (perhaps on account of some perversion of the words of the Lord's Supper), feasting upon the flesh of children (a rumor which was only too true in the case of certain heathen rites), and pledging themselves to deeds of wickedness, the destruction of the city or the overthrow of government.

> "Our enemies defend their hatred by the vain excuse that the Christians are the cause of every public disaster, of every common misfortune. If the Tiber rises to the city walls, if the Nile fails to rise over the corn lands, if there is a drought or an earthquake, or a famine or a pestilence, the cry is raised at once, 'The Christians to the lion!' "—Tertullian, Apology 40.

The victory that overcometh.—There was no way of overcoming such fanaticism, superstition, and bigotry but by living it down—living it down "even unto death." It has been said that the early Christian "outlived the pagan, outthought him, and outdied him." The spectacle of men and women, boys and girls, going to martyrdom without complaint, gladly choosing to suffer rather than deny their faith, at last convinced even the hardest-hearted that Christianity was not the infamous cult they supposed it to be. In spite of decimation, the church increased in numbers. "We multiply the more we are mown down," said Tertullian; "the blood of Christians is as seed." Or, as Justin, the converted philosopher, himself soon to become a martyr, wrote:

> "You can plainly see that when we are beheaded and crucified and exposed to wild beasts and chains and fire and every other torture, we do not abandon our profession; but just in proportion as such sufferings are inflicted so many more are added to our faith and religion through the name of Jesus. The gardener cuts off the limbs of the vine which have borne fruit in order that other branches may spring forth, and thus render them vigorous and productive. And so it proves with us. The vine which has been planted by God and our Saviour Christ is his people."—Justin, Dialogue with Trypho 110.

By the end of the third century, on the very eve of the last and bitterest persecution, to be followed soon by the open triumph of the church, Christianity had spread to the farthest limits of the empire. Not that Christians were everywhere in the majority. But they were in the majority in some of the chief centers; they were increasing generally; and the cross had been invisibly planted, along with the standards of the legions, upon the farthest frontiers of the Roman power. What had spread it in this way? The preaching and teaching of evangelists and clergy, the writings of apologists and scholars; but chiefly the simple, steadfast faith and honest lives and constancy even unto death of the humble rank and file of believers. "This is the victory that overcometh the world, even our faith" (1 John 5:4).

The word "faith" means also *faithfulness*.

STUDY TOPICS

1. Read over in your ancient history (for example, Breasted, *Ancient Times*, Chapters XXVIII, XXIX) the account of the Roman Empire from Hadrian to Diocletian. Were there any reasons for caution in dealing with latent political movements?

2. Study the map showing the expansion of early Christianity and compare it with a map of the Roman Empire. Draw one of your own to go into your notebook.

3. Look up "Catacombs," "Eucharist," "Antichrist," "Sacrament," "Blue Laws," and define them in your notebook. Who were Zeno and Epictetus?

4. Look up and read the story of Saint Perpetua (see the encyclopedia).

5. What were the rescripts of Trajan and Hadrian, and what rules did they lay down? Compare the two.

6. Explain the origin and growth of the legend of the "thundering legion." What is its value for our study of the spread of Christianity?

7. Explain the persecution of the early Christians (1) from the point of view of the emperors and civil authorities; (2) from that of the pagan population. How did Christianity spread in spite of persecution?

8. What effect had the testimony and the lives of "the humble rank and file of believers" upon the growth of Christianity? Has it a similar effect to-day? How may all of us bear witness for Christ in our daily lives?

CHAPTER XXIX

CHURCH WORSHIP AND MEMBERSHIP

In the early days of the church in Jerusalem, the Christians worshiped in the Temple like all other Jews. Outside Jerusalem, and even within the city, as the story of Stephen shows, they worshiped in the synagogues. Though arrested for preaching in the Temple courts, and though beaten and "cast out" of the synagogues, they continued to worship there until Palestinian Christianity and Judaism finally separated some time after the fall of Jerusalem.

Outside Palestine the Christian movement began, as a rule, in the Jewish synagogues. Here the gospel was preached on Sabbaths, and usually a few of its members or adherents (often the "God-fearing" Gentiles who had already accepted Judaism half way) were converted to Christianity and formed the nucleus of the new Christian congregation.

Hence it was only natural for the church's services of worship to be modeled very largely upon the services in the Jewish synagogue. The Greek translation of the Old Testament, used in the synagogues outside Palestine, was taken over by the Christians, and Lessons were read at public worship from the Law and Prophets. Certain of the Psalms were said at morning and evening prayer, just as in the Jewish services. Common prayers were likewise used, though their contents and wording were, of course, quite different from the Jewish prayers. These three elements in the synagogue services, Psalms,

277

Lessons, and Prayers, were also to be found in the worship of the Christians.

THE CHURCH'S WORSHIP

There were, however, two important exceptions, two services or sacraments for which the synagogue had no parallel. These were the administration of Baptism, and the Lord's Supper, or Eucharist.

The sacrament of Baptism.—The rite of baptism had been an essential feature of the Christian religion from its very beginning. Even before the ministry of our Lord, John the Baptist had preached "the baptism of repentance unto remission of sins." Jesus had been baptized, and his disciples. The early Christians in Jerusalem were all baptized: it was the normal way in which to become a Christian and a member of the church. The same procedure was followed in the Gentile mission by Paul and other leaders. It is sometimes said that baptism was taken over from the custom of the Jews in the *Diaspora* who baptized their Gentile proselytes. But this was not the same as Christian baptism, which admitted one to full-fledged membership in the church—a rite to which circumcision was the real Jewish parallel.

Its requirements.—The two requirements of the candidate for baptism were repentance and faith: repentance from his former sins, a "conversion" or facing about, turning his back upon his former life of self-indulgence, vice, or sin; and faith in Christ, confidence in his power over sin and evil and even death, and the resolute committal of all one's future happiness in this life and the next into the keeping of Jesus his Lord.

Very early some sort of creed or confession of faith was required. In the lifetime of Saint Paul it was little more than the words of acknowledgment, *Kyrios Iêsous* —"Jesus is Lord!" (See 1 Corinthians 12: 3.) By the middle of the second century this formula of belief had grown until it was approximately what we call, to-day, "the Apostles' Creed."

> "I believe in God, the Father almighty, maker of heaven and earth;
>
> "And in Jesus Christ, his only Son, our Lord; who was conceived by the Holy Spirit, born of the virgin Mary, suffered under Pontius Pilate, was crucified, dead, and buried; he descended into hades; the third day he rose from the dead; he ascended into heaven, and sitteth on the right hand of God the Father almighty; from thence he shall come to judge the living and the dead;
>
> "I believe in the Holy Spirit; the holy catholic church, the communion of saints; the forgiveness of sins; the resurrection of the body, and the life everlasting.   Amen." [1]

Baptism not repeated.—A description of the administration of baptism in the early church is found in the Apology of Justin Martyr:

> "I will also relate the manner in which we dedicated ourselves to God when we had been made new through Christ. As many as are persuaded and believe that what we teach is true, and undertake to live accordingly, are instructed to pray and

---

[1] "Hades," that is, the place of departed spirits, which our Lord visited and where he preached salvation, according to the early Christian belief, in the interval between his death and resurrection; see the creed-like passage in 1 Peter 3: 18–22. "The holy catholic church," that is, universal, world-wide; even at the beginning of the second century (see the epistles of Ignatius) this was the name of the Christian Church. It was universal, not in the sense of including the whole world, but as *spread throughout* it. "The communion of saints" was another name for the Church; Christians were "called to be saints," according to Saint Paul and other early teachers.

> intreat God with fasting for the remission of their
> sins that are past, we praying and fasting with them.
> Then they are brought where there is water and are
> regenerated in the same manner as we ourselves
> were born again. For in the name of God, the
> Father and Lord of the universe, and of our Saviour
> Jesus Christ and of the Holy Spirit, they then re-
> ceive the washing with water."—Justin, Apology 61.

So solemnly and seriously was this dedicatory sacrament received that many, like the author of the Epistle
to the Hebrews (see 6:4–6), believed there was no
hope for the wavering disciple who denied the faith
under stress of persecution. There were some who did
so, offering the incense and pouring the wine and calling
upon the gods, thereby saving themselves and their
families from banishment or death. They received a
certificate, or *libellus*, from the police, and were henceforth unmolested. But among the faithful they were
known as *libellatici*, "receipt holders," and grave questions were raised about their readmission into the
church after the persecution subsided. In some instances
they were rebaptized; but it became a rule, by the
middle of the third century, that baptism should not
be repeated. Once a person was baptized, he had "put
on Christ" and was "buried with him in his death and
raised up a new man in his resurrection," as Saint Paul
had taught (see Romans 6). Such a process could not
be repeated.

The Lord's Supper.—The other sacrament, for which
the synagogue offered no parallel, was the one which
commemorated the last supper of Jesus with his disciples, on the night in which he was betrayed. This too,
under the name, "the breaking of the bread," had been
observed constantly from the very first, in Jerusalem,

Antioch, Ephesus, Bithynia, Alexandria, Rome. Down in the catacombs beneath the imperial city may still be seen the altars where the early Christians celebrated this sacred rite; and to this day the lighted candles upon the altars of certain churches at the Communion service remind us of that dim yet glorious epoch of the long ago.

Justin Martyr also describes this service in his *Apology* addressed to the Emperor Antoninus about 150 A. D.

"Then there is presented to the president of the brethren bread and a cup of wine mingled with water, and having taken it he offers up praise and glory to the Father of all by the name of the Son and Holy Spirit; and he offers at length thanksgiving for our having been made worthy of these things by him. And when he concludes the prayer and thanksgiving all those present answer with acclamation, 'Amen'—which means in Hebrew, 'So be it.' After this those who are called deacons distribute to each of those present, for them to partake of the bread and the wine and water, and they carry away portions to those who are absent.

"And this food is called by us Eucharistia (Thanksgiving), and none may partake of it save those who believe our teachings and have been washed in the bath which is for remission of sins and rebirth, and who live as Christ taught; we do not receive these as common bread or common drink. . . . For the apostles, in the memorials made by them called Gospels, have related it to have been enjoined on them—Jesus took bread, gave thanks, and said, 'This do in memory of me; this is my body;' and likewise the cup, he took and said, 'This is my blood;' and he distributed to them alone."—Justin, Apology 66.

The prayer of consecration.—What was this prayer, offered by the "president" (that is, elder or bishop)? Justin does not say. It was a thanksgiving, of course, for from that prayer the service ("Eucharist") takes its name. Some light is thrown upon this question by a document discovered in 1875, after having been lost for many centuries, known as the *Didaché*, or "Teaching of the Twelve Apostles." It belonged perhaps to the north Syrian church, and was very likely written some time in the early second century. It is a little manual of doctrine, morals, and worship. After giving directions regarding baptism, fasting, and prayer, it continues,

> "Now concerning the Thanksgiving, give ye thanks thus (for the cup): We give thee thanks, our Father, for the holy vine of David thy servant, which thou madest known to us through Jesus thy servant; to thee be the glory forever. (And for the broken bread:) We give thanks to thee, our Father, for the life and knowledge which thou madest known to us through Jesus thy servant; to thee be the glory forever. As this broken bread was scattered abroad over the mountains, and being gathered together became one, so let thy church be gathered from the ends of the earth into thy kingdom; for thine is the glory and the power through Jesus Christ forever."
> —Didaché 9.

The importance of the Eucharist.—While their neighbors were feasting in the temple of Serapis, or undergoing initiation into the mysteries of Isis or the Eleusinia, or receiving the gory baptism of bull's blood in the cult of Mithras, the early Christians were gathering at the altar of their Lord to consecrate themselves afresh to his service and to receive the life-giving sacrament of his spiritual body and blood. We scarcely realize how much this service meant to them. It was jealously guarded from the eyes of unbelievers; it was received early in the morning, on the Lord's Day, the first food partaken on that day or in the new week; it was the sacred and divinely appointed means of communion with their present and all-powerful Lord; it was, in fact, in the words of Ignatius of Antioch, nothing less to them than "the medicine of immortality."

Development of the service.—There are some writers who hold that the Christian Eucharist was only a counterpart of the pagan mysteries, made necessary by the keen competition between the church and the heathen cults. This may be true of the love-feast, or common meal (see once more Pliny's letter to Trajan, referring to the common meal which they had given up), for it resembled in some ways the temple-banquets of the time; but it does not account for either the origin or the continued observance of the Eucharist, the "sacramentum" quite distinct from it.

As time went on, this service, which was thus from the beginning the central rite of the Christian religion, received more and richer adornment of devotional hymns, solemn ritual, rich ornaments and vestments. For example, the beautiful antiphonal words, called the *Sursum corda*, still used by many churches, are found very early in the liturgies:

> Priest: "Lift up your hearts."
> People: "We lift them up unto the Lord."
> Priest: "Let us give thanks unto the Lord."
> People: "It is meet and right so to do."

Yet nothing was allowed to obscure the central importance of worship and communion. Even as late as the fourth and fifth centuries there were some (see the *Confessions* of Saint Augustine) who objected to the chanting of psalms. The religion and the ritual of the early Christians were for the most part quite sternly severe in their simplicity. Men and women who might be called upon at any moment to bear witness to the faith in their own blood were not easily led to forget the vital truths of Christianity in the elaboration of pompous ceremonial.

MEMBERSHIP AND ORGANIZATION

Simple and solemn as were their services of worship, stern and heroic as was their temper of mind—though often relieved by a sunny and carefree happiness, and a profound, inalienable joy which possessed their hearts even in death—so also was their organization simple, and their conditions of membership were plain and unmistakable.

"Who are the Christians?"—The question was often asked, "Who are the Christians?" after the persecutions began. It became increasingly necessary to answer it as malignant rumors and false accusations spread abroad. The historian Tacitus writes that the Christians in Rome under Nero were convicted "not so much of arson as of hatred of the human race" (Annals 15:44). They were popularly accused of being men without a country, a charge which was admitted in a spiritual sense (see Hebrews 13:13-14); of representing a monstrous "third race," neither barbarian nor Greek; of intending the destruction of the commonwealth and sanctioning the foulest crimes.

One reply to the question, one of the earliest "Apologies" for Christianity, was that written by Aristides in the days of Antoninus Pius:

"The Christians know and trust God, the Creator of heaven and earth, in whom are all things and from whom are all things, and who hath no other God beside him. From him they have received the commandments which they have engraved on their minds and keep in the hope and expectation of the world to come. . . . If any of them have slaves, they persuade them to become Christians for the love they have to them; and when they become so they call them without distinction brothers. They do not worship strange gods. They walk in all humility and kindness, and falsehood is not found among them. They love one another. They do not refuse to help the widows. They rescue the orphan from violence. He who has gives ungrudgingly to him who lacks. If they see a stranger, they take him home and entertain him as a brother. . . . When one of their poor passes from this world, any one of them who sees it provides for his burial according to his ability. And if they hear that any one of their number is in prison or oppressed for the name of their Messiah, all of them provide for his needs. . . . Thus they labor to become righteous, as those who expect to see their Messiah and to receive from him the glorious fulfillment of the promises made to them. Truly this is a new people, and there is something divine in them!"— Aristides, Apology 15-16.

The church's organization.—As the Christians were "soldiers of Christ," so their organization was rigid and their discipline strict. In the days of the apostles local churches were ruled like the Jewish synagogues by "elders" (*presbyteroi*) under the leadership and direction of the apostles or their representatives. Such, for example, were the elders in Ephesus and Jerusalem. In addition to these were the "deacons," or "ministers," who either dispensed the charity of the church under the supervision of the elders, or bore the sacred bread of the Eucharist to those who were absent, sick, or in prison; or perhaps their duties included both.

After the time of the apostles we hear of "bishops," or "overseers," who were set over the local churches. Either they were appointed by apostles, as Paul appointed Timothy and Titus as his representatives, or they were elected by the elders to be their "president," or head. By the time of Clement and Ignatius, perhaps even earlier, bishops are found at the head of the various churches. Their commands must be obeyed. The Eucharist must not be celebrated without them. They are the "shepherds of the flock."

This simple, effective system of organization gradually spread over the whole Christian Church, and has with some modifications survived among the majority of Christians down to the present. Bishops of prominent churches or even whole cities came in time to enjoy greater power and authority than their humbler brethren. The archbishops of Alexandria, the metropolitans of Athens and Constantinople, the Roman pontiff, or Pope, became in the course of centuries the occupants of thrones and wielders of mighty scepters. But in the second and third centuries, in the days of the persecutions, the bishop was usually the father and shepherd of his flock, and the first to lay down his life for the faith.

Charity and education.—From the first the early church did not neglect the charitable relief of its poor. In the book of Acts we read of such provision, the sale of land and division of the funds, the care of the Hellenist widows, Dorcas' gifts, Paul's collection for the poor.

And in the second century we read of the rule, "In every congregation at least one widow is to be appointed to take care of sick women" (as the deacons cared for the men). And Justin Martyr says, "Those who are well to do give as they choose. The collection is then deposited with the president, who cares for orphans, widows, and those in want from sickness or other cause, those in prison, and strangers on a journey" (*Apology* 67). Celsus makes this a butt of ridicule when he writes, "What sort of persons do the Christians invite to their worship? 'Any one who is a sinner,' they say, 'or devoid of understanding, or simple-minded; in short, whoever is unfortunate will be welcomed to the kingdom of God.' " But at last the admiring comment was drawn from pagan lips, "Look how these Christians love one another!"

Not only the poor and the sick but also the ignorant were gathered into the fold. Schools were founded—for example, the famous one at Alexandria over which Pantænus presided and which educated a long succession of scholars and saints, among them Clement of Alexandria, Origen, Heraclas, and Dionysius. Their highest object was to bring all the treasures of Greek philosophy, science, and literature to the service of Christ and to the elucidation of the gospel message by means of theology and logic. The foundation of this school, some time in the second century, marks the point at which Christianity began to appeal more strongly than before to the intelligent and educated, the intellectually and philosophically trained minds of the Græco-Roman world. The foundation was already being laid for the rich development of Christian theology, literature, and history; a process which reached its culmination in the Greek Fathers of the fourth and fifth centuries, in the east, and in the west in the great schoolmen of the twelfth and thirteenth centuries—a process which kept learning alive through the long night of the Dark Ages when barbarism settled over most of Europe, and one which has been continued through the centuries down to the present.

STUDY TOPICS

1. Sketch briefly the origin and development of Christian worship.
2. Look up the references to the New Testament in this chapter. What was the earliest creed? How was it used?
3. See the picture of a *libellus* in Breasted's *Ancient Times*, p. 662, or in some other book.
4. If you can procure a translation of the *Didaché*, read the whole of it, and write a brief description of it in your notebook.
5. Explain the significance of baptism and the Eucharist to the early Christians. Refer both to the New Testament and the early Christian writers.
6. How did Aristides answer the pagan calumnies?
7. Describe the organization of the early church.
8. Have you been baptized, or admitted to the Holy Communion (or Lord's Supper)? If so, what is required of you? How does it compare with the requirements in the early church?
9. How ought educated persons to-day to use their advantages for Christ?

CHAPTER XXX

THE FATHERS OF THE EARLY CHURCH

BEFORE even the first century had been completed and Christianity had passed the first two generations of its growth (30–100 A. D.), the church had reached large numbers of various kinds of people. Even in Paul's day, "they of Cæsar's household" sent greetings to the far-away Christians in Philippi (Philippians 4:22). From Corinth, Erastus, the city treasurer, sends a greeting to the church in Ephesus (Romans 16:23; see Chapter XX). A list of the various trades and occupations represented by the Christians named in the New Testament, not including the literature of the second and third centuries, would be both interesting and informing. And in the second century the expansion of the church continued until its members were found, as Tertullian boasted, in all walks of life—in commerce, in industry, in the country, in the city, in the courts, the palace, the Senate. By another century paganism had begun losing ground on so large a scale that the most drastic measures were undertaken in the effort to crush out the new religion, under Decius and Diocletian.

THE FATHERS OF THE SECOND CENTURY

The various types of mind and outlook represented in the church of the second century are to be seen in such literature as has survived and come down to us. There were legalists and allegorists, like the author of the *Epistle of Barnabas*, who held that the Jews sinned in building the Temple at Jerusalem, since the Law referred not to a material but a spiritual structure! There were mystics and seers, like Hermas of Rome, who wrote a book called *The Shepherd*, a book full of visions and exhortations and stern rebukes for the sins of his neighbors. There were writers like Clement and Ignatius who emphasized obedience to episcopal authority so strongly that this almost appears the chief Christian virtue. There were wild visionaries, the Gnostics, who turned Christianity into a system of mythology and looked upon Christ as only one of many "emanations" from the Supreme Being. There were fanatical ascetics who forbade marriage and enjoined continual fasting and preparation for the descent of the New Jerusalem. These latter teachers, the Gnostics and Montanists as they were called, the church repudiated, for their teaching could not by any means be identified with her own. This was not done, however, without some controversy, as the "heretics" refused to admit that their teaching was false. The great writers who defended the true teaching of the church against such false interpretations and caricatures were numbered among the Fathers of the Church. Their writings were carefully preserved for later ages, though with some unfortunate omissions; and these writings, together with the writings of the apologists who defended the church against heathen attacks, form the bulk of the Christian literature of the second century.

Justin Martyr.—We do not know much about their lives. One of the best known is Justin Martyr, from whose *Apology* and *Dialogue* we have already quoted. He was born in Palestine, at Flavia Neapolis, the new Roman town on the site of ancient Sichem. His parents were pagans, and were compelled to leave Palestine about the year 100 on account of the unsettled state of the country. He had received the usual education of a Greek youth, but turned from one school of philosophy to another in the hope of satisfying both heart and mind. Only the philosophy of Plato seemed to give him any satisfaction; finally at Ephesus he met an old man who pointed him to the Jewish prophets and then to Christ. He was converted and went to Rome, still wearing his philosopher's cloak but teaching a new philosophy. Of his writings, some of which were against the Gnostics, only three survive: (1) the *Apology*, addressed to Antoninus Pius, about 150 A. D.; (2) a second *Apology*, or, rather, *Appendix* to the first, addressed shortly afterward to the Roman Senate; and (3) the *Dialogue with Trypho the Jew*, recording a conversation with a liberal Jew of Ephesus and showing vividly the early church's use of the Jewish Scriptures and their interpretation in a Christian sense.

The *Apology* is both a defense of Christians against the calumnies of their foes and a clear account of their teachings, worship, and political loyalty. Especially noteworthy is the assurance which he offers that Christians are not disloyal but, on the contrary, make good citizens, a fact which would appeal to an emperor.

> "More than all other men we are your helpers
> and allies in promoting peace, seeing that we hold
> it is impossible for the wicked, the covetous, the
> conspirator—and even the virtuous—to escape the
> notice of God; and that each man goes to everlasting
> punishment or salvation according to the worth of
> his actions."—Justin, Apology 12.

This argument was advanced more than once in the second century. Melito of Sardis argues that since Christianity was coeval with the empire, Christ having

been born under Augustus, the two powers were intended by God to be a mutual aid and support, and
therefore the government should prohibit the persecution of the Christians. Only wicked emperors like Nero
and Domitian had afflicted the church; good emperors
like Hadrian and Antoninus had protected it.

What impression the *Apology* made we do not know.
A few years later, about 165, seven Christians were
haled before a Roman prefect one morning, six men and
one woman, and commanded to throw the pinch of
incense on the altar before the bench. One of them was
Justin, still wearing his philosopher's cloak. The prefect,
Junius Rusticus, a gruff police magistrate, turned to
Justin and said, "Listen, you who are so wise and
pretend to know the truth! Do you think if you are
scourged and beheaded you will ascend to heaven?"
Justin replied, "Through prayer we can be saved on
account of our Lord Jesus Christ, even when we have
been punished; because this shall become to us salvation and confidence at the more fearful and universal
judgment seat of our Lord and Saviour." And the others
said, "Do what you will, we are Christians and do not
sacrifice to idols." Then the prefect pronounced the
sentence, "Let those who have refused to sacrifice to
the gods and to yield to the command of the Emperor
be scourged, and led away to be beheaded, according to
the laws." The trial had lasted only a few minutes, and
in an equal time Justin and his six companions had sealed
their testimony in death.

Saint Irenæus.—As Justin is the typical apologist,
so Irenæus, Bishop of Lyons in Gaul, is the typical
theologian. Born in Asia Minor about 130, perhaps in
Ephesus where he knew the aged Polycarp, and accom-
panying him to Rome (as some think), he formed a

living link which bound together the east and the west, Ephesus and Gaul, the life and thought of the post-apostolic age with that of the growing catholic church of the second century. Of his experiences in youth he writes:

> "I can describe the very place where the blessed Polycarp used to sit when he discoursed, his goings-out and his comings-in, his manner of life and personal appearance, and the discourses which he held before the people; and how he would describe his intercourse with John and with the rest who had seen the Lord, and how he would relate their words."
> —Eusebius, Ecclesiastical History 5:20.

Of his writings, the most important has survived, the one *Against Heresies,* written about 190. It is a criticism of various false doctrines held at the time, chiefly those of the Gnostics, but it includes a strong and thoughtful presentation of the teaching of the church. His central idea is that God and his world are not opposed—as the Gnostics taught, spirit and matter being incompatible—but there exists a true kinship between them. The Christian redemption consists in "the sanctification of nature and the exaltation of man to a new degree of union with God." Therefore the Son of God was incarnate: "On account of his infinite love he became what we are in order that he might make us what he himself is."

The spirit of his theology and of his life were one. He dealt gently and tenderly with those who were inclined toward Montanism, and so killed heresy by kindness. When some of his flock denied the faith during persecution, he hoped for their restoration, feeling that the prayers of the martyrs for the pardon of their weaker brethren would have great weight with God. He worked indefatigably in his diocese. In order to reach the Celtic people of the neighborhood he learned their difficult language and taught them the gospel. He died, according to a later writer, in the year 202.

The Epistle to Diognetus.—There is one writing which dates from the second century which ought to be quoted as showing the influence of the Greek spirit and of Greek philosophy upon the thought of the church. It is called the *Epistle to Diognetus*, a brief composition which has had a precarious history, the only surviving manuscript having been destroyed at Strasbourg during the Franco-Prussian war. Whoever its author, though anonymous, he belongs among the Fathers, for the spirit of his Christianity was destined to have a wide-spread influence upon the succeeding centuries.

> "What the soul is in the body, that are Christians in the world. The soul is spread throughout the body; so are Christians throughout the cities of the world. The soul dwells in the body, but is not a part of it; Christians dwell in the world, but are not of it. The soul is invisible, but remains in the body which is visible; so Christians are in the world, but their worship remains invisible. The flesh hates the soul, and wars against it; so the world hates the Christians, though it suffers no wrong, because they renounce its pleasures. . . . The soul, when severely disciplined, is made better; so Christians, when punished day by day, gain more strength. So grand is the fortress in which God has placed them, it is not right for them to decline to maintain it."— Epistle to Diognetus 6.

THE FATHERS OF THE THIRD CENTURY

When we turn from the second to the third century we come upon two writers of very different spirit than those we have just described. One is Tertullian, the fiery orator of North Africa; the other, Cyprian, Bishop of Carthage.

Tertullian.—The lawyer, Tertullian, was the son of a Roman centurion, well educated in Greek and Latin; he visited Rome and returned to Carthage as a teacher of rhetoric. Converted in 195, he married a Christian wife, was ordained a priest, and began at once to combat paganism in the strongest language of which he was capable. His numerous writings are apologetic and practical rather than doctrinal in character. He was a rigorous moralist and insisted upon Christians upholding the sternest and severest of standards. He even became for a time a Montanist and adopted the extravagant asceticism of that sect. The piercing irony of his attack upon the opponents of Christianity may be seen in such a passage as the following:

"Someone says, 'A good man, Caius Seius, only he is a Christian.' Or, 'I am astonished that such a sensible man as Lucius Titius has suddenly become a Christian.' No one reflects whether Caius is not good and Lucius sensible because they are Christians, or Christians because good and sensible! . . . A father who used to be patient has disowned a son who now obeys him. A master who used to be lenient has banished from his sight his now faithful servant. To be reformed by this name is to commit an offense. Virtue is less esteemed than hatred of the Christians."—Tertullian, Apology 3.

Cyprian.—The question of the discipline of those who fell away in the persecutions, especially during the terrible days of Decius, was a most vexing one in Carthage. A rich layman named Felicissimus, and a young presbyter named Novatus, insisted that the *libellus* of the apostates could be canceled by the *libellus pacis* of a confessor; that is, one who had "confessed" or borne testimony to Christ through suffering might write on a card, "Let the bearer and his friends receive communion," and the church would have to readmit them without any more ado. Cyprian and the clergy of Rome resisted this claim, though the result was the growth of a separate sect, the "Novatians," which lasted for two hundred years.

Cyprian himself was beheaded in 258, on the charge of being "the head of an accursed conspiracy, the enemy of the gods of Rome, and the cause and ringleader of the most iniquitous crimes." We wonder how it was possible for sane men to execute such a sentence upon a brave old man even then confined in the gardens which he had himself sold long before for the benefit of the poor, and who begged a moment's leave as he was led to the block to present his executioner with a few gold pieces for which he had no further use!

Clement of Alexandria.—We turn from the west to the east once more. Succeeding Pantænus, Clement became the head of the Catechetical School at Alexandria about 200 A. D. Referring to his master and predecessor, Clement called him "the Sicilian bee sucking the flowers from the meadow of the apostles and prophets." His chief writings are an *Exhortation to the Greeks*, the *Tutor*, and a collection of *Miscellanies*. He aimed to combine Greek philosophy and Christian doctrine, to reconcile faith and knowledge and show their inward connection. He looked back upon the history of the world and saw a gradual unfolding of divine wisdom, to the Greeks in the guise of philosophy, to the Jews and Christians as revelation. Christ, the divine Word, or Reason (*Logos*), of God, had been slowly educating the

world to reason and righteousness. The eternal Son of
God is the Tutor and Instructor of mankind.

One of the earliest Christian hymns was written by
Clement and has come down to us in the original Greek.

> "King of the holy ones,
> All-conquering Word
> Of the highest Father,
> Prefect of wisdom,
> Support of burdens,
> Rejoicing eternally,
> Of the mortal race
> Saviour, Jesus!
>
> "Let us sing together,
> Let us sing simply
> The mighty Child;
> We, the choir of peace,
> The Christ-begotten,
> The sober folk,
> Let us sing a psalm
> To the God of peace."
> —Clement, Hymn to the Word.

Origen.—But the greatest theologian of the early
church has yet to be named. He was Origen, born in
185 as the son of native Egyptian parents, educated in
the school of Clement and appointed his successor at the
early age of eighteen. His writings were voluminous in
all the various fields of theology, though his chief
interest was in the study of the Bible. During his exile
in Palestine he founded a school at Cæsarea which
produced several famous scholars and theologians of the
following generation. He was a master of both Greek
and Hebrew, and prepared a monumental work known
as the *Hexapla*, or sixfold Old Testament. In six parallel
columns were exhibited the Hebrew text, the same in

Greek characters, the translation of Aquila, that of Symmachus, the Septuagint, and the translation of Theodotion. Notes and marks were inserted to point out the variant readings of these versions. So enormous were the size and the costliness of the work that a second complete copy of it was never made, so far as we know, and it remained the chief treasure of the famous Library of Pamphilus at Cæsarea, probably down to the Arab conquest.

Other works of his were sermons, or *Homilies*, books of exegesis, commentaries, a reply to Celsus' *True Word Against the Christians*, and a great theological treatise known as *First Principles*. Origen employed a staff of skilled stenographers, and dictated his works—six thousand in all, according to Epiphanius (which may mean that many *rolls* or *tomes* of papyrus upon which they were written).

His influence upon later generations, even though he was charged with heresy on one or two points, is almost incalculable. He was easily the greatest scholar of his times; he was a friend of philosophers and kings; and he died a martyr, in a very true sense, if not literally. In the Decian persecution of 250–251 he was imprisoned and tortured at Tyre. His health was broken by sufferings, and he died there in 254.

Even the greatest, even the most learned, most virtuous, most holy, as well as the humblest and poorest in all the "motley company of Christ," were required to prove the last full measure of their devotion, and "die to live" in the fellowship of their dying, victorious Lord.

> "Marching with thy cross their banner,
>   They have triumphed, following
> Thee, the Captain of salvation,
>   Thee, their Saviour and their King.

> Gladly, Lord, with thee they suffered,
> Gladly, Lord, with thee they died;
> And by death to life immortal
> They were born and glorified."
> —*Bishop Christopher Wordsworth.*

STUDY TOPICS

1. Choose one of the Christian Fathers described in this chapter and look up his life in detail in the encyclopedia. Outline it in your notebook.
2. Make the suggested list of trades and occupations of the early Christians, as completely as you can, from the New Testament.
3. Who were the Gnostics? the Montanists? What is asceticism?
4. Does early Christian literature bear out the contrast between the Greek and Latin spirit, often noted in the history of classical literature? See your ancient history, chapter or section on Latin literature.
5. What was the Hexapla? Look it up further in the encyclopedia.
6. Look up and read the whole of the Epistle to Diognetus. Jot down its chief points in your notebook.
7. Many of the Fathers emphasized the value of Christianity as an influence for good in the Empire, even outside its membership. Is this true to-day?
8. Christians in the early days had to "count the cost" of discipleship, as their Master foresaw and forewarned them. Do you think we should be better Christians had we lived in those days? We are free from persecution, here in America and in other enlightened nations—a fact for which we ought to be grateful. However, Christianity still involves some sacrifice and service—can you describe some of "the cost" to-day?

CHAPTER XXXI

THE LAST PERSECUTION

It is sometimes said that there were seven persecutions of the early church. But in truth there was only one. In the long conflict of over two hundred and fifty years there were a few considerable intermissions, such as the long periods of peace before and after Decius in the third century. Nevertheless, paganism and Christianity were opposed and irreconcilable forces. No one recognized this more clearly than the official representatives of the Roman government, whose duty it was to defend the old religion with its rites and ceremonies; for paganism was intrenched within the most powerful political and military system the world has ever seen. Coming as a new faith, Christianity was forced to challenge the authority of this ancient system, and was answered with all the energy of a jealous and self-assured state religion. Inch by inch the church gained its ground, but at the fearful cost of innumerable martyrdoms. It purchased its victory with blood. Though widespread persecution was intermittent, the struggle was continuous. Like a forest fire, which dies down for weeks and even months at a time, buried deep in the roots of the trees that nourish and sustain it, then leaping up into a sea of flame as the winds fan and scatter it, so the fires of hatred and oppression burned in the heart of decaying paganism. The "persecutions" were only the conspicuous outbursts of a "persecution" which began as soon as pagans recognized the new religion and lasted until the reign of Constantine.

The life-and-death struggle.—It may seem almost monotonous, to-day, to go over the records of early Christianity. They are chiefly records of martyrdom. Their variety is only the variety of different forms of cruelty and of the various utterances of a common testimony to Christ. Many facts there are about the early church which we should like to know but which the church's historians overlooked, giving us instead the stories of the martyrs. But we forget that these were the stories which *they* learned, and were handed down until put in writing by Eusebius and his fellow historians. And we forget that the history of early Christianity is the history of a life-and-death struggle, a world-wide warfare, which Christ and his faithful were waging—and winning—over powers which seemed at first impregnable in the enjoyment of every conceivable advantage and resource. Its annals are, therefore, the annals of warfare. Each martyrdom was a victory of the spirit, won on "the field of honor." Unless we remember this, and discover the spirit in which this conflict was waged, we shall never understand the early Christians or realize how their victory was won. That spirit is best expressed by one who was himself a martyr, Cyprian, Bishop of Carthage:

> "It is he who once conquered death *for* us who conquers it always *in* us. . . . He is not simply the spectator of our conflict. It is he who wrestles in us; he wages our battles; in the conflict of our strife it is he who gives the crown and he who receives it."
> —Cyprian, Epistle 8.

Paganism might enjoy every outward advantage, but it could boast of nothing which might be compared with that spirit. The weapons of the Christian's warfare were not material, but they were invincible. Christianity, if it persisted, could not but win!

THE LAST EFFORT OF DEFEATED PAGANISM

Hence the mad desperation of those who sought to bolster up a lost cause, the fury of Decius and Diocletian and their confederates!

The long peace of Gallienus.—We have already noted the revival of persecution during the brief reign for two and a half years of the Emperor Decius. This had broken the long-established peace; but the gods of Rome, instead of blessing their advocates and rewarding the zeal of Decius, did nothing to defend the frontiers of the empire. Antioch, Tarsus, Cappadocia were captured by the Parthians. Gallienus, the new emperor (260–268), saw the uselessness of murdering innocent bishops and issued an edict which restored some of their rights to the Christian clergy. In certain districts the news was too good to be believed—as in Egypt, where the patriarch Dionysius of Alexandria wrote to inquire if liberty was really restored. The "religious places" of the Christians were opened once more; their cemeteries were restored; and the effect of this toleration was practically the recognition of the Christian Church as a legitimate body, entitled both to exist and to hold property.

Unfortunately, Gallienus was not a powerful ruler, and his brief reign was succeeded by those of emperors more narrowly devoted to paganism and more distracted by the declining power of the empire.

The persecution under Diocletian.—In the year 284 Diocletian, whose father and mother were slaves and who had risen to the command of the bodyguard of the Emperor Numerian, was chosen by the army as his successor. He was a courageous and clever ruler, and under the guise of restoring the republic and making its government more stable and democratic he transformed it into an absolute monarchy. For the first eighteen years of his reign the Christians were left undisturbed. Eusebius, the historian, says that the church grew worldly and satisfied in those years, the clergy ambitious, and the laity careless and lax. Some of the bishops even shared the civil government, and many Christians were to be found in the army, the court, and the administrative offices. But the church could not have been very worldly or it would never have faced the issue as it did a few years later.

Gradually Diocletian came to believe that in order to consolidate the empire and insure the undivided loyalty of all its component peoples, even to the very frontiers, it was necessary to establish one official religion. This would provide a bond of religious union throughout the empire whose highest sanction would be the divinity of the emperors at its head. In 297 Galerius, whom Diocletian had chosen as one of his colleagues, gained a great victory over the Persians and thus made secure the eastern frontier. This freed the emperors to devote their energies to internal affairs and apparently proved the reviving favor of the old gods, which Decius had lost.

The signal for persecution was given five years later when Diocletian and his colleagues were celebrating a public triumph in honor of their glorious reign. Some Christians who were present at the taking of the auspices were seen making the sign of the cross. The auspices were not propitious, and their failure was attributed to the presence of the Christians. At once it was decided to clear the court and the army of these disturbers. All civil and military officers were ordered either to sacrifice or resign their posts.

The four edicts.—The next step, in February, 303, was the destruction of the magnificent church at Nicomedia, just across the sea of Marmora from Byzantium. Immediately afterward were issued a series of edicts, the first ordering the destruction of Christian churches and sacred books, the loss of all civil rights and official positions by Christians, and the enslavement of any Christians at court who should obstinately refuse to give up their faith. Diocletian hoped the edict might be enforced quietly and without bloodshed; but he was sadly mistaken. The edict was torn down as soon as it was posted in Nicomedia—an offense for which the culprit was slowly roasted to death. In retaliation for burning the church the palace was set on fire twice within a fortnight. Diocletian became alarmed at the rebellion his tyranny had inspired, and ordered several Christians at court to be executed with hideous tortures. In April he issued his second edict, directing the arrest of all Christian clergy. The prisons were soon crowded with bishops, presbyters, deacons, and readers. Later in the year he issued the third edict, ordering the magistrates to "use every effort" to compel the clergy to sacrifice. The following March the fourth edict commanded all Christians everywhere to offer libations and sacrifices to the gods.

The horrors of the persecution are almost beyond imagining. It was the last effort of defeated paganism to crush out by brute force an adversary whose strength was every day growing greater and which was destined, if this last effort failed, to triumph completely before long. What military absolutism could not effect directly was undertaken indirectly. In 308 it was ordered to

sprinkle all food for sale in the markets with wine or
water which had been offered to the gods, thus giving
the Christians the alternative of eating food consecrated
to idolatry—which they had refused to do since the days
of Paul and the first Christians in Corinth—or of
starving to death. But even this measure failed.

The end of the persecution.—The persecution ended
much sooner in the west than in the east. By 305 the
two western emperors, Constantine and Maxentius, had
come into power; the former was an open friend of
Christianity and the latter was anxious to increase his
popularity by a reputation for mildness. In the east
Diocletian himself had retired even before the publication of the fourth edict, and was raising cabbages for a
pastime on his native Dalmatian farm. His colleague
and successor, Galerius, was stricken with a dreadful
disease, and before he died he came to realize the futility
of the persecution. On April 30, 311, he issued the Edict
of Toleration, permitting the Christians "freely to
profess their private opinions, and hold their assemblies
without fear of molestation." It may be that his own
sufferings from disease had taught him pity, or were
proof to him of the anger of God, for he added, "We
hope that our indulgence will induce the Christians to
pray to their God for our preservation and prosperity,
for their own, and for that of the Republic."

For two years, however, after Galerius' death, his
nephew Maximinus continued the persecution. Among
the martyrs were the great scholars and theologians,
Peter of Alexandria, Lucian of Antioch and Methodius
of Olympus. In order to bring Christianity into widespread contempt, there was produced a scurrilous
forgery called the *Acts of Pilate*, filled with slanders
about the death of Christ, which was ordered to be used

as a reading book in the public schools. It was not till the defeat of Maximinus in 313 by Licinius, who was now Constantine's colleague, that the Christians of the east were actually free to profess their religion.

THE CHURCH ON THE EVE OF VICTORY

At last the long struggle had ended. Though later efforts might be made to revive paganism as the imperial religion, they were belated and foredoomed to failure. Christianity had won, fairly and at immense cost, in a struggle that lasted more than eight generations, against overwhelming odds at the start; and it had won not by strokes of statecraft, not by intrigue and diplomacy, but by the slow, painful process of individual conversion and individual testimony.

By the beginning of the fourth century the church probably numbered well over a third, if not actually a majority, of the population of the empire. Its growth had been slow but steady. There was in it a power and an appeal against which paganism could only invoke the inertia of immemorial custom and habit, the "ancient use," and the apparent, easy-going prosperity of a world devoted, while its real strength waned, to creeds which had long been outworn. But with the gradual decline of the empire, with the lessening of its population through famine, pestilence, poverty, and continual war, and in face of the steadfast refusal of Christians to compromise their faith, doubts began to gather (especially in the third century) about the justice or usefulness—or success—of persecution. Men woke up and discovered, some time between the reign of Marcus Aurelius and Decius, that the empire was being honeycombed and undermined by Christianity. To the average pagan this was perhaps no occasion for alarm, but to the politically or financially interested pagan, to the priest of Jupiter or Ceres, the soothsayer or *haruspex*, the governor or magistrate, the fact was ominous and there was nothing to do, if the old religion was to be saved, but to stamp out the new faith at any cost. It was in a very real sense true, therefore, that the blood of the martyrs purchased the victory and peace of the church. They proved that Christianity was more than one among many cults, which a man might dabble in when fashionable or forsake when the government pronounced it unsafe. If the martyrs had refused to die, if they had yielded up their beliefs, their Scriptures, their freedom of conscience in an easy compromise with heathenism, there might not have been in our days a Christian Church, a New Testament, or the religious liberty which we prize so highly.

The extent of Christianity.—A glance at the map will show that Christianity at the end of the third century covered almost the whole of the Roman Empire. And if the records of the persecutions, the writings of the Fathers and the other documents which have come down to us from that period be read, and the regions and cities noted which they most frequently mention, it will appear that Christianity had remained true to its principle of expansion at the very beginning: it spread by cities and into thickly populated districts. It was not a country-religion, but urban, in those days. The pagans were the "rustics"—*pagani*—and heathenism survived in rural districts long after the cities were Christian.

Christianity in the east.—The church began its career in the east, a fact which the Fathers emphasized by comparing it to the rising of the sun. Its first conquests outside Palestine were in the neighboring countries along the Mediterranean coast. By the fourth century, some of these were thoroughly penetrated by the gospel. The church in Asia Minor probably numbered upward of half, perhaps more than half the population. Armenia was evangelized early in the second century, and was the first to accept Christianity as a nation. Syria and Egypt, Cyprus, Libya, Greece, Macedonia and Thrace were represented by a very strong minority of Christians. Farther east, in Mesopotamia and Persia, and even in India; in Arabia and Palestine, and along the east and west and even the north coasts of the Euxine sea, there were scattered groups of Christians. In Palestine the church was never strong; for the final breach between Jews and Christians had practically closed the gates against any further advance of Christianity within the borders of Judaism.

Christianity in the west.—In the west, Rome and southern Italy, Sicily, Carthage and its suburbs and the province of Africa generally, Numidia, Mauretania, and the Rhone valley were strong centers of Christian life. These include, of course, the most populous regions in the west. Northern Italy, Moesia, Illyricum, Pannonia, Gaul, Spain, Belgium, Germany, and the British Isles had some Christians, though they did not form the high percentage found in the east. In 314 a council was held at Arles in Gaul, attended by thirty-three bishops, probably chiefly from the western churches. Among these were three from England—the bishops of London, York and Caerleon, where there were martyrs under Diocletian—among them Saint Alban, the proto-martyr of Britain.

What impresses us most strongly in the early history of the church is the suddenness of its spread. Jesus was crucified in the year 29, unknown to the world, in a provincial capital on the eastern borders of the empire. Within quarter of a century his religion had won followers in the very capital of the empire, Rome itself, and "they of Cæsar's household" send greetings to fellow-Christians hundreds of miles away. The earliest Christian epitaph in Rome dates from the year 71, marking the grave of one who had lived and died a believer.

After this swift initial expansion, which persecution rather aided than hindered, we might expect a decline of enthusiasm and a period of stagnation or subsidence. So far as we know, no such reaction ever took place. Its rapid extensive growth was followed by two centuries of steady, intensive development. On the eve of its final triumph it had permeated every class and order of Græco-Roman society, had penetrated every part of the western world—and beyond—and was about to take over the whole of society and begin the formal task of Christianizing the laws and institutions and customs of men. If the Christians were not actually in a majority at the beginning of the fourth century, they were very nearly, and were soon actually to be; and they certainly possessed a moral superiority of influence and intelligence which was soon to be wielded for the good of mankind.

STUDY TOPICS

1. Can you recall any passages in the New Testament which reflect a similar spirit or express a similar thought to the quotation from Cyprian's epistle given above?

2. Show how the Christian victory was won "by blood." What might have taken place if the martyrs had declined to suffer and compromised with paganism?

3. Describe the edicts of Diocletian. What were they aimed to accomplish? Why did they fail?
4. Compare the effect of the edict of 308 with the situation at Corinth to which reference is made.
5. Trace on a map the expansion of early Christianity, noting particularly its growth in thickly populated regions.
6. How does the spirit of the church to-day, as you know it, compare with the martyr spirit of the early church? Can you name any modern martyrs for Christ? Would Christianity mean more to us if we had to risk all to follow Christ?
7. Who were Decius, Gallienus, Diocletian, Galerius, Constantine? Read over the account of the period, 250–313 A. D., in your ancient history.
8. Christians were only waiting until they were in the majority, or possessed sufficient moral influence, to change the customs and habits of the world, making it more like the kingdom of God. Is our world as Christian as it ought to be, considering the Christian majority of citizens? Is our neighborhood, our circle of friends, our playground and school Christian in spirit or only in name? Why do Christians sometimes neglect to make their voices heard or their votes count?—It is one of the sad features of American politics, social life, and industry.

CHAPTER XXXII

"BY THIS SIGN CONQUER"

CONSTANTINE the Great was born about 274 at Nish in Serbia, still an important city in the Balkans. As a boy he was sent to the court of Diocletian as a hostage for the fidelity of his father, Constantius Chlorus. In 296 he was taken by the Emperor on a military expedition, and he doubtless saw with his own eyes the outbreak of Diocletian's terrible persecution.

THE CAREER OF CONSTANTINE

When Diocletian died Constantine avoided the pitfalls of court intrigue and remained either with Galerius or with his father. The latter was a man with a high sense of honor, who favored the Christians and guaranteed them personal safety even while compelled to persecute them and destroy their churches. Though not himself a Christian he was a believer in one supreme God. Constantine inherited his father's faith, his sense of honor, and his tolerance of Christianity.

Constantine named Cæsar.—Constantius Chlorus died at York in 306, and immediately his soldiers placed themselves under the command of his son. Accepting the *fait accompli*, Galerius gave the new general the title of Cæsar, and appointed Severus as his coruler in the west. Severus soon after committed suicide, unable to put down the revolt of Maxentius; in his place Galerius now appointed Licinius. Four years later, in 311, Galerius issued the Edict of Toleration, already described, in his own name and the names of Constantine and Licinius.

The edict of Milan.—The unrest and weakness of the empire may be seen from the fact that there were now, for the first and last time, six emperors in power. Two were in revolt: Maximinus, the nephew of Galerius and champion of paganism, who aspired to rule alone the whole eastern half of the empire, and the rebel Maxentius, who had seized the city of Rome and laid claim to sole authority in the west. Licinius set out to defeat the former and Constantine the latter. Crossing the Alps in 312, Constantine defeated Maxentius at the Milvian Bridge near Rome. Shortly after, in 313, Constantine and Licinius met at Milan and issued the solemn edict of toleration which has taken its name from the city where they conferred. It provided that all civil and religious rights taken from the Christians by Diocletian should be restored; no interference should be offered the observance of their religion; their lands and buildings were to be returned. The tone of the edict is one of piety, of recognition of the divine justice, and a desire to propitiate for the crimes perpetrated in the persecution. It raised Christianity from a position of bare toleration (which had been granted by Galerius in 311) to one of equality with the established pagan religion. That same year, 313, Maximinus was defeated near Hadrianople; but even before he died in defeat, not waiting for the publication of the edict of Milan by his conqueror Licinius, he had issued a decree of his own making Christianity a recognized religion throughout the empire.

Constantine sole emperor.—Constantine and Licinius were now coregents of the whole empire, and Christianity was at last a fully recognized *religio licita*.

Neither of the emperors, however, was a professed Christian. Constantine leaned strongly in that direction, but Licinius leaned almost as strongly toward the opposite. But they both recognized the futility of persecution and the folly of attempting to crush out the religion of a vast minority (if not majority) of their subjects—especially a religion of such age and vitality, harmlessness and high character as Christianity.

But Constantine went further in his show of favor to the Christians. He became enrolled as a *catechumen*, or candidate for baptism, and received instruction from Christian bishops. This alienated Licinius, and thinking to make capital of a reaction in favor of paganism, he conspired against his fellow emperor. War resulted, and Licinius was left with only Thrace, Asia Minor, Syria and Egypt; Constantine held the rest of the empire.

Ten years later, civil war was again declared. Licinius began by persecuting the Christians, banishing his Christian court officials and soldiers in the army, and prohibiting public worship. Martyrs again came forward in great numbers. By now Constantine had made common cause with Christianity and took as his standard the *labarum*, a flag bearing the monogram of Christ in Greek; bishops accompanied his army, and a Christian field-chapel was moved along with his headquarters. Licinius was completely defeated, and Christianity became henceforth universally secure under the sole imperial headship of Constantine.

THE TRIUMPH OF THE CROSS

There is a story told by two Christian writers, Eusebius and Lactantius, according to which Constantine was led to favor Christianity through a vision which he saw at the Milvian Bridge. As his army was nearing the scene of battle, the Emperor gazed at the setting sun and saw plainly above it in the sky a shining cross with the words,

IN HOC SIGNO VINCES

—"By This Sign Conquer." Afterward he had a vision of Christ directing him to place this sign upon his banners.

The stories may well be true. A young general face to face with his first crucial battle, and already bearing some of the responsibilities and weighing some of the problems of a world-ruler, might well have been thinking of Christ and Christianity and the persecution still raging under Maximinus. What would *he* do about Christianity when his time came to decide? He was already pledged, as one of the signers of Galerius' decree, to tolerate the church. But what if Christ really was God, and Christianity the one true faith?—as his friend, Hosius, the bishop of Cordova, said. What if Christianity were made the one official universal religion, and the standards of the legions bore the symbols of Christ and the church? Such questions may have filled his mind as the troops drew near to battle, that late afternoon on the outskirts of Rome. In antiquity, men were not surprised to discover the solution of their problems in a vision.

At least, from then on Constantine's victories were successive stages in the triumph of the cross. Paganism was still alive, and had many advocates, learned and unlearned. One of them, the Emperor Julian, "the Apostate," who gave up Christianity and tried to restore polytheism, gave up the attempt at last and died in battle with the words (according to legend), "Galilæan, thou hast conquered!" That was fifty years later. Christ had already conquered, half a century before, only Julian and some others failed to recognize it.

The new capital.—However, there were signs of the Christian victory almost as soon as it was won. After the final defeat of Licinius in 323, Constantine transferred his capital, now the capital of the whole realm, from Rome to Constantinople. That is, a new city was built at Byzantium and named—perhaps by himself— for the first Christian emperor. A beautiful Christian church was built, known as the *Sancta Sophia*, or Church of the Divine Wisdom. The name survives to this day, for Constantine's church, destroyed by fire, was rebuilt in the sixth century by the Emperor Justinian, and still stands, though used by the Turks as a mosque.

Freedom of worship.—Here, and in the other great churches of the East which Constantine built or adorned, were now sung freely the hymns which Pliny's Christians had sung in secret before dawn. Here were now celebrated in broad daylight the Christian mysteries, here were said and sung the solemn, awe-inspiring liturgies, here were dispensed the church's sacraments, here at last men worshiped God without fear of the persecutor and tormentor, praising and blessing him for the peace which had been granted to his servants. One of those old Greek hymns is still used in many churches, known by the words of its first line in Latin, *"Gloria in Excelsis."*

> "Glory be to God on high, and on earth peace, good will toward men. We praise thee, we bless thee, we worship thee, we glorify thee, we give thanks to thee for thy great glory, O Lord God, heavenly King, God the Father Almighty.
>
> "O Lord, the only-begotten Son, Jesus Christ; O Lord God, Lamb of God, Son of the Father, that

> takest away the sins of the world, have mercy upon
> us. Thou that takest away the sins of the world,
> receive our prayer. Thou that sittest at the right
> hand of God the Father, have mercy upon us.
>
> "For thou only art holy; thou only art the Lord;
> thou only, O Christ, with the Holy Ghost, art most
> high in the glory of God the Father. Amen."

This ancient hymn is the Eastern parallel, in a sense,
of the majestic hymn of the Western church, the Latin
"Te Deum Laudamus."

The Council of Nicæa.—Soon began to be held the
famous *œcumenical* (or "universal") councils of the
church, the first of which was held in 325 at Nicæa in
Bithynia, not far from the Emperor's new capital. Over
three hundred bishops were present, from all parts of
the Christian Church—east and west. The leading
achievement of the council was the creed still known
(though subsequently modified) as the "Nicene Creed."
It sets forth the faith of the Apostles' Creed in more
expanded and definite form, in order to correct the
erroneous interpretation of those who looked upon
Christ as "merely a man," or "the chief of the angels,"
or something less than the Son of God. It is a classic
statement of the church's faith in Christ.

> "We believe in one God the Father almighty,
> maker of heaven and earth and of all things visible
> and invisible.
>
> "And in one Lord Jesus Christ, the only-begotten
> Son of God; begotten of his Father before all worlds;
> God of God, Light of Light, very God of very God;
> begotten, not made, being of one substance with
> the Father; by whom all things were made; who for
> us men and for our salvation came down from
> heaven, and was incarnate by the Holy Ghost of the

virgin Mary, and was made man; and was crucified also for us under Pontius Pilate; he suffered and was buried; and the third day he rose again, according to the Scriptures; and ascended into heaven, and sitteth at the right hand of the Father; and he shall come again, with glory, to judge both the quick and the dead; whose kingdom shall have no end.

"And we believe in the Holy Ghost, the Lord, and Giver of Life, who proceedeth from the Father and the Son; who with the Father and the Son together is worshiped and glorified; who spake by the prophets.

"And we believe one catholic and apostolic church; we acknowledge one baptism for the remission of sins; and we look for the resurrection of the dead, and the life of the world to come. Amen."

Reform of laws and customs.—Brilliant as were these outward signs of the victory of the church, there were still others, destined to be equally far-reaching. Christianity showed its real spirit in these ways as much as in the building of churches, the chanting of hymns and the writing of creeds. We ought to remember these also, for persons sometimes overlook them and say that the church failed to take full advantage of its success.

Almost the first token of the new order was the abolition of the penalty of crucifixion. The Emperor himself endeavored to discourage the exposure of infants—a practice older than civilization in the Near East, and one which even the philosophers of Greece had said nothing to discourage. He directed poor parents to bring their children to the magistrate and receive aid for their bringing-up. He established the most stringent laws against unchastity. He forbade the

branding of criminals in the face—since the face of man
is "made after the likeness of the heavenly beauty."
Legal business was forbidden on Sundays. A law was
made permitting the freeing of slaves at services of the
church. Gladiatorial shows were forbidden.

The world was not remade overnight when Constantine set the *labarum* at the head of his columns. But a
wonderful new step was taken in the direction of a
Christian civilization, a society ruled by the spirit of
Christ, when the first Christian emperor set free the
church from its bonds and proceeded to correct some of
the age-long abuses of justice. It was not the full noon;
it was only the dawn of the new day; but that glowing
dawn held the promise of still greater things yet to be
achieved in the name and led by the spirit of Christ.
To their achievement—since even to-day the full
promise of Christianity has not been attained—we are
called to labor as servants of the same Lord whom the
early Christians worshiped, and for whom great numbers of them laid down their lives.

STUDY TOPICS

1. Read over the account of Constantine's career in your
   ancient history or in the encyclopedia. Make an
   outline of it in your notebook.
2. Where was Nish? Hadrianople? The Milvian Bridge?
   Cordova? Byzantium? Nicæa? Locate them on
   the map.
3. Define *labarum; fait accompli* (see Glossary of Foreign
   Phrases at the back of the dictionary); *religio licita*
   (above, in this volume); *catechumen; œcumenical.*
4. Find a copy of the *Te Deum* in a hymnal or prayer
   book and compare it with the *Gloria in Excelsis.*
   Note that both are addressed to the Holy Trinity,

ARCH OF CONSTANTINE IN ROME

both make use of scriptural language (point it out); but the latter is briefer and more primitive than the former.

5. Compare the Apostles' and Nicene Creeds. Copy the latter in your notebook, and underline the words and phrases in it taken from the earlier formula. The remainder represents the additions made at Nicæa or later. Why were these made?

6. Make a list of the changes effected by the triumph of Christianity.

7. What were the forces which led to that victory in the course of almost three hundred years? Write down all those you can think of.

8. Note briefly some of the things you have learned in this course. Are there any lessons that you think will help you in your own life as a Christian? Are there any that give you a larger view of the purpose and mission of the Christian Church? Why is it worth while to study the early days of Christianity?

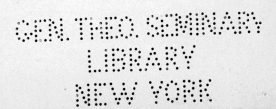

O ALMIGHTY GOD, who hast knit together thine elect in one communion and fellowship, in the mystical body of thy Son Christ our Lord; Grant us grace so to follow thy blessed saints in all virtuous and godly living, that we may come to those unspeakable joys which thou hast prepared for them that unfeignedly love thee; through Jesus Christ our Lord. Amen.